Himmler's Curtains

Himmler's Curtains

A Memoir of Loss and Concealment

SIMON WEISZ

HUTCHINSON
HEINEMANN

HUTCHINSON HEINEMANN

UK | USA | Canada | Ireland | Australia
India | New Zealand | South Africa

Hutchinson Heinemann is part of the Penguin Random House group of companies
whose addresses can be found at global.penguinrandomhouse.com

Penguin Random House UK,
One Embassy Gardens, 8 Viaduct Gardens, London SW11 7BW

penguin.co.uk

Penguin
Random House
UK

First published 2026

001

Set in 13.5/17pt Dante MT Std
Typeset by Six Red Marbles UK, Thetford, Norfolk

Printed and bound in Great Britain by Clays Ltd, Elcograf S.p.A.

The authorised representative in the EEA is Penguin Random House Ireland,
Morrison Chambers, 32 Nassau Street, Dublin D02 YH68

A CIP catalogue record for this book is available from the British Library

ISBN: 978–1–529–15484–9 (hardback)
ISBN: 978–1–529–15485–6 (trade paperback)

For my family

A tal colpa è nulla il pianto, non la terge e non la scusa.
(For such an offence, tears are useless, being powerless to efface it
or excuse it.)
Giuseppe Verdi/Antonio Somma, *Un ballo in maschera,*
Act III, scene 1

Even if we stay alive, we shall carry the wounds with us throughout
our lives.
Etty Hillesum, *An Interrupted Life*

What then . . . is me? . . . There is the me I have locked away out
of sight (my own sight) in a dark cupboard because it is too painful
to look at, since it is a me damaged and made ugly by the adverse
chances of life.
H. A. Williams, *Some Day I'll Find You*

The trouble with sweeping everything under the carpet is that,
eventually, there is so much stuff that you are bound to trip over it.
Ann Gulden

People lie for different reasons. Some lies are told in order to present
yourself in a more interesting or favourable light; others are told
to deceive people. Lies can hurt, but they can also save your skin.
Regardless of why they are told, however, lies most often lead to regret.
Toshikazu Kawaguchi, *Tales from the Cafe*

At the end of the day, we all remember for the same reason we try
to forget.
Elif Shafak, *The Island of Missing Trees*

Preface

Summer 1961

I am five years old. It is a hot summer's day, with a light breeze. Mother is hanging sheets on a long clothesline stretching diagonally across the garden. I am on board ship, sails flapping around my head – I am darting and ducking, sheet corners flicking, catching me, wrapping around my legs. I am laughing, tugging myself free. And then I trip over one of the wooden poles and the whole line of washing comes crashing down onto the muddy grass.

Mother is shouting at the far end of the garden, her face mottled with anger as she lunges towards me. I free myself from the ruined sheets, run in panic out of the garden gate and along the road. At the end of our street is an old house, to one side an alley leading to empty stables. I scramble up the stable stairs and hide at the back behind some sacking. If I don't move, if I just stay here very still in the dark, maybe Mother won't discover me. I don't want her to find me. Gradually my eyes grow heavy in the late-afternoon heat and I fall asleep. When I wake up it's dark outside. Now the empty stables scare me more than Mother's angry face. I know

I have to head home. As I walk slowly back up the road, scraping my shoes on the pavement, I see a black car outside our house. Lifting the door latch, I can hear low voices in the hallway, and inside I see two tall policemen reassuring Mother as she sits slumped on the stairs. Seeing me, the policemen relax and Mother hurls herself at me, 'What are you doing to me? What are you doing to me?', holding me at arm's length. I can't breathe, I wonder if everything will be fine, if the tall policemen will make everything fine. And yes, my mother is smiling prettily as the men leave.

As the door closes, she turns to me, eyes glittering. For the first time I notice that one grey iris has a slash of rust running through it. How had I not spotted it before? She raises her hand, then starts to slap me powerfully across my face, back and forth – slow, deliberate swipes that knock me to the floor. Her head thrown back, she is shouting three words in a deep monotone, one for each blow, three words exploding in my eardrums:

'No more loss. No more loss!'

Introduction

My mother, Ildikó Heimler, was born in 1926 in Eger, a county town in north-east Hungary, famed for its fine wines and a slender 115-foot-high minaret, a remnant of Ottoman occupation. Over the centuries an extensive network of tunnels was developed – a subterranean quarry providing building material for the town. These tunnels were subsequently repurposed as cellar storage – an asset but also, given the constant threat of subsidence, a liability.

Walking to school one summer morning in 1934, Mother found the road ahead blocked by hastily erected barriers – overnight the corner of a large baroque church had started to collapse into one of the tunnels below. As she approached, chunks of masonry from the building's elaborate cornice came crashing down into the street, clouds of dust and rubble choking the morning air. She dropped her school satchel and ran.

Eighty years later I am sitting with her in the hospice as she recalls this incident. She pulls a mohair shawl close around her shoulders. 'I couldn't know it then but looking back I wonder if it was an omen. Our world was about to come crashing down too.'

A survivor of the Holocaust, my mother died in 2017 aged

ninety-one. Throughout her long life she played a complex game of cat and mouse with the narrative of her wartime experience, at times rabidly secretive, at others overwhelmingly voluble.[1] This strategy was skilfully deployed so that one never knew what to expect, which was no doubt the desired effect.

For the first eighteen years of my life nothing was said, but I noted the absence of information, alert to the occasional, awkwardly veiled reference to the fate of my maternal great-grandparents, their children and grandchildren. It was as if the house was permanently charged with an unspoken energy.[2] In rare unguarded moments Mother would start to reminisce and then stop short, turn away. I remember heavy silences hanging in airless rooms, locked drawers and the absence of family portraits. A pulsating absence, hinting at assault, unnamed terror, crippling loss. But I knew I could not ask.

Between 15 May and 8 July 1944, some 440,000 Hungarian Jews were transported to the Judenrampe at Auschwitz. From here a railroad spur connected the ramp to the gas chambers and crematoria II and III. Disembarking from the trains, people were lined up in two columns – men and older boys in one column, women and children in the other. These columns were then inspected by Dr Mengele[3] and his staff. As a rule, all children below sixteen years of age (from 1944, below fourteen) and the elderly were selected for the gas chambers. As a statistical average, about 20 per cent of the people from the transports were chosen for labour. They were led into the camp, registered as prisoners and each assigned a number.

With a casual flick of his baton, Dr Mengele consigned Flóra Heimler, my grandmother, to instant death in the gas chambers. In that split second, there was no time for farewells. Mother, aged eighteen, was pushed to the right and stood by helplessly as her mother disappeared into the seething crowd. It was a defining moment and she would spend the rest of her life trying unsuccessfully to process that eviscerating loss – denial and despair jostling for supremacy.

Does history repeat itself? My mother certainly feared it might, a conviction which resulted in increasingly complex layers of subterfuge. The territory she inhabited was a fragile place, teetering between the past and the present. There was only one 'truth' – the need to protect herself from her unbearable pain and loss. There was only one answer to the question 'Is it safe enough to exist?' – 'Only by becoming someone other than me.'

Years after her death, I still hear her voice. In particular, this statement floats back to me, among the many pieces of wreckage that refuse to sink: *One should always know one's limitations.* A convenient get-out clause, suggesting both defeat and defiance, it released her from all responsibility except survival. Perhaps it was also a plea for lenience – there was only so much that could be demanded of a person, by her or anyone else.

Mother's principal preoccupation, to which she devoted considerable energy, was the cult-like preservation of her looks. Freud, in his 1914 paper 'On Narcissism: An Introduction',[4] observes that the narcissist will keep from his or her ego anything that might diminish it – for the narcissist the ego is sacrosanct. While it could be sustained, Mother wore her beauty as a badge of honour, the very definition of her identity, an unblemished self-image defiantly blotting out the privations of her earlier trauma. But with the passing years, she gazed with increasing bewilderment at a face staring back at her from the mirror which she could not, or would not, acknowledge. As her looks faded and collapsed, so did her claim on the world. No longer admired for her physical attraction, she felt she had nothing else to offer and found herself once again – as in her youth – abandoned, without identity, stateless, left only with the shadows of what she had endured and lost. This image of Mother, peering in despair at a reflection she could no longer own, brings to mind John Rothenstein's description of Francis Bacon's portraits: '. . . to look at a painting by Bacon is to look into a mirror, and to see there our own afflictions and our fears of solitude, failure, humiliation, old age, death and of nameless threatened catastrophe.'[5]

Appearance, public perception, orderliness – these were Mother's gods, fiercely worshipped throughout her adult life, and with good reason. For one terrifying year as a young girl she had cheated death on a daily basis, continually alert to the possibility of arbitrary attack. The rules of the game were implacable: never step out of line (literally), never falter, never say the wrong word. No coincidence then that in later life the highest praise she could bestow on someone was that 'he [or she] never puts a foot wrong'. Having escaped the hell of Auschwitz, Ravensbrück and the brutal death march from the ruins of Berlin, she devoted the remainder of her life to the pursuit of external order at any cost – how else to silence the annihilating demons battering at the door?

From my earliest years I found myself drawn into a web of dependency and collusion as co-conspirator and acolyte. Fetching and carrying creams and bottles of scent, the paraphernalia with which to mask, camouflage and console, I knew, without knowing why, that I must sustain her fiction of equilibrium whatever the cost, with all the sinuous deceptions and betrayals that entailed.

Since her own needs were paramount, my mother's disturbed perception of the parenting template demanded that I adopt the role of the parentified child, in effect an inversion of the traditional mother/child relationship. The psychotherapist Graham Music describes his own childhood as follows: 'I honed my skills in understanding distress in the cauldron of a dysfunctional family in which adults relied on children to help manage their own feelings. I learnt early to be hyper-responsive to mood changes, and how to make others feel better.'[6] This passage exactly echoes my own bewildering experience of childhood. It was not possible to establish a healthy relationship with my mother – my role, as her support act, was to smile and reassure. John Bowlby, a British psychiatrist and psychoanalyst notable for his interest in child development and for his pioneering work in attachment theory, provides a similar gloss on the unrealistic expectations of the traumatised parent: '. . . a parent, having had a traumatic childhood, is apprehensive of being reminded of past miseries . . . as a result her children are required always to appear happy.'[7]

Throughout my childhood I watched Mother's every move, calibrating each twist and turn – valuable lessons for me as it turned out, ducking and diving in a dangerous world filled with ghouls, within and without. It is only now, some years after her death, that I have been able to pick my way through the confused intersections of our relationship and acknowledge the profound impact of transferred trauma.

I am tracking two journeys here – Mother's and mine. This book uncovers the dark spaces of her memory and the ways in which the trauma of her wartime experience found new resonance in my developing consciousness. As a gay child growing up in the 1960s, I too was familiar with the imperative of hidden identity: in the art of dissimulation I could not have wished for a more skilful guide.

I have found it impossible to create a narrative arc framed within a neat chronological continuum. Instead, interwoven episodes of secrecy and subterfuge reveal our separate strategies for survival and – finally – acknowledgement and acceptance of our true selves.

CHAPTER I

June 2017

A dream, or perhaps a nightmare, cutting through the fog of early-morning sleep. She has been dead for a little over a month, but here she comes, sailing into view swathed in a full-length mink coat. She appears as she was in her mid-forties, plumpish but nonetheless with a triumphant gleam. 'Mother, what are you doing scrabbling through the bin bags I'm taking to the dump? You don't need this stuff any more.' She is clutching a large honey-coloured snakeskin handbag, reaches inside and retrieves a gold-plated powder compact. She sits on the edge of my bed and powders her nose with brisk, well-practised movements, then clicks the compact shut again, turning to face me with an aggrieved expression. 'So, what shall we talk about today? More of your furtive little interrogations, after the fact? Just tell me, who is indulging whom here?' So proud of her command of English. I rise to the bait: 'The day I dared to contradict you in public, aged five. Shall we start there?'

May 1961

We are walking home from the high street, Mother and I. It is a bright spring morning. I am trotting along in new leather shoes, of which I am very proud. They are navy blue so I have decided to call them my Danish Blue shoes, Danish Blue cheese being my latest enthusiasm. We meet Mr Milburn, who lives in our street – a widower, long tweed coat, trilby, walking cane. The old man doffs his hat, chucks me under the chin, engages Mother in conversation, enquires about our shopping expedition. Mother, adopting a lofty tone: 'We have been to buy new shoes for this young man. Good shoes are so important. I should know . . . ' She falters, checks herself. 'And to the fishmonger's to buy trout.' I look up at Mother, piping up brightly: 'No, we didn't, you said the trout was much too expensive, so we got kippers instead.' Mother's eyes dilate with sudden fury, masked quickly by a brittle peal of laughter. 'Silly little boy, what nonsense! Now we must be getting along, goodbye!' We turn the corner in silence. I sense something is wrong but I'm not sure what.

Mother opens the front door, slams it shut behind us and drags me to the foot of the stairs, flips me over her knees and starts to thrash me. 'Never contradict me in public – NEVER, NEVER, NEVER!' Heavy blows fall with each repeated word. 'Now go to your room, and don't ever tell lies again, do you hear?' I retreat up the stairs, howling, fearful of her anger, indignant, uncomprehending.

Later that morning the doorbell rings – our neighbour

Miss Robson stands beaming on the front path, bearing a newly baked cake. Mother calls up to me from the hallway – I am to come down and say thank you. I shuffle downstairs reluctantly and stand silently in front of Miss Robson, my lips primped into what is expected, demanded – the tight, obedient smile of the well-behaved little boy, colluding in this party game of denial and make-believe. Miss Robson has hairs sticking out of her chin and I don't want to touch her rotten cake. Mother pushes me forward with a conspiratorial wink: 'Simon and I have had a little disagreement this morning, but now we are the best of friends again, aren't we, darling?' Her fingers prod me in the small of the back and I know better than to disagree.

Mother prepares coffee – I am told to sit at the kitchen table. The hairs on Miss Robson's chin twitch energetically as she talks. Mother, relishing the Englishness of this neighbourly exchange, is determined to make a good impression. She gives me a meaningful glare. 'Eat up your cake, then you may disappear.' I stare glumly at the slice of Madeira cake on my plate, each dry, hairy mouthful clawing at the back of my throat.

In my dream, Mother looks suitably affronted. 'I remember NOTHING of this, not one word. All these years later and you are still telling lies! This meeting is at an end.' Gathering her mink coat closer around her shoulders, she throws me a final look of reproach and leaves.

CHAPTER 2

February 1953

In the early 1950s Mother met Paula Katz at a garden party hosted by mutual friends. Chatting with other guests, she saw a taxi draw up and a short but formidable figure with a prominent Roman nose, wearing a well-tailored suit and vermilion lipstick, slowly dismounted. Mother noticed immediately that Paula walked awkwardly, both legs encased in calipers, and as she made her way towards the terrace she suddenly tripped, sprawling face down on the gravel path. Mother rushed forward and years later Paula would wryly observe: 'The first thing your mother offered me was lint and disinfectant – which says it all!'

Paula's life was colourful and glamorous, an attractive contrast to Mother's more humdrum existence as a new wife and mother, marooned in a north London suburb. Despite her disability – she contracted polio as a small child – she went up to Oxford to read English and during the war was a probation officer for the Citizens Advice Bureau in the East End. At the end of the war, she worked briefly for an obscure publishing house alongside Quentin Crisp, who became a close friend – 'we bonded over nail varnish, darling' – but it

was her work with young Holocaust survivors that would
have lasting impact. She ran a refugee scheme for several
years, placing children from the camps with Jewish families
in London. Inevitably, the outcomes varied markedly. These
children were profoundly damaged by their brutalising experiences and many families, who had signed up with the best
of intentions, found the challenges overwhelming. With tact
and diplomacy, Paula juggled and cajoled, rearranging place-
ments, rescuing children from disgruntled foster parents
who had naively anticipated perfectly behaved additions to
their well-ordered households, deriving great satisfaction
from those children who did manage to adjust and thrive
in happy environments. Some of these children were to
become her lifelong friends, among them academics, rabbis,
politicians, cooks and couturiers. For Paula, the lives these
children forged for themselves as they grew into adulthood,
in Europe, America, Israel and beyond, and the happiness
they found with new families of their own, were a matter of
intense pride. They became her extended family.

Mother, however, was dismayed. She had welcomed this
chance encounter with an older woman who could offer her
affection, wit and – above all – loyalty, but now this friendship
was about to drag her back into the trauma she was trying
so energetically to forget. She froze as Paula recounted the
horrors witnessed by the children under her care, the psychological issues they were grappling with. For Mother, this was
forbidden territory: encouraged by my father, she had done
her best to obliterate such memories.

'He was right – what was the use of dwelling on those

horrors? And anyway, nobody really wanted to know.[1] When I met your father, I felt obliged to try and talk to his mother, to say something of what I had experienced. I thought she had a right to know. But she clamped her hands to her ears, couldn't bear to hear about it. Perhaps it was guilt, that they managed to escape it all? But to be silenced in that way – it was annihilating. And yet there I was, doing exactly the same thing to Paula. She never really forgave me. We skirted around it, both of us infinitely well mannered, but the damage was done.'[2]

My arrival three years later provided Mother with the perfect opportunity for bridge-building, although with a subtle twist. Paula was invited to be my godmother, and whatever misgivings she may have had about assisting at the Anglican baptism of a Jewish child, she accepted. For Mother, this was a significant victory, a tacit acknowledgement that her friend was prepared to collude in her careful strategy of assimilation.

Clearing out my father's study after he died, I found my baptism card, with its saccharine watercolour of Christ at the baptismal font, meticulously filed away in a leather folder in his safe – further documentary proof, should my parents ever be challenged, of the cultural anonymity they claimed as their own.

HOLY BAPTISM

Called into His marvellous light (1, Peter, 29)
He took them up in His arms, put His hands upon them
& blessed them.
24th June 1956

However fraudulent the ceremony, Paula assumed her role as indulgent godparent with inventive gusto. By the mid-1960s she had established herself as a prolific and successful author. My parents may have been privately scathing about the historical romances she wrote in quick succession, usually a minimum of two every year, but they applauded her energy and invention. When I turned ten, I was allowed to take the train down to London to stay with her. Her small flat in Marylebone was crammed with antiques inherited from her Scottish mother – a fine Hepplewhite chair, a bureau by Thomas Sheraton, the tapering legs decorated with faded flower garlands, a graceful Georgian silver wine jug. Bookcases were wedged against every wall – her father's 1926 edition of the *Encyclopaedia Britannica*, fragile, leather-bound copies of the *Gentleman's Magazine* from the 1730s and '40s, a 1904 edition of Pepys's diaries and an extensive library of historical reference books. She worked at a large table under the window in her bedroom, pride of place given to a vast Remington typewriter, piles of manuscripts on either side, weighed down by anything that came to hand – an ebony eighteenth-century snuffbox, a lump of desert rose from a trip to Morocco, or random mementoes from her travels to Martinique (by banana boat), Australia, the United States, Greece and Israel. But my most potent memory is the heady mix of tandoori chicken, Chanel No. 5 and the swirling smoke from her habitual Café Crème cigarillos.

I recently found a typed note she sent Mother regarding my impending fifth birthday:

11th March 1961 – suggestions:

a) flick-knife
b) knuckleduster
c) bicycle chain
d) truncheon
e) broken bottle

Or perhaps not? If a car, kindly state make, i.e. Rolls-Royce, Bentley, Mercedes-Benz or Citröen etc. Owing to income tax demands, gold, platinum or diamonds will not be considered. Alternatively, a small dog collar, or a bottle of whisky? The matter now being URGENT, kindly take this as a final demand and answer by return.

In later years Paula took me to the original production of Lionel Bart's *Oliver!*, to the Angus Steak House across the road from her flat for rump steak and chips, to the top of the Post Office Tower, and to explore the treasures of the Wallace Collection, just round the corner, introducing me to *The Laughing Cavalier* by Frans Hals, Boucher's *Madame de Pompadour*, Rubens' *The Rainbow Landscape* and Fragonard's *The Swing*. She would send me long typed letters, peppered with glorious swear words. No question of talking down, her letters were full of caustic observation, diatribes about dodgy politicians, the erratic plumbing in her flat, detailed accounts of dinner parties with her rackety actor friends. I read and reread them, feeling hugely privileged.

Autumn 1966

A parcel arrived containing Paula's newly published book – a memoir recounting her time with the children from the camps. Mother, unwrapping the parcel at the breakfast table, suddenly froze as she read the dedication to us on the title page. 'How could she? How dare she?' Tears coursing down her face, she ran from the room.

Mother's outrage blinded her to the real impulse that had prompted Paula's dedication: acknowledgement of a significant friendship, certainly, but also the recognition that Mother had, against all the odds, survived and made a new life for herself. Instead, Mother saw the gesture as an unforgivable act of betrayal. As far as she was concerned, the friendship was at an end. The two women never spoke again.

When I moved to London in 1979, I rang Paula and our relationship resumed. Mother was mortified but, realising that I would not be dissuaded, chalked it up as yet another of my many betrayals.

Paula could be garrulous and demanding, but she was consistently supportive of me, took me out for a celebratory supper at Rules when I won a scholarship to the Guildhall School of Music & Drama, bought me a subscription to the London Library, purred when I returned from a trip to Paris and presented her with a bottle of Chanel No. 5, fiercely challenged my political affiliations if they deviated even slightly from her passionately held left-wing views, posted me clippings from the *Guardian*, especially the racier reviews by

Nancy Banks-Smith, and even when we bickered retained an unshakeable faith in the restorative power of a glass of whisky and a cigarillo. She had a collection of battered LPs and introduced me to Piaf, Dietrich and Ella Fitzgerald, her favourite being Ella's rendition of 'Don't Fence Me In', which she would sing along to with gusto. This was her torch song, and she wanted it to be mine too.

Paula wrote some sixty novels over a forty-year period – but in old age her energy deserted her and the money dried up. Without telling her, I rang my parents in the hope that they might help in some way. Mother was adamant – no help would be offered. Forced to sell the flat, Paula moved into a nursing home which I found for her. With typical generosity, she gave me most of her library, her father's stopwatch and pewter whisky flask, as well as some of her antique furniture, including the Hepplewhite chair that I am sitting on as I write this.

On my last visit, in pain and resentful, she lashed out at me: 'Why in God's name did you park me here, of all places? The food is loathsome, the staff treat me like an imbecile and there's not a goddam soul I can talk to.' The empty whisky bottles in her waste bin signalled her growing despair. She wanted out and two weeks later she was dead. Loyal friendship poorly repaid – we failed her, all of us.

CHAPTER 3

After Mother's death I found a typed card, slightly dog-eared, dated 4 April 1960. Originally placed in the window of our local newsagent, it was tucked inside a compartment of her leather writing case. Mother kept everything.

CLEANING LADY SOUGHT
Hard worker, good character, impeccable references

I was four years old, but aware that something important was about to happen. I sat on the top stair, watching a steady stream of women shuffle into the morning room to be interrogated by Mother. These interviews became increasingly brief as the morning wore on. The last person to arrive was a small, slight, neatly dressed woman. She paused as she passed along the hallway below and looked up at me for a moment, her eyes locking with mine, pursed lips hinting at a smile. At lunch I made Mother promise she would engage the last person on the list. 'But why?' 'Because she had a kind smile and I think she will become my friend.'

Pearl Robson arrived the following week. It was a cold spring morning and she let herself in through the back door to find me perched on a stool, waiting for her. 'Why, it's bitter out! That Jack Frost has been working his magic.' She carefully removed a headscarf, folded it neatly with her coat, pulled a perfectly ironed cotton pinny from her bag and tied it round her trim waist. The tip of her sharp nose was pink with cold, her grey eyes were calm and steady. With a conspiratorial wink, she dipped one hand into the pocket of her pinafore and pulled out a toffee.

Pearl came to the house three days a week for the next fifteen years. A wise presence, unfazed by Mother's mood swings, she offered unobtrusive, consistent support. She was proud of her husband Mal, a train driver for the local colliery, and of her daughter, their only child. Her council house on the coast was spotless, filled with carefully burnished knick-knacks and, as the years rolled by, cast-off furniture from my parents' house, which she polished with due reverence.

Pearl was both ally and co-conspirator. One of the many arbitrary rules devised by Mother was that we were only allowed to take broken biscuits from the tin, leaving the whole ones for visitors. Mother spent a good deal of her time on the telephone, berating hapless staff at her favoured department stores. She had perfected the art of pouring withering scorn down the telephone receiver: 'I distinctly asked for Hungarian salami and you have sent me German!' Or: 'As a loyal customer, I really expected better of you – you have sent me a girdle in rayon when I specifically stipulated silk: you will replace the item FORTHWITH or I shall take my custom elsewhere – is that understood?' While Mother, enthroned in the hall, dragged the entrails from the quaking assistant at the other end of the phone, Pearl would reach for the biscuit tin in the kitchen cupboard, break a biscuit into two pieces and silently pass them to me with a wink.

When I was small, we had a special ritual if Mother was absent. The runner stair carpet left large areas of dark-stained oak exposed on either side. Once a week Pearl had instructions to dust and polish the staircase, so we would tackle a side each, the wooden box with dusters and polish sitting between us. Starting at the top landing, we would kneel either side, and as we descended backwards, step by step, Pearl would sing the chorus from her favourite Geordie song:

> *Keep your feet still, Geordie hinny, let's be happy through the neet*
> *For we may not be sae happy through the day*
> *Oh give us that bit comfort, keep your feet still, Geordie lad,*
> *And divn't drive me bonny dreams away.*

The first two lines accompanied our careful application of beeswax (woe betide if we should smear the carpet in the process), the third line was the signal to polish the step energetically with our brushes, while the fourth line was the cue for a final buff with a soft yellow duster, with a triumphant flourish on the word 'away!' When we reached the last step, we would solemnly shake hands: job done. On a sunny day I could see the dust motes flying up and then gently descending again onto the steps we had just polished, but I didn't care – time spent with Pearl was good, and safe.

Pearl's steady presence was a necessary support act for Mother, as she began to carve out a new identity for herself as matriarch and hostess. Pearl was backstage at every large social gathering, washing dishes, tidying the drawing room when the guests moved next door to the dining room, stashing away the silver when dinner was over. With the guests once more installed in the drawing room, she would roll up her apron, survey the restored order in the kitchen and, satisfied that not a pin was out of place, quietly let herself out of the house.

When the colliery closed down, Father – at Mother's instigation – found Mal a job in the factory store. This arrangement appealed to Mother, a reassuring echo of the paternalistic structure of her childhood, when the local villagers tended her father's vineyards and their wives were sent to work in her mother's kitchen.

When she was seventeen, Pearl almost died. As she stood by the open fire one evening, a burning coal rolled from the grate and her nightdress caught alight. She had the presence of mind to rush out of the front door and hurl herself to the ground where neighbours, hearing her screams, managed to smother the flames. She lay in the intensive care unit for a year and Mal came to sit with her every day until she was well enough to come home.

Two women linked by early trauma. Over the years the relationship became more subtly layered – shifting from employer to needy child, from housekeeper to trusted confidante. Impossible to know how much Mother spoke of her wartime experience but watching Pearl handling the elaborate Hungarian china and heavy silver trays, dusting and polishing with particular care, it was clear she was intently aware of their emotional significance. Perhaps this reversal of roles was unsustainable in the long run; perhaps Mother felt she had revealed too much, depended too much?

One afternoon, home for the school holidays, I could hear their raised voices from the kitchen. As I walked in, Pearl – her face tense with anxiety – confronted Mother: 'Mal's in trouble, you have to help him.' Mother's riposte – on safe ground now, relishing her reclaimed status as Pearl's employer – was glacial: 'There is nothing I can do for you – my hands are tied.' It had been brought to Father's attention that items of significant value had gone missing from the factory store. The three men who worked there were all questioned, but it was Mal who was summarily demoted, taking a lesser role as gateman, signing visitors and deliveries in and out of the factory compound. Three weeks later he suffered a fatal heart attack. Pearl never came to the house again.

We kept in touch. I would secretly visit her and we wrote to each other. Years later I visited her in hospital when she was dying. The pale grey eyes were sightless now, but her mind was clear. 'I'm glad you came, pet. Look after yer mam. What she saw, what she lived through. You have to forgive.'

CHAPTER 4

Summer 1965

Mother's first return to Hungary since 1944. Although post-war communist rule ostensibly disregarded racial difference, in reality its legitimacy was based on pre-existing ethnic nationalism. The Communist Party ranks were largely populated by members of the former Arrow Cross – the fascist organisation that controlled the Hungarian government from October 1944 to April 1945 and enjoyed considerable popular support. Twenty years later, political opportunism, or pragmatism, meant that Communist Party officials were willing to forgive and forget in order to secure a broad base of political support.

Mother told me, many years later, that as we stepped out of the airport we came face-to-face with the prevailing mood. Unaware of the identity of his passengers, the taxi driver launched into an enthusiastic anti-Semitic diatribe – 'Things are bad here. Those filthy Jews! Infiltrating every section of society all over again . . . just when we thought we had finally got rid of them!' I spoke no Hungarian and of course at that time knew nothing of our family background, but I do remember Mother's ashen face, my parents' stunned silence as the driver prattled on.

We spent the first week in Budapest, visiting my father's relatives. Life for Jews in Budapest during the German occupation had been perilous, but it had been possible for many to hide, or at least to move from one apartment house to the next, in order to avoid detection. Most of my father's family had survived the war in this way, reclaiming their large, grandly proportioned apartments, now sparsely furnished, with empty rectangles on the walls where paintings had been removed, bartered for food when times were hard. These were emotional reunions – portly great-uncles and -aunts who spoke no English cuffed me under the chin and then left me in a corner with the Hungarian radio at full blast while the adults talked quietly in a different room. Much wringing of hands, tears shed and prodigious amounts of food consumed. I remember a long table covered with a stiff damask tablecloth, the centrepiece a vast white tureen filled with steaming chicken soup. Plates were circulated with great solemnity, each one swimming with golden globs of chicken fat. Mother gave me a warning glance from the other end of the table as I toyed reluctantly with my spoon. Refusing to eat was clearly not an option – these heavy meals were proof of survival, the greasy aromatic soup obliterating loss and heartache.

Years later, I reminded her of those lengthy, formal meals, watching her focus shift away from the conversation around the table. 'They were your father's relatives, perfectly decent people, but I felt such irrational rage that they had survived and my family had not. Going through the motions, the small talk, hearing of their struggles through the war, their judicious adjustments as the communists took over. Some, naturally, took up the communist cause, championing the new reforms, the push to end poverty, while at the same time grieving that they could no longer obtain silk shirts and handmade shoes. And of course, so careful to make no reference to the fate of my parents, or indeed my own experience. Nothing unpleasant at the dinner table, please!'

At the start of the second week, we hired a car and set out for Eger, Mother's home town in north-eastern Hungary. The road across the great Hungarian plain cut through fields of tall maize stretching to the horizon. I looked out of the back window of the car, the air above the tarmac rippling in the mid-morning heat haze. In the far distance I could just see a small black dot on the road far behind us, neither growing nor receding. We stopped at a petrol station but no car passed us along the road. Twenty minutes later we set off again, and when I looked back out of the window there it was again, the same small black dot. By the time we reached our hotel I had a raging sore throat and was running a fever. My father called for a doctor who arrived carrying a shiny black briefcase. He examined my throat and established that I had severe tonsillitis (*mandulagyulladás* in Hungarian, which sounds more impressive) and I was put to bed with a course of penicillin.

Mother had arranged to meet Erzsébet, her mother's former housekeeper, now very elderly and living in an alms-house. After much fussing at the prospect of leaving me on my own and reassurances from Father, they left, locking the door behind them. I sank back under the large white duvet and slept. I woke later, hearing low voices at the door, and blearily opened my eyes to see the door handle turning slowly. Two men slipped into the room – my bed was partly screened by a curtain and instinctively I ducked down out of sight under the duvet and lay very still.

They worked their way around the room methodically, opening drawers, rifling through the suitcases, checking the pockets of Father's suits in the wardrobe. And then, just as silently, they left. After a while, I risked peeking out from underneath the duvet, but the room was empty. Still feverish, I was unsure if I was dreaming, fell back against the pillows and slept again.

On their return, I told my parents about the two men. Mother initially dismissed my story – 'You have a fever, it must have a been a dream.' Nevertheless, they exchanged nervous looks and rang down to the lobby. The hotel staff professed to know nothing about any intruders, the manager bustling into our room. 'The little boy has been ill, no? A confusion maybe?'

No doubt it was simply a routine check – at the height of the Cold War two Hungarian-born British nationals would automatically have been of interest to the secret police. When we drove to Baja the following day I kept checking out of the rear window, but there was no little black dot on the road behind us.

In old age, Mother recalled that visit to Erzsébet in the almshouse in Eger. 'She was very welcoming, talking fondly about my parents, their many kindnesses to her and her family. And then, glancing around the room, I noticed a small ebony figure of a prancing horse, carefully placed on top of a vitrine. I recognised it at once – it was a gift to me from my mother when I was recovering from a mastoid operation. I loved it, kept it on my bedside table always. And there it was, staring at me in this strange place. I guess she meant no harm, but I felt suddenly sick – that little horse, casually removed from our house once we had gone, it spoke to me so powerfully of our loss, our shattered family life. For me it was like a final slap in the face, just in case I had forgotten. But what could I say? I made our excuses as soon as I could and we left.'

Baja lies some two hundred kilometres south of Budapest, on the banks of the Danube. Here we visited Mother's only surviving aunt Edit (my grandmother Flóra's elder sister) and her husband Béla, a retired civil engineer, responsible for building roads and bridges over a huge territory. Always travelling, he knew everyone and was well liked. In 1944 he was tipped off about the imminent deportations and the family went into hiding.

After the war, Edit and Béla settled in a large, rambling house close to the river. It had a covered veranda and a garden filled with lush plants and creepers. At the end of a winding path I found an apricot tree, and hanging from its lower branches an old hammock. I lay there, reaching up to pluck the sweet fruit warmed by the sun – my happiest memory of that holiday. Returning to the veranda, I found Mother sitting with Edit. On the table, covered with an embroidered cloth, Aunt Edit had laid out pastries, a dark and delicious cake, and glasses of golden Tokaji. Uncle Béla reclined in a wicker chair at a tactful distance, letting the two women talk and grieve. He gave me a wink, crooked his finger and practised 'magic', plucking coins from my ears, showing me card tricks. We had no common language, just humour and affection. It was enough. We walked slowly down to the banks of the Danube where Béla kept a rowing boat, tied up at the bottom of steep steps. I took a photograph of him with my Kodak box camera, the old man looking up at me, squinting slightly against the strong afternoon sun, the waistband of his trousers almost up to his armpits, hands crossed over his comfortable belly. For a few years afterwards, he and Edit wrote to Mother in England, their italicised Gothic script growing more tremulous with the passing years. And then the letters stopped.

At the end of our trip, while we waited at Budapest airport for our flight to be announced, two officials approached with glassy smiles. There was a 'problem' with Mother's paperwork – would we please to kindly follow? We were all ushered into an interview room and my parents were then taken away for questioning. They came back looking shaken and lighter of wallet (after protracted negotiation, a significant payment to the airport police secured our seats on the flight back to London). Even Mother's British passport – that most cherished of documents – could not completely protect her, it seemed. Twenty years after she left, the country that betrayed her still had the power to threaten her new, hard-won identity.[1]

Summer 1983

Béla and Edit's daughter Lilla, Mother's cousin, visits me in London. She gives me a letter she has found among her mother's papers. It's from Flóra to Edit, sister to sister, written in the summer of 1943, by which time my grandfather Ede was already dead and life must have felt increasingly threatening for the family, with the German invasion of Hungary only a few months away. Lilla has thoughtfully translated it for me. Rather than commenting on the turmoil around her, the daily humiliation and deprivation she must have been experiencing, Flóra instead chooses to describe, with some pride, her newly acquired skill – the grafting of roses in her garden.

> Kedves Edit! The rose garden I planted last year around the house at the vineyard is really flourishing. Gabi, one of the villagers who tend the vines, has been showing me how to graft roses. Keen to learn more about this, I wrote off to the Somogyi Library in Szeged – the librarian there has very kindly sent me an extract on rose grafting from the *Rózsa-Újság* [Hungarian Rose Journal], so with luck I will become quite the expert! First, with a sharp pruning knife you cut a neat inverted 'V' into the chosen rootstock, then you dip the stem of the new shoot in honey and tuck it inside the flap of bark, binding it tight with a strip of rag. It isn't exactly foolproof, but mostly it does take. I find it magical, grafting

new life onto old. I have tried to teach Ildikó the tricks of rose grafting, but she doesn't seem to be dexterous enough. Of course, she loves the end result, prancing from bush to bush, sniffing the various scents, but she has no curiosity to learn the magic herself. Anyway, I am very excited because I have had some success with a beautiful climber called 'Madame Alfred Carrière' – it has almost white petals, the centre deepening to a pale apricot tint. The blooms have a heavenly scent and this year I have had a repeat flowering. So you see, despite everything, life could be worse.

One afternoon we are standing in my kitchen and Lilla is instructing me in the preparation of *paprikás csirke*. I am jotting down specific quantities of sweet and hot paprika, red pepper, tomato purée, chicken stock, soured cream, Lilla encouraging me to be more generous with the olive oil as I brown the chicken pieces. 'This is how my mother Edit prepared it, in our kitchen in Baja. In the summer holidays your mother Ildikó used to come visit us and we would sit together in the hammock under the apricot tree in the garden and pretend we were sailing far, far away over the ocean . . . to America.' Her eyes crinkle up in sorrow. 'To lose everyone and live with such guilt afterwards – it destroyed my mother. Me too . . . We should have gone to America, all of us.'

CHAPTER 5

Spring 1982

I am twenty-six. The train pulls into the station and I step down onto the platform cautiously. I am regressing with every minute that passes, becoming once more a schoolboy of twelve returning 'home' for the Easter holidays. Mother is waiting at the barrier, dressed for the occasion in a full-length mink coat, clutching a large black crocodile handbag.

She oozes affronted hauteur as we navigate our way to her new BMW. 'Good of you to come' – the tone of voice is acid. Firing up the engine, she presses home her grievance: 'Of course, you only put in an appearance when it's to your advantage, please don't imagine I hadn't noticed.'

Mother's opening salvo. I have been offered her old car, the reason for my trip north, but there is no such thing as a free car, it seems. She is right of course, or at least partly. I pay homage at the maternal shrine as rarely as is decently possible. Unnerved by Mother's feverish attempts to 'fit in', the house seems to me a bewildering stage set bristling with contradiction and subterfuge. Elaborate herbaceous flower beds border the path leading up to the solid oak front door – to the passer-by, the perfectly composed English home, complete with mock-Tudor beams and herringbone brickwork. But on stepping inside, there is no connection with the outside world – Mother has hung every window with net curtains, so nothing stirs, only memories. And these are of her choosing – edited, saccharine, sanitised. Unless she decides otherwise.

Building bridges after her outburst, Mother offers coffee, which I dread, knowing it will be the bitter, watery rerun of her breakfast brew. She launches in: 'Do you remember when you were chosen to deliver the reading at the school Christmas service? I have to confess it secretly amused me, but of course I was proud of you – you were only seven but played your part so well!' And indeed, I remember feeling intensely proud to have been chosen. The week before the service, Mr Cherry, the headmaster, collected me in his Wolseley and drove me over to the church to rehearse. We went through the text in the vestry, Mr Cherry suggesting where to place emphasis on particular words, where to insert a pause. And then the church warden led me up to the pulpit and switched on the sound system. Standing at the back of the church, Mr Cherry nodded in approval as my high-pitched voice rang out clearly in that cavernous space.

Finally, the day of the service arrived – for Mother a moment of almost delirious deception, duping Mr Cherry, the congregation and of course me, the unwitting Jewish boy with my neatly brushed hair, adopting a suitably pious air as I trotted up into the pulpit. Although I was unaware of the trickery being played out, I do recall a strange sense of empowerment as I looked down on the rows of neatly dressed families, with their upturned, expectant faces. Stepping forward to the lectern, I found the silk ribbon marking the verse from Matthew 1:21 and began to read: 'And she shall bring forth a son, and thou shalt call his name Jesus: for he shall save his people from their sins . . .'

I remember a similar feeling of priggish superiority as we filed into school assembly each morning, passing the five Jewish boys who stayed outside as we launched into 'All Things Bright and Beautiful'. They always looked pasty and sad, eyes lowered, huddled together under the sweep of the stairwell. As the heavy doors closed behind us, excluding those five boys, I felt a tingling pleasure of belonging. And why would I not? After all, I had the baptism card to prove it. I still have it, tucked at the back of my desk drawer as I write.

Mother's bitter-sweet delight as she enthusiastically engaged in this charade of shifting identity was anchored in an urgent and persistent need to assimilate. Indeed, it was hard-wired into her DNA. Her father Ede was a leading barrister in Eger and a member of a group closely associated with the ideology of the Freemasons; he was on the bench of the city council and sat as a judge for Eger's legal disciplinary court. Bull-headed and charismatic, he had a penchant for fine wines and good cigars and was jokingly referred to as Winston by friends and family. Aware that his professional standing was precarious in a country that was becoming increasingly anti-Semitic,[1] Ede was careful to establish friendly relations with the Catholic clergy and enrolled his three daughters at the local Catholic convent school – the Sancta Maria Általános Iskola és Leánygimnázium – an elementary and high school for girls, established by Mary Ward, a seventeenth-century Englishwoman with an enlightened approach to the education of young women.[2] Sending his girls there was clearly a strategic move by my grandfather to demonstrate the family's ongoing commitment to cultural assimilation. The school was run by Mother Ulrich, dubbed by Ede (no doubt with a wry smile) as a 'decent anti-Semite'. It seems she was also a shrewd businesswoman, with an eye for the main chance: Catholics were charged a nominal fee and Protestants paid half as much again, but Jewish pupils were obliged to pay twice the going rate.

In 1930 tragedy struck – the middle child Edit, aged only eight, contracted miliary tuberculosis. In the absence of antibiotics there was nothing to be done – her distraught parents brought the child home from the hospital and within a week she was dead. Although the family was in the process of converting to Catholicism[3] (substantial bribes to church officials had already been paid) the paperwork was far from complete and the only option was a Jewish funeral, reinforcing their religious affiliation just as they were attempting to distance themselves from the Jewish community.

Visiting Eger recently, I found the Jewish cemetery locked and overgrown. I tracked down the warden, who for a modest fee was prepared to open the rusting gates and let me in. 'No one comes here any more. There are only three Jews left in the town, the fourth is over there,' pointing to a freshly dug grave. Everywhere I looked, tombstones toppled beneath choking weeds. Many were cracked or smashed, their inscriptions mostly indecipherable. Edit's stone, half strangled with ivy, stood alone in one corner, below her name these words in Hebrew:

HER SOUL WILL BE FOREVER LINKED TO
THE CHAIN OF LIFE.

Back in his little office, the warden pulled out a large crumbling leather-bound ledger. 'It says here your grandparents purchased two adjoining plots for themselves, alongside Edit's grave. But of course . . .' He shrugged and showed me out. It seems that Ede decided to hedge his bets, despite the family's application to convert to Catholicism.

Sitting in Mother's kitchen, I push the acrid coffee to one side and shift the conversation to the territory of Mother's pre-war childhood, usually off-limits. Surprisingly, Mother engages, purring like a cat. 'I was the baby. Zsuzsi was eight years older, regarded as something of a bluestocking, and unfortunately rather plain.' Mother contrives a pitying look and then continues in an oddly girlish voice: 'Whereas I was, I have to admit, the pretty one, the preferred child. My father just adored me! He used to take me to the best café in town and buy me glasses of delicious ice cream. Sometimes his colleagues joined us – I did so enjoy being made much of, such delightful memories.' She is getting into her stride, the accusation of my neglect forgotten as she pats her hair into place, eyes flashing with enthusiasm, happily recounting her youthful beauty, the only attribute about which she has ever been entirely confident. 'I had thick shiny plaits – they were so long I could sit on them! Your grandmother Flóra used to wash my hair every week with lemon juice, to bring out the blonde highlights, you know?' Indeed, photographs of my mother as a young girl suggest, ironically, the perfect Hitler-Jugend – dressed in an Austrian dirndl, with pale grey eyes, freckles and those thick blonde plaits hanging down to her waist. In one photo she stands proudly astride her British Raleigh bike.

Years later, newly arrived in London, Mother was walking one morning along Sloane Street on her way to an appointment with a dentist in Knightsbridge – after the privations of her time in the camps, her teeth were in a precarious state. Suddenly, she heard a voice calling her name, a hand lightly touching her shoulder. She wheeled around in panic to see a Polish officer standing before her. 'Miss Heimler, I thought it was you. But where are your plaits?' This soldier was one of the Polish military elite who fled over the border into Hungary after the German invasion of Poland. Grandmother Flóra would offer hospitality every week – my mother, dressed in traditional Hungarian costume, handing round strudel and coffee. 'Can you imagine, standing there on a busy London street that morning, trying to explain to this man what happened to my plaits?' A tear falls slowly down her cheek, her broken smile recalling the terror, humiliation and loss. I reach out and hold her hand.

The next morning, as I start to reverse down the drive, Mother comes to the window: 'Take care of my car, it is

in perfect condition – not a mark on it, not a blemish.'
She smiles, painted lips framing her perfect teeth, skilfully
remodelled by the Hungarian dentist in Knightsbridge. 'And
next time, perhaps you will deign to visit without an obvious
incentive, do you think?'

CHAPTER 6

My parents met on 15 January 1950 at the house of Endre Meister, a Hungarian sculptor and commercial artist. Always known in the family by his nickname Bandi (pronounced Bondi), he and his wife Klára were close friends of Mother's parents in Eger. Bandi was also a member of a photography club in Budapest where he had met and befriended my paternal grandfather. After the war, now settled in London, Bandi and Klára became surrogate parents for my mother and the couple arranged a Sunday lunch in order to introduce the two young people. Mother almost failed to turn up. She had just started working for the Hungarian Legation and the previous evening had attended a reception at the Dorchester. Her earnings were scant, but she had saved up enough to buy the essential little black dress – 'It was a Jacqmar design in shot silk and cost fifteen guineas, a small fortune, darling, but I felt like a million dollars wearing it.' One of the luminaries attending that evening was the Austrian artist Oskar Kokoschka, who apparently took a shine to Mother, insisting she sit for him. Initially she agreed, but friends, aware of the artist's lively interest in beautiful young women, warned her away. Years later, during one of my visits home, she proudly showed me the dress. As she carefully packed it away in its yellowing tissue paper she said, rather wistfully I thought, 'This could have landed me into all kinds of trouble!' She was probably right, but nonetheless it would have been an intriguing portrait. Giddy with her success that evening, she stayed too long, returning to her Earl's Court bedsit in the early hours.

When her alarm went off at eight the next morning she was sorely tempted to roll over and ignore it, but good manners prevailed, and she dragged herself out of bed. Father, then a young research chemist in the paper division at Kodak, had competed in a fencing tournament the previous day and he too woke up that morning cursing the idea of a formal Sunday lunch. In error, he boarded a direct train to Brighton, sailing through East Croydon where he was supposed to alight. He arrived an hour and a half late, to be met by Mother's icy gaze. It was a rocky start, but – bowled over by Mother's beauty – he rose to the challenge. They discovered a shared love of Sándor Márai, whose books charted so acutely Hungary's moral collapse in the interwar period as the country slid enthusiastically towards fascism. They talked of their respective childhoods – Mother described idyllic summers at the family's vineyards and at her grandmother's estate in western Hungary, and Father told her about his early childhood on the Rózsadomb.[1] When he was very small, the family rented the upper half of a villa, with Béla Bartók and his wife occupying the lower half. My grandmother was no fan of the maestro's music – I remember her telling me, 'When he was warming up with Mozart, then I was quite happy to stay home, instructing the cook,

preparing lunch and so on. But when he started composing –
*unglaublich, schrecklich** – I went straight out shopping.'

Apparently Bartók would appear at Grandmother's door
periodically, clutching a small bag of toy cars that Father had
rolled over the balcony edge: history doesn't relate whether
Grandmother gave him a piece of her mind about his com-
positions. The Bartóks were also avid naturists and took to
lounging naked in their garden during the summer months.
This was the last straw for Grandmother – she found a villa
for sale nearby on Vérhalom utca and the family moved
within a month. Father recalled the day they took owner-
ship: 'Your grandfather was inordinately proud of the new
house – strong as an ox, he opened the front door, flipped
upside down and began to process from room to room on
his hands, roaring like a demented monster, shedding keys,
pocket watch and small change as he went, with us boys following behind, squealing with delight.'

My grandfather was no sentimentalist – unlike Mother's
father Ede, he had developed a keen international perspec-
tive. A self-made industrialist (his factory produced chemicals
for international export), he travelled widely, attending annual
trade conventions in Paris, Berlin and London, making
useful business contacts along the way. With anti-Semitism
in Hungary on the rise, he saw the writing on the wall and
by the early thirties was exploring opportunities to transfer
his production activities to France or Great Britain. Negotiations with the Hungarian Board of Trade dragged on into

* unbelievable, awful

the late thirties, despite increasingly generous bribes paid out by Grandfather to a long list of corrupt civil servants. By 1938 my father's elder brother was already in England, courtesy of Hungary's *Numerus Clausus* Act of 1920, which firmly restricted the percentage of Jews permitted access to a Hungarian university education. In December 1939 the contents of the villa were packed up and dispatched to Rotterdam, awaiting shipment to England, but the villa itself, Grandfather's handsome Mercedes saloon and the factory remained unsold, and Grandfather lingered, hoping to secure a deal. The family stayed in a grand hotel on the fashionable Margaret Island while Grandfather harried officials at the Treasury without success. Still hoping to salvage some capital, he had retained a skeletal staff to run the various chemical processes, headed up, unusually, by a young woman. Judith Meyer was an outstanding industrial chemist, hand-picked by Grandfather, but she was also a Jew and painfully aware of her precarious position. She became increasingly despondent once she realised that Grandfather – her close friend and mentor – was intent on leaving. One morning he walked into his office and found that she had hanged herself from the rafters. Profoundly shaken and overcome with guilt, he abandoned all hope of a deal and the family left Budapest for England in January 1940. I still have their dining-car tickets from the Magyar Állam-vasutak (Hungarian State Railways), discovered in Grandmother's bureau after she died.

The week before they left, Grandmother went into town and bought considerable quantities of platinum jewellery, then hopped into a taxi and visited a trusted furrier on Váci utca, who sewed the jewels into the lining of her long black Persian lamb coat. On the day of departure, weighed down by her heavy coat, she teetered along the station platform. Aged thirteen, and completely unaware of the danger they faced, Father began to giggle. There was a tense rejoinder: 'Shush! Don't say a word – just keep walking.' The jewels proved a lifesaver, providing an income during the first year in England, as Grandfather set about establishing his new business.

Mother must have felt instinctively that she could trust my father and as they walked to the station following the lunch at the Meisters, she found herself confiding in him. Sitting with her in the hospice towards the end of her life, I asked about that first meeting. 'He was very sweet and attentive, and right away I felt intensely safe in his company – much to my surprise, I found myself recounting the horrors I had been through, right there on the platform at East Croydon station.' Following this first encounter, Father wrote to his parents announcing that he had just met the girl he intended to marry. As I learned years later, he also made fleeting reference in the letter to some of what Mother had shared with him. Their response was typical of Jews who had escaped the horror – a confused mix of guilt and suspicion. I have the letter from Grandfather: 'Please proceed with caution – I am sure she is a lovely girl, but you must be aware that, given her appalling experiences, she is likely to be unstable and emotionally disturbed.' Father was incensed and, unaccountably, told Mother. It was not an auspicious start.

Undeterred, Father continued to pursue his quarry. He

knew he had competition, notably the wealthy heir to the Floris confectionery empire, famed for their elaborate cakes (favoured by Winston Churchill) but in particular for their sensational griottes in cognac. One evening Mother took Father to a cocktail party hosted by well-to-do Hungarian émigrés, probably aware that the young Floris would be among the invited guests. Soon Mother was flirting outrageously and Floris, sensing his advantage, insisted on taking down her telephone number. Father, thinking swiftly on his feet, intervened: 'It's Whitehall 1212.' Floris solemnly inscribed the number into an elegant leather-bound notebook, not realising that it was in fact the number for Scotland Yard. Mother no doubt relished the situation – two eligible young men vying for her attention – and Father's quick thinking amused her. 'He was no oil painting your father, but I adored his sense of humour.' They married a month later.

Father, appalled to learn of his young wife's traumatic year in the camps, was determined to shield her from any further assault. It was understandable that he should seek to protect her, but his strategy of concealment would have repercussions affecting all of us. In one of his first letters to her, he insisted that she concentrate on their future together, encouraging her to 'batten down the hatches'. Their compact was complete denial – they would make no reference to her wartime experience or of their shared Jewish ancestry. Once Father joined the family business and became more prosperous, he dissuaded Mother from filing a claim for compensation from the German government. His argument was that in order to prove her eligibility she would have to relive the horrors of the camps – a protracted process that he felt would destroy her. In a letter sent while on a business trip to Denmark, he added 'in any case, happily we don't need the money', which was hardly the point. Quite consciously, he set about infantilising his young wife – she would be the little woman at home, the trophy wife upon whom he could lavish all manner of creature comforts in order to permanently obliterate the horrors she had experienced. On his return from the Danish trip, he presented her with a superb platinum and moonstone choker, the first of many extravagant gifts. His motive was clear, if naive – if he showered her with enough fine clothes and jewels, she need never look back.

In many ways it was a good marriage – he was loving and protective, she in turn was delighted, at least initially, to accept the security he offered. Theirs was a richly layered relationship – Father was a gifted pianist, Mother had a pleasant singing voice, and they made music together, went to concerts, occasionally to the opera, loved dancing. I remember as a small boy watching Mother leaving for a dinner dance – long brocade evening gown, pearls and a mink stole, hair piled high, trailing a waft of perfume as she glided down the stairs. They knew how to amuse themselves and they had the money to do it. In the mid-seventies Father acquired a new Bristol, an absurdly expensive hand-built British motor car, of which he was hugely proud. They took it on touring holidays along the Loire Valley, visited the Italian Lakes and frequently Zurich, where Father had business dealings. They dined at La Tour d'Argent in Paris, took the Blue Train from Pretoria to Cape Town, flew to New York in the early sixties, attended the Bayreuth and Salzburg festivals, went to Wimbledon (Father was a particular fan of Arthur Ashe and Evonne Goolagong) and were regular theatregoers. To the casual observer the perfect couple – widely read, amusing and generous hosts, secure in their extensive circle of similarly well-to-do friends.

But behind closed doors, Mother battled with her ghosts. As stipulated by Father, she attempted to banish her horrors, hiding them in a dark cupboard and throwing away the key. But those demons refused to lie low, persistently clamouring to be let out. In the mid-sixties Mother evidently decided to ignore Father's earlier diktat and revisit the idea of claiming compensation. After her death I found some correspondence filed away in her writing case, including various letters from a Dr S. Roth who presumably acted as an intermediary between claimants and the German government. On 27 August 1964, he wrote: 'You would certainly be entitled to compensation for deprivation of liberty and any damage to health which your persecution has caused – not only physical injuries are eligible but also psychological or neurological complaints (anxiety states, nightmares, depression, headaches etc.) which are so often the aftermath of persecution and degradation. Such a claim could still be submitted.' A subsequent letter offered Mother an appointment at Roth's offices in Cleveland Square, near Paddington, on 1 October at 9 a.m. but there is no further communication. Travelling by train to London to meet with Dr Roth would have meant a two-day absence – Mother would have had to tell Father and almost certainly he vetoed the idea.

There was a further price to pay for accepting Father's protection, and the financial stability that entailed came at a cost: in effect it required her to abandon all hope of personal agency. Perhaps relinquishing all responsibility was a relief – perhaps the rigours of survival had exhausted all resilience. The skewed power dynamics that characterised their marriage was a mirroring of wider forces at play. For Father, the honouring of identity was too dangerous a game – his instinct to protect my mother was both an expression of control and also prompted by the fear of exposure.

When she died, I set about clearing her bedroom. At the back of a drawer in her dressing table, I found a few crumpled sheets of paper on which she had scribbled some notes in pencil. My parents had always presented an implacably united front but here was bitterness and resentment scrawled across every page, written in a shaking hand towards the end of her life. She railed against the terms of the marriage, the constant control he exerted. 'Where is my independence, where is my freedom? He has turned me into a child. I am made a prisoner – again.'

CHAPTER 7

Throughout my childhood, Father felt excluded and increasingly concerned by the intensely symbiotic relationship between Mother and me. He watched us with tacit disapproval, recognising that her hold over me was apparently non-negotiable. As a result, my relationship with him was conflicted and contradictory – at times I turned to him as a necessary escape route, but more often I resented his intrusion.

He spoke fondly of his own father as 'the benign dictator' and this clearly influenced his own parenting style. A firm disciplinarian, his mood could switch in an instant if I stepped out of line, his default jocular affection erased by an icy, terrifying stare. At breakfast he would erect the morning edition of the *Daily Telegraph* as a barrier to conversation – occasionally his hand would reach round for his coffee cup, but it was clear that no other distraction was to be countenanced.

When I was small, I used to dread the sound of his car on the drive in the early evening. As he entered the hallway, I could hear Mother's voice recounting in minute detail my latest misdemeanour. His firm allegiance to Mother in all things meant I had no room for manoeuvre and reprimands usually took the form of a scathing telling-off and no pocket money. On one occasion (I can't remember the specific crime) he marched me down to the garden house, grabbed a flimsy bamboo stick and attempted to cane me with it. It broke almost immediately (much to his relief, I suspect) and I got away with 'Go to your room and no supper!' which seemed to me a reasonable outcome.

His insistence on academic success was relentless. Aged five, I was enrolled at a private preparatory school. It was a gloomy place, formerly the home of a nineteenth-century shipping magnate. Solidly built in stone in the Victorian High Gothic style, it was surrounded by dark shrubberies of laurel and tall beech trees. Father drove me to school on my first day – there is a picture of me taken by him, clutching my shoe bag, trying to put on a brave face. As he left me at the front door he whispered in my ear: 'You can be anything you want to be, remember that.'

As my education progressed through subsequent schools, he would prepare me for end-of-term exams by setting me weekly tests. Maths was my greatest failing. 'How can you not understand?' he would ask, his voice rising in irritation. 'There is poetry in mathematics, if you would only look!' My inability to grasp even the basic concepts was particularly frustrating for him, as was my ineptitude in science. By way of encouragement, before I set off for the exams he would present me with what he called a 'DO IT'. On the reverse of one of his business cards he would write 'SIMON CAN DO IT, AND HE WILL DO IT VERY WELL!' This instruction, tucked into my blazer pocket, tended to have variable results. As a very small boy, when indulgent adults asked the inevitable question 'And what do you want to be when you grow up?' Father had coached me to respond confidently 'I am going to be an engineer!' I think he had fond notions of my joining the family firm in due course, but since I spent most of my time sketching ladies in elegant evening dresses, this seemed an increasingly unlikely outcome. After his death, when I started to empty the contents of the house, I came upon several dusty boxes of unopened Meccano sets stacked on a high shelf in the garage, no doubt purchased by Father in the forlorn hope that I might develop an interest in construction.

I remember, aged six or seven, sitting on the edge of the bath one morning as Father shaved, listening to stories about his various eccentric Hungarian relatives. Aunt Kitty was a case in point. Rather plain, she was left on the shelf (Father's words) until in desperation the family scouted around and found her a husband. Their choice turned out to be a bit of a chancer.

Suspiciously good-looking, Zoltán absconded with Kitty's dowry shortly after the wedding and was never heard of again. Quietly accepting her lot, she spent the rest of her life traipsing from one set of relatives to the next. Despite her straitened circumstances, she would arrive for lunch with a couple of herrings wrapped in paper, bought that morning at the Nagycsarnok, Budapest's central market. Father and his elder brother Laci would run down the hill to meet her, a tall, ungainly figure dressed in black, trudging up the Rózsadomb in the blazing heat of a Hungarian summer's day, the herrings stuffed into one of the pockets of her long coat. And always, trailing behind her, a long line of hopeful alley cats. 'Poor Kitty. Mother would politely accept the packet of half-rotten fish and throw it straight into the garbage.' 'What happened to her?' Father, standing in front of the shaving mirror, his razor poised in mid-air: 'I don't know. We left and then the war came.' I must have been about eight when he told me this story and I remember wondering how people could be left behind like that, just forgotten, like discarded luggage. It occurred to me that if he could so casually jettison an aunt, what about me? If I failed in some way to please him would I too be dropped by the wayside? 'Come on, I'll finish up here, then we can head out for a walk.' His matter-of-fact manner scared me. I made up some excuse about homework, retreated to my bedroom and shut the door.

On Sunday mornings Mother would have breakfast in bed. Father had a limited repertoire – either a greyish mound of scrambled eggs with mushrooms or a fancy alternative of tinned asparagus, each stem rolled up in a wafer-thin slice of Brunswick ham, presented alongside a large cup of coffee and a glass of freshly squeezed orange juice. Mother's tray was pale pink with a scalloped edge and a print of an Audubon rose beneath the varnish; my job was to pick a posy of flowers to complete the ensemble.

In later years, when travelling home for the weekend, I would always buy a bunch of flowers and present these to Mother. This was expected, indeed obligatory, but Mother would always feign surprise. 'Oh, DARLING, how lovely, but you really shouldn't!' A week later I would receive, without fail, a follow-up call. Always the same formula: 'Do you know, your lovely flowers are still going strong!' On one occasion my train was late (already a crisis looming) and I forgot to stop at the florist. Mother's stony face when she opened the door and saw me empty-handed spoke volumes. I never made that mistake again.

Once the tray had been delivered upstairs, we were temporarily off the hook. Father and I would sit in the breakfast room and he would tell me about the exotic cars he saw in pre-war Budapest – Packards, Buicks, Lancias and, best of all, the fleet of sumptuous automobiles belonging to the Chilean ambassador, whose residence was right across the street. Father, aged about eight, made friends with the chauffeur who allowed him to polish the ambassador's Isotta Fraschini limousine: the Tipo 8A Castagna Transformable was a vast beast with an impossibly long bonnet housing a powerful straight-eight engine. It was painted a midnight blue, the passenger seats upholstered in velvet, and the internal furnishings – handles, door sliders, interior light fittings – all nickel-plated; better still, the dash instrumentation was backlit with a soft violet glow and the radiator surmounted with an illuminated winged goddess.[1] Growing up in the 1960s, I felt keenly that I had been born in the wrong era – the humdrum Rovers, Vauxhall Crestas and the occasional Jaguar burbling around our neighbouring streets seemed poor substitutes.

Father was an enthusiastic photographer and instructed a carpenter to modify his study so it could double as a darkroom. His teak desktop incorporated a hatch neatly concealing a sink below and at the far end stood his enlarger, with photographic paper, chemicals and trays stashed in a cupboard below. He and I would retreat there on Sunday evenings, a safe haven off-limits to Mother who knew better than to intrude and potentially ruin the light-sensitive printing process. To me, the darkroom felt like the setting for a sci-fi movie, with Father issuing whispered instructions, as if somehow our voices might disturb the mysterious processes at play. He taught me the technique known as 'Dodge and Burn' – manipulating an image by holding a cardboard template over the photographic paper as it was exposed under the enlarger, so that a particular area, for instance a cloudscape, could be enhanced. 'It's a bit of a cheat, but a little cheating never did anyone any harm.' Once the photographic paper had been dipped into the tray of developing liquid, my job was to nudge it from side to side in the tray, the gentle rocking motion accelerating the chemical reaction. The soft thudding of the paper, as it collided first with one side of the tray and then the other, lulled us into a sort of stupor as we stood there, waiting under the dull red light for the ghostly image to emerge. Once it was sufficiently developed, Father would take a pair of large wooden tongs, transfer the dripping paper into a tray containing fixing solution and then hang it up to dry. We were making magic, and Mother was not part of the equation.

Looking back, however, I wonder if Father's lessons in visual trickery in some way echoed Mother's persistent attempts to rearrange reality – 'a little cheating never did anyone any harm'. In their different ways, they both offered a template for disguise, encouraging me in my adult life to present to the world an 'acceptable' version of myself in order to avoid any possibility of detection – either of my Jewish identity or of my sexual orientation.

Mother had a weekly appointment at the hairdresser's every Saturday, so Father would drive me into town to spend an hour or two in the decaying calm of the town library. An imposing stone staircase ascended to the first-floor reading rooms, top-lit and grandly proportioned, with wrought-iron spiral stairways leading to upper galleries and committee rooms. At the far end of one of the reading rooms was a small hatch in the wall, presided over by an old lady who always wore the same lavender-coloured crocheted cardigan. Father would give me a thruppenny bit for a glass of milk and a chocolate biscuit, then settle me down in one of the alcoves with a stack of books that he had carefully selected – *Tarka the Otter*, *White Fang*, *King Solomon's Mines*. These Saturday expeditions to the library were, as with our photography sessions, part of Father's strategy to remove me at least temporarily from Mother's orbit, introducing me to the tales of endurance, heroism and adventure he had enjoyed as a boy. Instead, my attention would wander, the pile of required reading unopened as I wriggled into the deepest part of my wicker chair, breathing in the stillness, the smell of old leather bindings on the shelves around me, the watery light from the distant skylights forming dappled patterns on the worn parquet flooring.

Meanwhile, Father would scan the stacks in the neighbouring room, hunting out suitable reading matter for Mother, avoiding anything that might be deemed too disturbing. The novels of H. E. Bates were firm favourites – *The Jacaranda Tree* and *A Moment in Time* in particular – as well as E. F. Benson's *Mapp & Lucia* series, and of course all the Miss Marple books, principally because St Mary Mead reminded Mother of village life in the late 1940s, her first experience of England. Later, she read Karen Blixen's *Out of Africa*, loved *The No. 1 Ladies' Detective Agency* series by Alexander McCall Smith and, perhaps not surprisingly, Willa Cather's *My Ántonia*, with its overarching theme of nostalgia and exile.

On country walks, Father would cup his hands together and blow gently, making a noise that perfectly mimicked a hooting owl. He tried to show me, but Mother would grow irritated and hurry us along, so I never learned his trick. He also swam the crawl with great style and one summer when I was about eight years old decided to teach me, but I panicked every time I had to rotate my head below the water, so after a few sessions he gave up. There were further efforts to coach me in tennis, squash and fencing – I fared moderately at the first two, but instinctively loathed wielding a fencing foil, finding the aggressive parry and thrust both terrifying and pointless. As a regional fencing champion, Father was not impressed – his disappointment was palpable and I recognised from an early age that I couldn't compete. I used to dread the school sports day each summer. All boys had to run at least one race and I always came last, without fail. One year Father filmed the occasion with his cine camera, princi-pally I suspect to record Mother looking stylish in a new hat, but also in the hope that I might surprise him. Weeks later he set up the projector and, much to Mother's uncontrolled merriment, played the film in reverse so that I appeared to win the race, albeit backwards. An affectionate tease perhaps, and yet I knew that for Father winning was, in the end, the only option.

During school holidays I was sometimes allowed to accompany Father to the factory. The business was diverse in output – with satellite companies in Holland and Greece, and licensees in the USA, Singapore and China – but one of its core specialisations was marine electroplating. As a small boy, I used to stand at the factory gates, watching the lorries as they arrived in their livery of sage green. Vast piston rings would be slowly craned onto the loading bay and then deliv-ered to the factory floor to be lowered into electroplating tanks. The air in the plating hall was thick with acrid chemical fumes, scraping the back of my throat till I almost gagged. I remember my intense embarrassment as Father and I walked between the towering vats, the workers touching their cloth caps as we passed by.

During one visit to the factory, the foreman came up to discuss a technical problem with Father, then turned to me with a wink. 'So is the wee laddie coming to work here, eh?' I smiled weakly, Father's hand clamped firmly to my shoulder. 'Ah yes, we'll make a chemical engineer of him yet!'

One evening Father arrived home ashen-faced. A young lad at the factory had been walking along the edge of one of the towering vats of acid to adjust a plating rig. Overcome by the fumes, he lost his balance and fell. Father paced up and down, dinner untouched. I left the table as quickly as I could but for weeks after dreamt that I too was falling, unnoticed, into a vat of acid.

Overlooking the factory floor, Father's office had a touch of Scandinavian elegance – teak-lined walls and elegant bronze-framed bookcases filled with technical books, a long rosewood conference table, and above it an illuminated alcove proudly displaying the firm's Queen's Award to Industry. On these visits Father would let me choose a pencil from one of the many compartments in his imposing desk. The Telex machine in the adjoining office was another excitement, spooling out its tickertape messages from Hong Kong, Basel, Singapore and New York. Mary Perkins, Father's secretary, all sixties bouffant and sharp spectacles, would leap to her feet as they came through and snip them into manageable lengths, taking them through to Father on a black leather tray. She made me mugs of hot chocolate and fed me biscuits, and away from the stench and the noise below I would fantasise about working here when I grew up. But in reality I knew that the two spaces – the chairman's office and the factory floor – were indelibly linked, one dependent on the other. When Father was on the phone in his office next door, I would sidle into his tall-backed leather chair at the head of the gleaming conference table and pretend to hold a meeting, making imaginary notes with my trophy pencil. But I knew I had no interest in what was happening down on the factory floor. I was an impostor – there was no place for me here.

The idea that I might have some kind of agency, even a degree of personal choice, was never part of Father's mindset. He saw it as his mission to scrutinise every aspect of my life with forensic energy. One of the first things he turned his attention to was my handwriting. By the age of six or so, my writing had developed into a neat, upright and slightly rounded script. I was rather proud of it and that year won the school handwriting prize, but Father would have none of it. 'This will never do – you need a more forward-slanting script, else you will never write sufficiently fast in examinations.' And so he set to, devising daily exercises to recast my script into a form that he felt was more practical, efficient and no doubt more masculine. As a result, my handwriting is, to this day, a carbon copy of his own.

When the A-level results were announced, my headmaster called us into his office. Father had decided that I should read History at university, but it transpired that I had a better mark in English than History, despite both being A-grades. Perhaps I should reconsider? Father intervened immediately, without hesitation: 'Simon can read novels in his spare time, he is going to read History.' And that was that.

A few weeks later, for my final school concert, I was chosen to play the solo in Mozart's 3rd violin concerto. I practised for weeks beforehand and knew the score by heart, but at the last moment I panicked and took a music stand out onto the stage. Father had assembled a large group of friends, family and business acquaintances for the occasion, and afterwards everyone gathered in the school foyer. He clapped me on the shoulder: 'Not bad, not bad – although, shame about the music stand.'

There were moments when I redeemed myself. After sitting the entrance exam for Cambridge, I went to work in a small country hotel. One morning Father telephoned me: I had won an exhibition (not quite as stellar as a scholarship, but nonetheless a recognition of merit). I remember so clearly – once I'd recovered from my initial disbelief – hearing the excitement in his voice, and feeling intensely pleased for him rather than for myself.

By my early thirties I was working in a reasonably senior position for a PR agency in London. Father knew that my salary was fairly modest and would make studied references to the successful sons of friends and neighbours. 'The Dickson boy has just landed a plum job as a research engineer at Rolls-Royce. I always knew he was a bright lad.' Or 'Did you know that Jonathan [a contemporary of mine at prep school] has been made a junior partner at his law firm?' The subtext was clear: 'What about you? Where is your success?' I began to scour the job pages of the *Guardian* more carefully and, to my relief, was appointed to run the communications team for a large architectural practice. I immediately picked up the phone and rang home. Father launched in: 'What do you know about this outfit? Are they sound?' I was taken aback: 'Father, this place has an international reputation – it's a big deal!' 'Very well, I'll do some research and get back to you. I hope you haven't been rash enough to accept the job yet.

What salary are they offering, by the way?' He called me back the next day. 'I have taken some soundings, seems kosher – go ahead.' And then, as an afterthought: 'Well done.'

No accident that I proved reasonably adept in this role – my early training in deference, prioritising the needs of others, was a valuable asset as I navigated the competing egos of more than a dozen directors. Mother and Father were quick to visit – I gave them a tour of the studio and then took them to lunch at the restaurant next door. I had arranged a company Mercedes to drive them back to their London club, and as Father settled into the plush leather seat, he turned to Mother: 'Do you know, I think our boy might come good after all!' As time went by, he came to revise that opinion, puzzled by my subsequent career moves and dismayed at my inability to earn 'real money', the inevitable, inescapable benchmark of success in his terms.

7 July 2019

I get a call from Father's friend Sam. Arriving to collect Father for their usual Sunday swim, he rings the doorbell but gets no reply. Anxious, he calls the police who turn up and force an entry. Father is bemused to find a young police-woman interrupting his morning shower and has no recollection of any arrangement with Sam. 'You had better head up on the next train, your father seems very confused.' The first sign that all is not well.

3 August 2019

The sound of the stairlift wakes me at 3 a.m. Father, bundled in his dressing gown, is making a slow descent to the hallway below. 'Pa, it's the middle of the night. Where are you going?' Shifting in his throne, he giggles like a schoolboy who has been rumbled on his way to raid the tuck shop. 'I honestly don't know . . .' And then he begins to weep. I get him back to bed. He has no memory of this escapade the following morning. He sits at the breakfast table staring at his coffee cup, avoiding my eyes. I know the moment has come for the conversation I have been dreading: 'Pa, you know the power-of-attorney document we drew up? I think, maybe, it's time I assume that role, don't you?' He stares into the distance, then his eyes swivel back to me. Does his crumpled smile suggest defeat, resignation – or can I detect a whiff of irony? 'I think, maybe, you're right.' He totters to his feet and leaves the room.

1 September 2019

Father is lying in a hospital bed which has been installed in a downstairs room facing the garden. I listen to his jagged breathing, his head cradled in a mound of soft pillows. His dark eyes are open, unblinking, perhaps unseeing now the morphine has kicked in. I moisten his mouth with a sponge, adjust his covers, small acts. A few months before, processing the results of the MRI scans that confirm the tumours lodged in his brain, he turned to the doctor with a cool eye: 'I want a dignified death, if such a thing is possible. I have no more projects. It has been a good life.'

A late-summer afternoon, Glenn Gould playing Bach, Father's breath faltering, as if waiting for the closure of a particular cadence. I hold his hand and watch the feeble pulse at the base of his neck. And then it stops.

CHAPTER 8

Mother is in her late eighties, manoeuvring her way along the hallway. She pushes a Zimmer frame, dragging her legs slowly behind, each move accompanied by loud cracks from her disintegrating hips. Her progress is precarious and painfully slow, and as she passes the hall table she loses her balance and starts to fall. I catch her, but one of her flailing hands sweeps a vase crashing to the floor. Once I have settled her in her chair, I gather the broken fragments. 'Ah, we bought that in Portugal, I gave the exact same one to Marie-Ange, do you remember?'

Summer 1969

I do remember. We were staying in a family hotel in the hills above Porto. Guests with children of similar age gravitated to one another, my mother striking up conversation with a woman from Geneva. Marie-Ange was the complete opposite of Mother – small and spry, a teacher of eurythmics. Her husband, Aubrey, was a tall, angular Englishman, his manner awkward, somehow tortured. He looked as though he would only ever be truly happy on a cricket pitch, far away from his family. There were three children, sixteen-year-old Jean-Luc and much younger twins. The women chatted eagerly and I watched as an intense friendship developed. I was surprised, and flattered, that Jean-Luc seemed in some way protective of me. One morning I lost my footing, bumping my head on the side of the pool and tumbling into the water. Jean-Luc was practising dives and I watched him quite calmly – his arcing torso distorting strangely as his body sliced through the surface above me, growing more distant as I sank slowly to the bottom. Then I was lying on the cool paving slabs. I saw his mouth moving, but I couldn't hear him – he was shaking me and something snapped in my ears. He was shouting: 'Xavier, Xavier – talk to me!' But I didn't understand – why was he calling me that name?

Over the following two weeks my father and Aubrey played tennis, the wives drove to the local town in search of embroidered linen, often sitting together at one end of the terrace sipping cocktails, talking intently, hands clasped. One evening Mother asked me to bring her a wrap from her room as there was a slight chill in the evening air. As I approached their table, Marie-Ange stood up abruptly, walking away to the terrace railing, dabbing her eyes with a handkerchief. Mother turned to me, her eyes puffy and red. She snatched the wrap from me – it was clear I was not to intervene.

Later that evening, Jean-Luc suggested we go to the village to buy ice cream. As we walked past the hotel gates, he looped an arm over my shoulder and began to talk quietly. 'Seven years ago we were on holiday, driving over the Alps – me, my father, mother and my little brother Xavier. We were singing some ridiculous song, Father conducting us, his arms waving like a crazy person, showing off as he steered round the tight hairpin bends. Xavier was screaming with delight as Father fooled around. I remember Xavier, turning back to me, sticking his tongue out, you know, the usual kid brother stuff. And then there was this huge bus right in front of us and Father had no time to swerve. It hit us head-on. They said the car just snapped in two. Mother and I were found about eighty feet away, lying together on the back seat. There was nothing really left of the front part of the car. So, Aubrey' – his face wincing slightly as he said the name – 'Aubrey is my stepfather, the twins are my half-brothers. I just thought you should know.' As we sat in the village square eating our ice creams, I began to wonder why he had decided to share this sad story with me – after all, we barely knew each other. We walked back in silence. Entering the hotel lobby, Jean-Luc sprinted up the main stairway two at a time – when he reached the first landing, he leaned over the banister and called down to me: 'Goodnight – Xavier!' His face creased into a kind of crooked smile, and then he disappeared.

The two women agreed that I would join the family in Chamonix for a skiing trip the following Easter. On our last day of the holiday Mother and I went into town. We walked along a shady boulevard, my forefinger held in the cool crook of her forearm, our favourite connecting gesture. 'Mother, I'm not sure about this idea. For one thing I can't ski. And for another, something feels wrong. Somehow, I don't think these people are very happy.' 'Nonsense, darling, Marie-Ange could not be more charming. She already refers to you as her "borrowed treasure" – isn't that nice?' Mother propelled me into the cafe on the main square and ordered ice creams. All was well, it seemed.

A few weeks later, a letter arrived for me at home: 'Dear Xavier, we miss you . . . Until next Easter, yours – Marie-Ange and Jean-Luc.' Two strangers drawing me into their cat's cradle of loss and make-believe – a sinister seduction that flattered my thirteen-year-old vanity. I knew I should say nothing about this and stuffed the letter quickly to the back of my desk drawer.

April 1970

A few days after the end of the spring term, I was on a train to London. Rosamund Grantham, an aunt of Aubrey, was standing by the barrier at King's Cross – short grey hair, tweed suit and sensible shoes. 'Be on your best behaviour, darling,' Mother instructed me. 'She used to work at the Foreign Office. Something frightfully important.' Rosamund's manner was brusque, with a genial chuckle that I didn't entirely trust. 'Come along now, chop-chop, else we shall miss the boat train from Victoria.' Once installed on the train, I remembered Mother's instruction: 'Be sure to make lively conversation, it's so kind of Rosamund to take you under her wing.' I launched in dutifully: 'Rosamund, what did you do at the Foreign Office? And what IS the Foreign Office exactly?' Pale grey eyes flickered in my direction. 'I say, we're just passing Chatham Docks. That's where HMS

Victory was built, did you know? I assume you've learned about Nelson and Trafalgar at school?' I was being put on the spot and forgot that Rosamund had neatly avoided my question.

The chalet, enveloped in crystal-white snow, sat high above the village, wide verandas offering spectacular views over the mountains. Marie-Ange greeted us at the door, but I immediately sensed that something had shifted since last summer's seductive hijacking of my identity. Secretly, I was intrigued at the prospect of slipping once again into the shoes of the dead child, but now there was no mention of Xavier. Nothing was said but it was clear I had been invited under sufferance. Another family had joined the party and Jean-Luc's focus was elsewhere; I was put in a room with the twins. Marie-Ange occasionally threw me a distracted smile while coordinating meals for fourteen guests. The first evening I saw her talking in a corner with Rosamund and I walked over to join them, but seeing me approach, they got up pointedly and moved away. I remembered Mother's instructions at the train station and offered to help, but carrying a salad bowl to the table I tripped, throwing the contents over a white woollen rug. Aubrey leapt to his feet, thrusting me aside to clear the mess, hissing angrily in my ear, 'Ruddy little fool!' In the evenings, the conversation rattled along in French which I found hard to follow and we played board games which I didn't understand. The skiing was a disaster. No lessons were organised for me, so I slithered, terrified, over the icy snow in blinding sunshine, watching the others dart down the slopes, their every movement assured and stylish. On the last day in Chamonix, Rosamund and I shared a ski lift. At the top, she zipped up her ski suit and adjusted her goggles. 'Right, young man, see you at the bottom. Chop-chop!' I watched as she competently negotiated the first bend and disappeared from view. Almost immediately, I careened clumsily into a snowdrift and landed, crab-like, my sticks and skis embedded vertically as if I had been hung out to dry. A passing skier rescued me half an hour later and I trudged in misery down the mountain, my face erupting in spectacular blisters from the fierce mountain sun.

Looking back, I suspect that Aubrey and his aunt must have rumbled the game of substitution that was playing out before them and tackled Marie-Ange – how else to explain my feeling of being kept firmly at arm's length?

A week later we left for Geneva and the dynamic shifted yet again. Rosamund returned to London and Aubrey was occupied with work. No longer under surveillance, perhaps Marie-Ange felt she had free rein to step through the looking glass. The family house, on a wide avenue in a well-heeled suburb, was surprisingly formal – antiques, Persian carpets, an imposing eighteenth-century tapestry hanging in the hallway. Marie-Ange bustled about, organising the children's luggage, preparing supper. 'You're up on the second floor, my dear – perhaps you would like to go unpack?' I knew, immediately as I pushed the door open, that this was his room.

The walls were a dusty sky blue, with wisps of painted clouds flitting across the ceiling. There were posters of Batman and a bright red Ferrari, small ski boots and skis stashed in one corner, a shelf with neatly arranged model cars, a desk with a pile of *Tintin* books. I flung myself onto the bed, staring up at the ceiling where a model RAF Spitfire, suspended by a thread, circled slowly in the breeze. Except for the ski boots, this could have been my room. I fell asleep and dreamt I was back on the ski slope, sliding out of control over the glistening ice.

I woke to the sound of a bell tinkling in the hallway below. When I stumbled downstairs, everyone else was already seated at the dining table. Marie-Ange gestured to an empty space beside her: '*Dépêche-toi, chéri.*' I mumbled apologies and scrambled into my chair, embarrassed. I reached for my napkin, tightly rolled in a silver band engraved with the single letter 'X'. Marie-Ange gave my hand a light pat, the meal continued.

The week passed quickly. Jean-Luc introduced me to his cousin Francine who was studying at the music conservatoire. I borrowed a violin and we played duets together, Jean-Luc listening with that same crooked smile I remembered from last summer. Marie-Ange took me to one of her classes and I noted how completely she commanded the space, minutely directing the children's movements, how they responded instinctively to every inflexion of her voice – authoritative, coaxing, triumphant. At a certain point she flicked a glance in my direction, then demonstrated a subtle arabesque with catlike grace. As we walked to her car, she turned to me, her eyes dancing. 'Oh, Xavier, *chéri*, that was perfect – such a good class!' Immediately she gasped, her face torn into thin strips of pain. 'I must stop this. I'm so sorry, really.' We drove home in silence. As we entered the house, she said, 'Can you forgive me? I have no right, I know . . .'

On the last evening it began to snow. After supper Marie-Ange seemed distracted, agitated. I offered to help clear the dishes but she waved me away. 'You had better go upstairs and pack.' Dismissed, I slowly climbed the stairs to Xavier's bedroom and lay on his bed, pinned down by her anger: I was leaving and she was losing Xavier, all over again. Smudges of grey snow started to stick to the windowpane and suddenly the room seemed stifling.

I threw open the door and clattered down the stairs, two at a time. Aubrey was in his study. 'I want to go and say goodbye to Francine, can I borrow the Solex?' He was writing, lifted his head briefly and refused as I knew he would, but I persisted and was surprised when he suddenly spat out: 'OK, take it, just leave me in peace!' I hurried out to the garage before he could change his mind, cranked up the moped and set off. Somehow, I navigated my way across town, the snow swirling softly against a dusk-red sky. It was a relief to find refuge in a happy, shambolic household, away from Aubrey's terse disapproval. When I next looked at my watch it was past ten o'clock and, reluctantly, I knew I should head back. Francine was anxious – it was dark and the snow was thicker, more persistent. I assured her I would be fine, although secretly I wasn't convinced. Halfway home, I came to an intersection that I had to cross diagonally and waited in the central reservation for a gap in the oncoming traffic. There was a Peugeot heading towards me but it was a long way off so I decided to chance it. The Solex tyres flailed, spinning in the slush, and too late I realised that I couldn't pick up enough speed and then the car was bearing down on me, headlights blinding. There was a searing pain in my right leg as the car smashed into me and after that everything froze into separate snapshots. I arced upward into the night sky and watched calmly as the horizon flipped a quarter-turn, then flipped again, and now the street lights were hanging downward. Then I was lying in a thick snowbank at the side of the road, a huddle of faces bending over me, all shouting at the same time in excitable French. At the hospital, an X-ray revealed a hairline fracture – when the ambulance took me back to the house a couple of days later, one leg in plaster, Marie-Ange was waiting at the door, her face drawn and grey. Jean-Luc carried me upstairs, laying me gently on the bed. The next morning, I shuffled awkwardly into the taxi, the family standing tight-lipped to watch me leave. At the last minute, Marie-Ange darted to the car, handing me a small package which I stuffed unopened into my coat pocket, waving as the car pulled away. As I settled into my seat on the plane, I remembered and pulled it out. Removing the tissue paper, I found a small box covered in dull red leather and released the catch. The lid snapped open to reveal the silver napkin ring engraved with the letter 'X'.

On the flight home, the stabbing pain in my leg grew more intense, as did my sense of humiliation. Shivering in my seat, I was trying to fathom what Mother might have intended, as I recalled the two women weeping together on that summer evening. The middle-aged lady beside me, noticing my distress, placed a comforting hand on my arm.

'Are you all right, my dear, first time flying, eh?' I nodded and pretended to read my book but the page was a blur – why had my mother offered me as a temporary substitute for that dead boy? The more I thought about it, the grubbier the game appeared to be, if it was a game at all. I sensed I had been used, but my fourteen-year-old self couldn't work out why. I felt the beginnings of anger now, frustrated by my inability to fight my way through this maze of her making, and ashamed too, knowing I would never find it possible to confront her.

I never did, and fifty years later I am still trying to make sense of this dark episode. An impulsive act on Mother's part, or a chance to demonstrate her complete control? Was the trip an elaborate set-up, a test to see how skilfully I could slip from one life into another – as she had done? Certainly her gesture had little to do with generosity, given that the commodity she offered was on temporary loan, to be returned to sender. Whatever her motive, I suspect she had no idea of the damage she inflicted on both Marie-Ange and me.

At the airport I could see Father standing at the barrier, his face full of thunder. Spotting a rubbish bin, I stuffed the small package inside – I wonder now if I should have handed it to Mother, as a lasting reminder of what she had done.

CHAPTER 9

April 1969

One morning Father found Mother and me earnestly discussing what outfit she should wear that evening, riffling through her jewellery box to pick out the perfect ensemble. Clearly, he felt something had to be done. A few days later I overheard a particularly heated exchange as I walked downstairs: 'You are turning our son into a little pansy – I won't have it! A different environment is called for.' And then an ominous silence as I entered the room, Mother darting a meaningful look at Father. Father cleared his throat. 'Simon, you'll be sitting for the Common Entrance Exam quite soon and your mother and I have been discussing various options. On balance, I feel boarding school might be the best way forward.' Cue a sharp intake of breath from Mother. I said nothing but immediately thought of Richard, one of my best friends from prep school, who had been sent away at seven and wrote me letters describing the horrors of early-morning runs and cold showers. The prospect was not a happy one.

Over the next few days there were increasingly bitter arguments between them, but Father won the day – I was to be sent away. Father retired to his study, quietly triumphant, while Mother – distraught at the prospect of a protracted separation (I was not on temporary loan this time) – dissolved into paroxysms of grief. I retreated to my room, numb with panic. None of us prepared for what was to follow.

During the first week at the new school, I discovered the tennis courts in a far corner of the school grounds, shielded from view by a tall yew hedge. I came here to weep, lonely, scared and ashamed of the jeers and taunts from the other boys. A failure at every type of sport, I was not popular.

I had been dispatched to school with a typed card pasted onto the inside lid of my tuckbox. Mother's baffling instructions read as follows:

> Be punctual
> Don't contradict
> Don't be cheeky
> Know your place
> Don't speak out of turn
> Be attentive
> Don't stick out like a sore thumb
> Succeed!

My sense of dislocation was total, overwhelming. I took refuge in the art studio, presided over by Mr Dees, who wore a large garnet ring and encouraged me to take up tapestry. I knew I was not making a success of school, but each week when I rang home I rehearsed my patter in advance, arranged my pinched face into something approximating a smile, lifted the receiver, dropped the coin into the slot. 'Hullo, Mother. Yes, yes, school is huge fun. I've made loads of friends, it's going really, really well!' I walked away down the long grey linoleum corridor, slipped out of a side door and made for the tennis courts.

Above all, I dreaded the encounters with bullying older boys. One winter afternoon, showering after rugby (which, of course, I hated), I was kicked and pummelled to the floor by one of them, while others crowded round shouting, 'Filthy Jew, go home!' Trying to escape the onslaught of freezing water and vicious kicks, I yelled at them: 'I'm not Jewish! Leave me alone!' That riled them even more – a couple of them yanked me to my feet while the tallest one punched me repeatedly in the face, then hurled me to the floor. 'That'll teach you to answer back, filthy Jew-boy!' I lay there, dizzy from the blows, watching the cold water turn red as it swilled into the drain.

That evening, getting ready for bed, I made an inventory of my pasty, bruised face in the bathroom mirror: thick, curling hair, dark eyes, a small squared-off nose. I knew I didn't look typically English – how could I, with Hungarian parents and a name like Weisz – but why did they think I was Jewish? Pulling on my pyjama bottoms, I looked down at my foreskin with a rush of gratitude – were they too stupid to notice that I wasn't circumcised? Or was calling me a Jew just a convenient pretext to rough me up?

No call home on that occasion – I remember desperately wanting to but knowing instinctively I couldn't. 'Know your place' – Mother's diktat. Suddenly, I felt unmoored, fearful. Who was I? What was my place? Clearly I didn't fit in, but I had no idea why. Even at the age of thirteen I sensed there were things my parents were hiding from me but I knew that any enquiry was out of the question. Impossible to admit that I had been beaten up, and equally impossible to say why – my role was to shield them from any hint of unpleasantness. This humiliation had to be my secret, darkly held and far more damaging than the bruises, which soon faded. Father's mantra ricocheted around in my head – 'You can be whatever you want to be.' But not weak, anything but that.

The school swimming captain, Sandy Gibson, was assigned as our dormitory prefect. In theory he was supposed to keep eight young boys in check, in practice he spent most of his time mooning over photos of Lara, the current girlfriend who attended our sister school. His success was sporadic, given the frequent outbreaks of acne, which transformed his face into a plate of pink porridge. No doubt his fine physique compensated – one afternoon I stumbled on them groping behind the chemistry labs. I lingered, curious, but Sandy spotted me. 'Bugger off, you pathetic little runt!' Despite the alarming acne, he was my first crush. One winter evening, as we scrabbled into our beds, he was practising pull-ups on the door lintel, wearing only his pyjama bottoms. As I stared at him, transfixed, he caught my gaze and scowled. 'What are you looking at, you little pervert?' Snide whispers passed from one bed to the next; someone aimed a slipper at my head which caught one eye with a stinging blow. Gibson dropped down to the floor and yelled: 'Lights out, scumbags – all of you, NOW!' I lay in my narrow bed, frozen in the dark, cradling my humiliation, listening in my misery to grunts from bodies shivering beneath threadbare bedclothes. Suddenly I heard the rasp of worn mattress springs and one of the boys sat up, shining his torch right in my face. The others swiftly followed suit with enthusiastic yelps, until there were seven blinding torches pinning me against my bedhead. And then they began to chant: 'Weisz is a WOMAN, Weisz is a WOMAN!' On and on, louder and louder – I covered my head with my pillow, trying to block out their taunts.

After what seemed like an eternity, Gibson kicked open the dormitory door and flicked on the main light, hollering at everyone to turn off their torches and shut up. An uneasy silence followed, punctuated by occasional sniggers. Later, I quietly eased open the top drawer of my bedside locker, fumbling for the bottle of aspirin stashed below a pile of socks. I knew there were twenty tablets. I carefully counted out five – was that enough? I stuffed them quickly into my mouth, crunching into the sour-sweet mess which fizzled on my teeth, swallowing hard. I lay there, waiting in my dark tunnel of shame and despair. What would happen to me? During the night I woke up feeling nauseous. I slipped across the cold floorboards, out into the corridor and dived into the bathroom, retching half-digested acrid globs which spattered into the lavatory bowl.

In the spring term, my status shifted. One of my few talents was that I could draw, and smutty sketches were always popular. Added to which I now discovered I had my uses in the dormitory – furtive encounters under the bedclothes gave me agency, of a kind. I knew I was navigating a precarious path, but I learned to exploit this new-found power. Years of training, anticipating and accommodating Mother's every mood swing, had fine-tuned my negotiating skills. The antennae flicked back and forth, reading each moment, intuiting the extent of required support. And now I was discovering these skills could be usefully deployed in the outside world – I was becoming savvy, duplicitous beyond my years, a promiscuous operator.

In front of me is a short, typed note from Mother, dated 27 May 1970 and posted to me at school, announcing her arrival by train. 'Just a very brief note to ask you to meet me in the lounge of the Station Hotel as soon after 1 p.m. on Wednesday as you can make it. My train arrives at 12.55 p.m. so I shall book a table and wait for you.' A summons. When I arrived, I spotted Mother enthroned at the far end of the ornate hotel lounge. She had dressed as if for a royal garden party – large floral hat, silk dress, white gloves. Brushing aside the assistance of the maître d', she sailed across the vast and almost empty dining room, settling on a secluded window table. Small talk and prawn cocktails were followed by gelatinous lumps of haddock doused in a parsley sauce, and then a poor attempt at a sherry trifle. After the plates were cleared away, she pulled out a gold compact and began dabbing powder on her nose. The studied ritual of repair never altered, her mouth stretching into the approximation of a wide smile as she applied a fresh coating of lipstick. 'Now, I wanted to have a talk, darling, possibly something we should have discussed earlier, but here we are, better late than never.' I looked at her blankly, and then it dawned on me, the streetwise fourteen-year-old. I rolled my eyes. 'If this is what I think it is, Mother, the train has already left the station.' Undaunted, she launched into what was clearly a rehearsed patter, navigating her way around 'unwanted attention', 'natural urges' and 'raging hormones'. The stretched lipstick smile shifted somewhat to accommodate these uncomfortable phrases, and as she prattled on, I wondered if this visit had been prompted by one of her monthly coffee mornings, a gaggle of anxious mothers all fretting about the 'goings-on' at expensive public schools. 'So you see, darling, nothing to worry about, all perfectly normal – oh lord, is that really the time?' She hailed the waiter with an imperious flourish of her lipstick-smeared napkin. 'I say!' the vocal tone taken down a notch to indicate gravitas. I knew this routine all too well and tried to hide behind the menu – I'm not with her, nothing to do with me.

The waiter duly produced our bill, tucked discreetly inside a leather folder. Father would have spent several minutes carefully scrutinising the bill, a habit which she hated. On one such occasion she snapped at him: 'Do you have to? It makes you look like a vulgar little shopkeeper!' His response was cutting: 'As you well know, my dear, I don't relish the prospect of being cheated. Always worth checking . . . ' He paused, adding with a sneer, 'Or perhaps you would rather settle the bill yourself?', knowing full well that the only money at her disposal was the monthly allowance he chose to give her. I well remember the collapsed look that flashed across her face, pulling out her powder compact to mask her humiliation.

Today, however, Mother was in full command. Diving

into the recesses of her handbag, she produced several crisp pound notes, placed them inside the folder and rose majestically. The waiter bobbed deferentially, opening the double doors as she bustled through the lobby and straight out onto the platform. The train pulled slowly out of the station, Mother in typically regal fashion waving a gloved hand from the carriage window. I waved back and then, in defiant mood, jabbed a Stuyvesant into my mouth and headed back to school.

CHAPTER 10

September 1972

Sixth-formers at school were allocated rooms up on the attic floor and, intoxicated by this new-found independence, four of us set about covering the bland walls of our study with black paper, enlivened by psychedelic Ban the Bomb posters and photos of Bob Marley. I became obsessed by David Bowie in his Ziggy Stardust glam-rock phase and, free from parental scrutiny, slavishly copied (as far as I dared) his outrageous sense of style – beaded jackets, flared jeans and platform boots. We jammed the study door shut and played music at full volume (*Close to the Edge* by the group Yes was a firm favourite), pumped out a 'radical' weekly school magazine using an old Gestetner machine and smoked copious amounts of weed. My status seemed to shift, I acquired a new following, and not just among my peers.

Julian Portmore was head of the history department. He wore his black hair, thinning slightly, slicked back and touching his shirt collar. I was in his class and occasionally he would stop me in the corridor to chat – chance meetings at first. Then he started to set me additional work, told me I had Oxbridge potential and arranged a meeting with my parents.

Mother, enthralled by this whiff of potential academic glory, dressed for the occasion – large mink hat, crocodile handbag and shoes. We assembled in the headmaster's study and it was agreed that I should have a new work schedule, with Mr Portmore as my assigned tutor. As the meeting concluded, Mother extended a gracious hand to Mr Portmore and reeled off a well-rehearsed patter of effusive thanks. Sweeping out of the door, she whispered to me: 'Did you see the frayed cuff on his jacket? I almost offered to fix it.' Next on the agenda was a celebratory lunch at the Station Hotel, my parents excited that their boy should have been singled out for such personalised tutoring.

Our weekly sessions were designed principally to prepare me for the general paper – my reading list included, inevitably, excerpts from Cardinal Newman's *Idea of a University*, A. J. P. Taylor's *Origins of the Second World War* and a sprinkling of Apollinaire, Verlaine and Rimbaud. Tutoring continued by correspondence during the Easter holiday; letters arrived, ostensibly about schoolwork, but I noted that Mr Portmore was adopting an increasingly easy, personal tone and, eagerly, I responded accordingly.

Back at school, the lessons were often held at Mr Portmore's house. My unguarded letters to my parents referred to a growing friendship, to which my father responded with pointed questions about the progress of my schoolwork. 'We didn't send you to an expensive boarding school to have you socialising with teachers. Some focus is required.' But in my school pigeonhole, littered with circulars about fire drills and the school cinema club, I began to find an occasional cream envelope from Mr Portmore, usually a marked essay with a note scrawled on the back of a carefully chosen postcard – a view of the gardens at Sissinghurst, a Pugin pencil drawing and, once, a bust of Antinous which I immediately pinned to my study wall.

At the start of the summer term, it was announced that the school play would be *Romeo and Juliet*. Ignoring Father's diktat regarding extracurricular activities, I signed up for an audition and spent the next week memorising the Queen Mab monologue, desperate to secure the part of Mercutio. As I walked out onto the school stage, Mr Portmore's voice echoed up from the back of the hall, which was in darkness. 'Could you just walk up and down for me? Now, can you rush in, as if breathless? Oh, and can you do a cartwheel by the way?' I had to admit that I couldn't and – wilting under the overhead lights – stuttered my way without much conviction through the prepared lines and left, dejected.

I was cast as Benvolio. In my arrogance, I asked to see Mr Portmore: 'But, sir, it's a non-part, he's a complete drip!' Mr Portmore smiled sympathetically, reassuring me I was well cast. 'Benvolio is a kindly chap, supportive, a peacemaker. The part is perfect for you, believe me.' Leading me to the door, he turned, gripping me by the elbow: ' "Alas, that love, so gentle in his view, / Should be so tyrannous and rough in proof!" You see? Perfect!' I hovered in the corridor outside his room, trying to understand the meaning of his conspiratorial smile, reliving the sensation of his touch, wanting to run back into the room. And then what? Instead, I walked away feeling foolish and scared.

Rehearsals began the following week. I arrived, sulking, going through the motions of the little I was required to do. Mr Portmore took me to one side at the end of the session. 'I know you're upset. Please don't be. And to cheer you up, I've chosen the most delicious outfit for you.' Raising his voice: 'Come and check your costumes, everyone!' There was a stampede to the long rack at the back of the stage. Mr Portmore handed me a deep burgundy doublet with slashed sleeves, striped tights and soft leather boots. The other boys were larking about, stripping down to their Y-fronts, breaking voices shrieking and yelping as they shimmied into their tights. Mr Portmore whispered in my ear: 'I want you to shine . . . try it on.' I wriggled into my costume and felt immediately transformed, a delirious peacock, strutting out to the forestage in my high boots. There was a long mirror positioned in one of the wings and I caught sight of a Renaissance youth, long curling hair tumbling to padded shoulders, a cinched waist with pleated velvet folds cut short at the crotch. I hammed it up, striking an exaggerated pose. Who cared if Benvolio was a non-part? Mr Portmore leaned over to adjust a sleeve, a lock of hair falling over his face, and for a split second his hand brushed my wrist. Standing back, he nodded approval, then turned to check Mercutio's costume. Irritated, I started to walk away, but he called me back. 'Simon, we need a babysitter next Wednesday, might you be free?' I was startled – he had made a point of asking me in front of the entire cast. I felt strangely proud.

Approaching the house, I could see three faces peering out of an upstairs window. As I walked up the front path the door was flung open and a gaggle of children surveyed me solemnly. I shouted 'Boo!' and they ran away shrieking. Mr Portmore appeared in the hallway and ushered me into his study. 'I'm glad you're early, and call me Julian by the way, can't be doing with all that "sir" nonsense. Now, there's something I want you to listen to.' He was waving an LP box set. 'Live recording of *Rosenkavalier*, conducted by Kleiber. Do you know the work?' He opened the lid of a stereo system, delicately placed one of the discs on the turntable, squatted on the floor. 'Florence is giving the kids their tea, we have twenty minutes or so. Come, sit down.'

I had never heard a note of Richard Strauss before. Nervous, I shut my eyes and focused on the dazzling fanfare, which faded immediately, leaving only the plangent notes of an oboe. In a conspiratorial whisper, Julian talked me through the music: 'This is the prelude to Octavian's arrival at the start of Act II, the pivotal moment – the presentation of the silver rose. Wait! Here it is . . . Sophie is accepting the rose, the symbol of betrothal, from Count Octavian Rofrano, Rosenkavalier to Baron Ochs.' Julian leapt to his feet, reached for the printed libretto and read the relevant text: '*Ist wie ein Gruss vom Himmel. Ist bereits zu stark, als dass mans ertragen kann . . . Wo war ich schon einmal und war so selig?* So, a rough translation would be "It's like a greeting from heaven – too strong to be endured . . . where have I been so blissfully carefree?" You see?' He paused, smiled at my blank, frozen face. 'Do you know, I think I shall call you Rofrano from now on.'

At that moment Florence put her head round the door.

'Hullo!' Her eyes flickered over us momentarily, then she walked over to the record player and lifted up the arm. 'Time for the children's bath, Julian – hurry up or we'll be late!'

There was the usual kerfuffle of three competing bedtime stories, pleas for one more. I heard the front door slamming shut, the house wrapping itself in the gathering dusk. I wandered down into the study, pulled out the boxed set, took the Act II disc from its sleeve and placed it on the turntable. Adjusting the volume to the lowest setting, I lay down beside one of the speakers and listened again.

A week later Julian suggested we go for a walk along the river with the kids – Florence was at an orchestra rehearsal. Instead of his school corduroy jacket, he was wearing a long Afghan coat which flapped in the wind. Even his walk was different – at school he strutted along the corridor with his head held high and his hands thrust behind his black gown, but now his pace was slower, turning occasionally to look at me quizzically. 'That meeting with your mother, it almost felt as though she was trying to seduce me, her fingers stroking the frayed edge of my sleeve – did you notice?' He laughed. 'I was quite taken aback. And those eyes of hers – she's quite something, isn't she?' I giggled awkwardly, wondering what Mother would think if she could hear this, imagining her disapproval if she could see us walking together. 'She does that – it's a kind of instinctive seduction routine. It's how she operates.' This exchange made me uneasy, so I raced after the kids, scooping up the little one, chucking him over my shoulder.

I became willingly enmeshed in their family life, helping

the eldest girl with her homework, making paper boats with the middle one, building mud pies in the garden with the smallest one. But each time I caught sight of his gaze, sensed his despair, I felt a sharp jolt of vertigo – how long could we ignore the taut wires of alarm careening through the house?

Florence seemed increasingly preoccupied – pummelling bread dough on the kitchen counter, thumbing intently through a psychotherapy journal in her study, jotting notes, battling with an ever-growing mountain of clothes on the ironing board, making a shopping list for me, grateful but at the same time wary.

The end of the spring term approached and with it a suffocating terror at the prospect of monotonous weeks at home, separated from Julian. Leaping down the main stairs at school, two at a time, I bumped into Mr Dees the art teacher, who threw me a strange sidelong glance. He had long ago perfected the language of the arched eyebrow. 'Why the hurry, young man, hmmm? Off out again? Shouldn't you be working for your exams?' Pursing his lips, he proceeded up the stairs exuding a stately air of disapproval. I met Julian outside school and we walked without speaking down to the river. I wasn't sure how to navigate this silence, and began to mimic Mr Dees, rather successfully I thought. We passed under a vast lime tree, its lower branches enveloping the walkway in shade. Julian spun me round, his hands on my shoulders. 'Stop, please – I can't bear it.' Elated, I slipped from his grasp and walked out into the sunshine – Julian had tears in his eyes, because of me.

One evening, brushing my teeth in the bathroom, I caught

sight of my reflection and froze, somehow unable to recognise the face staring back at me. In panic, I slumped down onto the floor, feeling lost and frightened. The next morning I phoned home. Mother answered but I could hear women's voices in the background – I guessed she was hosting one of her monthly coffee mornings. There was a sudden peal of laughter and Mother's tinkling voice at the other end of the phone: 'I have to go, darling, this isn't the best time. You'll be home in a few days, we can talk then.' What was I about to tell her? What could I possibly say? I replaced the receiver, feeling abandoned, fearful of what was happening to me.

Despite the evident risk, Julian wrote to me at home, often twice weekly. I listened keenly for the postman, rushing downstairs to retrieve the post before my parents could find it. One morning, Mother cornered me, brandishing three envelopes, their thick cream paper and spidery handwriting immediately familiar. 'I want you to tell me about this friendship, let us talk.' I followed her into the drawing room, where she sat in icy silence. I gazed at the envelopes lying in her lap, longing to snatch them and escape. 'Well?' My mouth was dry, scrabbling to find the right placatory words. 'There's nothing to say. We enjoy each other's company, that's all . . . really.' She flashed me a caustic look. 'I have no doubt you are flattered by the attention, but I hope you would tell me if you felt there was something, you know – not quite right? When I was your age, I was completely mad about one of the nuns at my convent school. A natural infatuation, one is impressionable at this age, but a distraction, nonetheless.' I fled to my bedroom, locked the door and devoured the letters, one by one. Retrieving the borrowed LP of *Rosen-kavalier* from its hiding place, I flicked on the turntable and played the start of Act II at full volume, elated with the giddy knowledge that I was needed in this way. I could hear Mother rushing upstairs but chose to ignore her remonstrations as she pounded on my locked door.

As the summer progressed, I lurched between the euphoria of being chosen and the terror of uncharted territory, any sense of order now in free fall. When we passed each other in the school corridors, our eyes locked briefly. Sometimes I deliberately turned away to talk to friends, enjoying this small act of cruelty, the power I could exert over him. At the end of that term I woke one morning with a burning throat and a high temperature. I was transferred to the sick wing and the doctor diagnosed glandular fever. The next few days were a blur, occasionally aware of the matron bustling about changing my sheets, encouraging me to sip water. And Julian appeared, sat by my bed. 'I'm going to phone your parents – it's obvious you're not in a fit state to travel yet, so I'm going to suggest we put you up for a few days.'

Florence answered the door. Seeing me on the step, her eyes narrowed. She let me pass without a word and then stomped down the basement stairs back into the kitchen. The door banged shut, leaving her cold fury echoing in the hallway. Julian showed me to my room, then sprinted down the stairs. I heard the harsh back and forth of their voices, then his slow steps returning. As he came frowning into my room, the kitchen door was flung wide open again, Florence hurling her anger up the stairway: 'How do you think I feel, with your fancy boy paraded so blatantly in our house?'

I burrowed down under the heavy bedcovers, fearful of what was unfolding, wishing I was anywhere but here. The high-ceilinged room was lined with books – trying to block out my panic, I scanned the shelves, but my eyes hurt too much. Propped against a carafe of water on the bedside table was a get-well card drawn by the children. Through a slit in the dark velvet curtains, a ray of sunlight snaked its way across the bed, but even that was too bright. I slumped back against the pillows – I was falling down Alice's rabbit hole, down and down.

When I woke again it was dusk, and Julian was standing at the end of my bed. 'Your father's arriving tomorrow morning to drive you home.' He faltered, his voice dropping to a whisper. 'What we found, you and I, no one can take that from us. I believe that. And you must too – so that's a kind of victory, don't you think?' Lying there in the dark, all I could hear was the defeat in his cracking voice.

The next morning Father arrived – there was stilted conversation as Florence made coffee and Father presented Julian with a bottle of Tokaji by way of thanks. On the long drive home, I lay on the back seat, wrapped in my confusion and shame.

Once I had recovered, my parents decided to send me to a summer school in Annecy – ostensibly to improve my French language skills although I was to discover they had another motive entirely. I had written to Julian giving him the time when my train would stop at the nearest station and he was there on the platform, together with the three children. I leaned out of the window, the children crowding round brandishing a model aeroplane, a new football, the little one showing me his drawing of a house, with six people poking their heads out of separate windows – one of them was clearly me. Julian and I hadn't exchanged a word, the train began to move, and all I could do was wave as the four specks on the platform disappeared into the distance.

For two weeks I sat blankly in a classful of other teen-agers, hung out in coffee bars and went for aimless bike rides around the lake. Eventually, the language course dragged to a close. I had written Julian a couple of letters but, strangely, received nothing from him. My father met my train. He seemed preoccupied and we drove home in silence. Mother went through the motions of welcoming me home, but the atmosphere during supper was oddly subdued. After we had cleared away, they sat me down in the drawing room. Father's voice was dry, businesslike: 'This matter of you and Mr Portmore – we found the letters in your desk – we have had to put a stop to it.' I leapt to my feet, screaming abuse at them, damned in that moment by my own raw, defensive fury. Mother pulled me back into my chair. 'Sit down and listen. These things happen, you will grow out of it. And if you don't, well . . . ' She paused, looking pointedly at Father. Important to say the Right Thing. 'Your father and I . . . we will find it in ourselves to love you, despite everything.' I stormed out of the room, that caveat – the unspoken acknowledgement of their deep disappointment – hanging heavily in the air.

Hours later, Mother knocked on my door. 'Come downstairs please, Dr Halewood is here to see you.' I already knew I had lost, steadying myself as I walked slowly downstairs. Mother propelled me into the dining room, then left, closing the door behind her. The doctor was sitting at the dining table and gestured me to join him. His quiet voice was a blur of disjointed questions and phrases swirling around my head: 'When did you first experience such feelings? . . . This may be just a transitory phase . . . You are not to blame for what's happened.' I tried to focus but felt somehow outside my body. I registered his words, welcomed them even, but at the same time couldn't quite believe them. I found myself slowly naming my confused feelings, realising as I spoke that surfacing alongside my misery was an intense feeling of relief. Dr Halewood listened calmly, making entries in a black notebook. As he filled each page with his neat, italicised script, I wondered if my memories of the past few months might magically evaporate as I spoke, captured now only in his notebook. His carefully modulated voice was strangely compelling and the suffocating weight of subterfuge began to shift. 'I think a short course of sedatives would be wise.' He handed me a small bottle filled with pale blue capsules: one to be taken every evening.

There was a brief murmur of voices in the hall and the doctor was ushered out. I sat pinned to my chair, clutching the bottle of pills as my parents came into the dining room. Father laid down the law: 'There is to be no contact between you, is that understood?' He paused, looked at me steadily, his voice softening slightly. 'You should know that we don't consider you the guilty party. There is no blame here.' I glanced across the table at Mother, dabbing her eyes with a crumpled handkerchief. I got to my feet, started to scrabble for some kind of apology, but Father waved me away with a weary smile. 'I think we're done for now, don't you?'

As I climbed the stairs to my room, a shrill voice started screaming in my head: 'No blame? No blame? You wanted this, admit it! What have you done to Florence? What about the children? What will they think of you now? And the school, you can just hear them, can't you? Jeering and snickering behind your back!'

Late one afternoon during that long, bleak summer, Mother knocked on my bedroom door. As she slumped dejectedly onto the bed, I could see she had been crying. 'I wonder if this is my fault. Am I to blame somehow? Tell me!' I found myself mumbling the reassurances I knew she needed to hear. 'Please, Mother, it's nothing to do with you, I promise.' The necessary lie. 'I hope you're right. I can't bear to think that I, that I . . . ' Hands clasped to her bosom, a slight pause for dramatic effect. Then, exonerated, she stood over me, her voice shifting in register: 'Now, where are the rest of the letters? Give them to me, all of them.' Numbed by the daily dosage of pale blue capsules, I reached for a shoe box on top of my wardrobe and meekly handed it over. Later, an insistent, acrid smell woke me. From the window I could see Mother savagely stoking a brazier at the end of the garden and I watched as the thick plume of grey smoke rose up into the evening sky.

July 1978

Five years after we last saw each other, I spot Julian walking towards me along a crowded London pavement. He is with a group of people. Not knowing what to do, I walk past him, then turn to look back. I see he has also stopped, is quickly fabricating some excuse, walking back to me. We find a bench in Temple Gardens and talk. It is a stilted conversation. I chain-smoke while he asks me about my university life, tells me about his new job, talks about the children, and then mentions – his voice matter-of-fact, almost defiant – that he now has a partner. I feel suddenly detached, remote – I find myself noting the receding hairline, beads of sweat running down his face as he tries to gauge my reaction. And in that moment I realise, with dismay, that we have nothing more to say to each other. Fumbling for another cigarette, I make my excuses and walk quickly away.

June 2007

Twenty-nine years later, I am working as publicist at a small publishing house. We are bringing out a new biography of Oscar Wilde, and for the launch party I have managed to negotiate the use of one of the rooms in the National Portrait Gallery, which happens to be exhibiting a large model for a sculpture of Wilde by Maggi Hambling.[1] The evening is a success – good photo opportunities for the press and a cluster of influential guests. Afterwards Claire, the editorial director, hosts a dinner at her house, to which I am invited, along with the author, an agent, some friends and a literary critic. I manage some small talk but feel painfully out of my depth so retreat, a mute observer, tracking the various conversations circling around the table. We are finishing supper, the author debating Wilde's destructive obsession with Bosie Douglas and the disastrous lawsuit that followed, while the critic at the other end of the table is having a heated discussion about Jeremy Thorpe and the alleged attempt to murder Norman Scott. There is a pause while Claire tops up our glasses. 'I find it baffling,' she says, 'how celebrities – people in public office or positions of authority – somehow regard their dalliances as off-limits, assume they have earned some kind of immunity. It's the most extraordinary, delusional sense of entitlement, don't you think? I had a friend at Oxford who after graduating went on to teach at a boarding school in Gloucestershire. He was married, with young children – and there was a beautiful young boy in his class. The infatuation ruined him – he lost his job, his marriage, and who knows what happened to that poor boy . . .'

The guests begin to fiddle with their wine glasses, mute in their collective disapproval, struggling to find a well-judged bon mot. It looks as though the dinner party may break up at this point. I am unable to breathe, the walls appear to be undulating weirdly, I lurch to my feet, knocking over my wine glass in the process, scrabbling to mop up the mess, glancing at the surprised faces around the table. Claire looks up at me in alarm – 'Simon?'

I stare down at the blotched stain of Burgundy spreading out over the tablecloth. 'I was that boy.'

The room erupts into lively chatter, everyone eagerly firing questions at me. I look around the table at their astonished faces and hesitantly begin to offer up my account – a young boy mesmerised by a charismatic older man, my confused, excited complicity. As I talk, I am filled with a growing sense of anger – anger for what happened to that boy, ashamed also that I have offered up his story as end-of-supper tittle-tattle. Exhausted, I feel myself floating above the wreckage of that dinner table, looking down in bewilderment at the gesticulating figures below, like so many vultures picking over a corpse.

September 2015

Claire emails me to say that the tenant of her top-floor flat is leaving: might I be interested? A few weeks after I move in, she knocks on my door. 'Florence and her partner Moira are arriving today – they would be happy to see you, so why don't you join us for drinks?' I accept the invitation – principally because I cannot, in that moment, think how to refuse it – and spend the rest of the day dreading the encounter to come. But when I walk into Claire's sitting room that evening, a small white-haired figure rises from a chair by the fire, moves towards me, arms held out in greeting. 'Claire and Moira are preparing supper in the kitchen – let's sit together, shall we? So here we are, more than forty years later . . .' I sense this is her invitation to revisit that summer, to finally confront our shared pain, and I launch in awkwardly, trying to describe the overwhelming shame I felt then – the deceit, the damage I must have caused. She stops me. 'You were just a young boy caught up in our misery.' 'And the children?' I am not sure what I want to hear. 'For a while they asked about you, what had happened. Of course, now they're grown-up with families of their own.' She pauses, takes my hand. 'The guilt you felt back then, or still feel now – there is no need, I can assure you. Yes, I could have wished for a less brutal way to end our marriage, but . . .' glancing towards the kitchen, 'later I found Moira and so, as you can see, all is well.'

I am struck by her calm poise, grateful for this quiet absolution, as she carefully steers our conversation to safer ground. She tells me about the old farmhouse that she and Moira have restored together, the joy she finds in her many grandchildren – it is a moment of generosity and repair.

July 2023

What do I feel now, looking back on that summer, all those years ago? Compassion for a precocious young boy, dancing on the knife edge of what might be within reach. Compassion too for my parents, whose principal concern was to avoid a scandal. Compassion even for a doctor's faith in a small bottle of blue pills. Conventional wisdom might well pass judgement on what happened that summer. And yet, two lives briefly converged, sparking a moment of truth.

Julian is in his eighties now. Each year we mark our respective birthdays, occasionally suggesting that we should meet, secure in the knowledge that we won't.

CHAPTER II

23 March 1974

I am living in my parents' house, studying for my A levels. It is my eighteenth birthday – because a great deal hangs on my exam results, it has been decided there will be no party, but I may choose what I would like for dinner. My mother busies herself with her recipe books but something else hangs in the air. I can't place it, but at breakfast I notice looks passing between my parents. I go upstairs, collect my books and leave for school. That evening we are to eat in the dining room, to mark the occasion. Mother has set the table with the best Rosenthal porcelain, my father has filled the wine decanter. I remember the stifling decorum, my parents more silent than usual. I long for the ordeal to be over. We clear away the plates and then my father says quietly, 'Come and sit down, we have something to tell you.'

June 1964

I am eight years old, curled up on a stool next to the stove, reading. My mother, her back turned to me, is standing at the other end of the room, peeling apples at the kitchen sink. I carefully mark the page, close the book. I have been waiting for the right moment. I am very scared, but there is no going back now. 'What happened to my other granny, how did she die?'

My mother's body is tense as she spins round to face me, her face mottled. Caught off guard by my question, she begins to choke on a loop of apple peel. In her panic, she scrabbles at the back of her throat, her eyes locked on mine, pleading with me, but I can't move. The next moment her whole frame is heaving, as she takes in great gulps of air. 'How could you ask such a thing? How could you?' She slumps into a chair, her breathing slowly becoming calmer. 'Not now, maybe later. Much later. Go to your room . . .' I run to the stairs.

23 March 1974

By keeping everyone guessing, Mother could construct a certain mystique: you might approach the oracle as supplicant, but you could never be sure how much would be disclosed, and on what terms. Now, sitting in front of my parents, I feel a heavy curtain is about to be lifted, a curtain which has muffled years of half-guessed truths. It dawns on me that the formality of the birthday meal is a farce – this is not a celebration for me. Instead, Mother is about to take centre stage.

Glancing at my father, she pats her hair and launches in: 'We feel that, now you're eighteen, there are things you should know. You're an adult now, and it is right that you should be told about your family history. You're old enough to deal with this information responsibly.' Another piece of coded instruction, no doubt much rehearsed. I cannot in this moment compute the transactional nature of this gift, so intricately wrapped with subtle conditions. But I do know that something is being given and at the same time something is being taken away.

Mother begins: 'You should know that our family is Jewish. On both sides. When you have heard my story, you will understand why this is strictly private information. *You may not tell a soul.*' She places heavy emphasis on each word, a forefinger levelled at my face. Her bloodshot eyes pin me to my chair, accusing before the fact, ever alert to the possibility of betrayal.

My father breaks in: 'On the other hand, you can be secretly proud.' He recites a list of eminent Jews. 'Disraeli, Einstein, Mendelssohn, Mahler, Marx, Herzl, Pulitzer, Lubitsch, Weill, Arendt, Freud, Menuhin.' The names shift uneasily in my head, pale figures forming in the shadows, clasping hands in a silent dance as they circle around me. 'We should celebrate the extraordinary contribution they have made and – privately – we can allow that we are, as a race, in some ways special, very special.' Father's words box me into submissive silence. He allows himself a hollow laugh. 'And that is our downfall, our fatal flaw. We humans are inherently jealous, embittered creatures – Jews have been persecuted over the centuries for their intelligence and creativity.' His hands grip the table, his voice wavers. 'What the Nazis devised was, of course, in a different league – the systematic, industrialised extermination. The Germans have the perfect word – *Vernichtung* – it means rendering into nothing. Now, listen to your mother's story.'

She turns to me, any pretence at composure abandoned. 'The Germans occupied Hungary on 19 March 1944. I had just turned eighteen, about to finish my baccalaureate – I was planning to be a doctor. On 22 March laws were passed enabling the seizure of all Jewish assets. A Jew could no longer drive a car or take public transport, phones and radios were confiscated. Jews were totally removed from economic, professional and public life. At a stroke we were wiped off the map.

'My father, your grandfather Ede, had been transported as a forced labourer to a remote part of Ukraine, a place called Shostka to the north-east of Kyiv. He was diabetic – at first, we could send packets of insulin, then the rules changed. Eventually he was too sick to work so they sent him on a stretcher to the station. Apparently, he was lying on the platform waiting for the train back to Budapest when the stationmaster intervened. He said he had no interest in transporting sick Jews. And so Father died a few days later, on 2 March. The note we received stated he had died of a heart attack.

'On 1 May new legislation came into force. Only pregnant Jewish women and children under the age of three were allowed to obtain milk. We could no longer buy butter, eggs, rice, poppy seeds, paprika. In any event, we were not allowed to go shopping until 11 a.m., by which time most of the food in the market had long gone. So we realised they were hell-bent on starving us. I guess we were luckier than many – we still had revenue from Father's office, and from the vineyard. At night we would close the windows, draw the curtains and tune into the BBC world news – *verboten* of course, but at least this way we could keep track of what was happening.

'I was standing in my mother's pantry when they came beating on our door. It was early May. I could hear my mother running to the front door but I stood still in the dark, my hand hovering over the marble shelf where pastries and chocolate truffles used to be set to cool. I closed my eyes, one finger brushing the marble surface, then lightly touching my lower lip, willing myself to remember. I knew it was all over, the life we had lived. Nothing left – just a few packing cases in a secret room behind a fake wall.

'Imagine, almost half a million Jews from across rural Hungary all swept up in a matter of months.[1] And be under no illusion that this was solely courtesy of the Germans – Eichmann's *Sonderkommando* consisted of just two hundred men, maximum. So, the willing complicity of the Hungarians was crucial in this process, and very efficient they were too. Hundreds of local officials and gendarmes oversaw the ghettoisation and deportations – with great energy and zeal.[2] The old Jewish quarter was cordoned off as a makeshift ghetto, and several neighbouring Gentile families were also ordered to vacate their homes, they were furious about it – the idea that they should be forced out so that their houses could be occupied by Jews! On 5 May we were moved into a small house – me, my sister Zsuzsi and my mother Flóra. There were six rooms, two families per room, a toilet in the yard – we were barely allowed to leave the house, the stench of unwashed bodies was insufferable.

'There was an old woman in our room who smuggled in a piece of sausage. She lay in her bed, staring at the wall, chewing – the stink of garlic made me retch, but the sadness in her eyes was worse. She had already given up hope. Every day came a new order – give up your wedding rings. Then the next day – hand over your silver. A few days later – all fountain pens to be handed in. It was a kind of slow torture, a war of attrition if you like. Little by little we were being dehumanised.

'After the first week, they sent us out to work in a brick factory, about ten kilometres outside the town – I say "work" but in fact it was a deliberate denigration: no sooner had we finished building a wall than they would make us knock it down simply to break our spirits, and we would start all over again. The gendarmes would watch us work, chain-smoking, laughing at us. There was a young lout in charge. One day he gave us his cap and made us pick up all their cigarette stubs, littered over the ground. So we scrabbled around, collecting the stubs on our hands and knees, and one of us took the cap over to him. He just sneered at us, chucked the cap up into the air and ordered us to pick them up again. Another time a bunch of us were sent to clear out a chicken pen – you can imagine the stench, and we were not given shovels, we did this with our bare hands. One gendarme knew of my father, his reputation as a respected barrister, so he gave me an extra hard kick in the ribs as I knelt in the chicken shit.'

Summer 1962

I am six years old. There is a gang of boys in our street and I badly want to be allowed to join. I tag along but am repeatedly turned away. Why can I not belong, why am I not good enough? One afternoon I decide to try one last time. I pitch up at the garden shack the gang use as their HQ and knock nervously at the door. It opens a crack and Jonathan, the leader, peers out at me. He is taller than me, with blond curly hair and blue eyes. I wish I could be like Jonathan – I don't want to be me, small, dark, slightly pudgy, awkward, bad at games. 'Please let me join!' 'Why would I do that?' he says. I have no answer, I can think of no good reason why they should agree to let me in. 'Wait outside,' he snaps, and the door slams shut again. I hear the gang members muttering inside, a muffled guffaw, some giggling, then the door reopens. 'You have to do a test first.' I eagerly agree. I am to dig a trench at the bottom of the garden. Jonathan produces a spade. 'Take your shorts off, and your shoes and socks.' The other gang members sidle out from the shack and watch me as I dig away. After an hour or so, sweating in the afternoon sun, the trench is about four feet wide and three feet deep. 'Get in!' comes the next command. I step down nervously. Jonathan has unfurled a garden hose and starts to fill the trench with water. Soon I am standing in thick, swirling mud, almost up to my knees. 'Now you need to make some mud pies.' I set to work and soon there are about a dozen sodden clay balls lined up along the edge of the trench. 'Now!' shouts Jonathan and the first mud pie slams into my face, knocking me backwards. With yelps and whoops the others join in, hurling mud missiles at every part of my body. But my feet are rooted in the mud, I can't escape the onslaught. And then they are gone, running out into the street. I don't know what to do, pinned down in the trench as the mud begins to cake on my face, my clothes. I claw the greasy clay from my eyes, and when I manage to open them, I see Jonathan walking back towards me. I hope he is going to help me up out of the trench, but he stops at the edge, looking down at me with a sneer. 'What a shame – have we made your clothes all dirty? Just piss off, you little creep!' He walks away.

23 March 1974

'We stayed in the ghetto for a month or so, then on 12 June[3] we were told to pack our things. We were allowed only one suitcase weighing no more than twenty-five kilos. Of course, we had no means of weighing the luggage, and they knew that – yet another way of terrorising us. People were frantically going through their belongings, trying to select what to take, what to leave. Upstairs there was a heavily pregnant woman, Éva, with a little girl, maybe five years old. I went and helped her pack, and we stuck together as the Hungarian soldiers marched us down to the train station. Walking past the Orthodox synagogue on Kossuth Lajos utca[4] I spotted

Mrs Farkas,* a neighbour of ours. She saw me too, thrust herself forward, her face contorted with fury and a kind of triumph, shouting, 'It's about time!' and then, with a snarl, spat right in my face. I couldn't take it in, this woman who until recently was quite happy to exchange pleasantries with my mother when they met on the street. At the station, there was a huge crowd, the air heavy with heat and fear. As we approached, people were starting to panic, the soldiers using their rifle butts to maintain order. And the train – this unending line of gaping cattle trucks towering above the platform: was this for us? And yet, this is so hard to explain, but after all the fear, it was almost a relief – no more responsibility, no more decisions, all we had to do was climb up into this train to God knows where.[5]

'A whistle blew and the soldiers' dogs lunged forward on their short leads, their teeth bared. Sounds of anguish sliced through the summer morning – mothers shrieking for children lost in the surging crowd, the cries of the elderly trampled underfoot. It was . . . inhuman, savage. Everyone began scrabbling up into the trucks. Once my mother had struggled up I turned to help Éva and her little girl. There must have been over a hundred people in our truck, no room to turn, let alone sit down. In one corner there was a pail, that's it. Éva and I edged our way to the door opening, desperate to turn our faces away from the crush of people around us. There was no time that morning to

* Farkas is an old Hungarian name meaning wolf.

use the water pump in the yard – we were already parched, faint. Éva's face was drawn and grey, her little girl a ghost clasping her arms around her mother's large belly. Then the doors slammed shut and we were thrown into almost complete darkness. There was a small grating on the far side of the truck, but those near it blocked any passing air. With a great grinding of wheels the train began to move and . . .'

My mother's fists are twisting the tablecloth into a sweaty ball, her body heaving, her face contorted, staring back into the darkness. 'As the trucks jolted forwards, people were thrown against each other and I remember this sound – a great moan, like a tidal wave of grief and defeat rolling from one carriage to the next.

'Hours passed. We were all numbed, hypnotised by the rhythm of the wheels pounding over the tracks. Many slept where they stood, mouths gaping, starved of air, propped against their neighbour. Night fell.

'In the early morning the train slowly screeched to a halt. Zsuzsi was standing near to a grating and peered out – we were in a station siding, heaven knows where. The stench from the overflowing pail was unbearable and we badly needed water. Someone shouted, "Who here speaks German?" Zsuzsi lifted her hand, pulled me over to the grating, then whispered to me, "You're pretty. When the guard comes by, shake your plaits. I'll do the talking." Soon a soldier came strolling by, so I arranged my blonde plaits and smiled, and Zsuzsi called out in her best *Hochdeutsch.* "If I may, please, sir, might we have some water?" He was young, rather handsome, I smiled at him again and I thought he smiled back as he leapt up onto the footplate. His face was near mine, but now I could see he wasn't smiling at all, his lips stretched into a grimace. "Get back, you whore bitch, there's no water for you Yids." I fell back against the other bodies, numbed by the force of this hatred. Mother had barely uttered a word the entire journey but in that moment she whispered, "Explain to me, a nation that could produce Goethe, Schiller, Bach – and now this?"[6]

'That evening Éva went into labour. I remember my mother comforting the little girl as Éva shook and twisted, howling in pain. I begged for some space, people grumbling as they shifted a few inches. I knelt beside her – of course I hadn't a clue what I was doing, mopping the sweat from her face. It was over quite soon, as if she didn't want to cause any bother. I watched the tiny head emerge, then with a great heave Éva gave birth. I held the child, wrapping it in a scarf, while Flóra cut the cord, mopping the blood as best she could, there seemed to be a great deal of it. "Slap it!" hissed my mother. "Quick!" I tried, I tried, but the little rag of a child was already dead. Éva followed her a few hours later. My mother pulled the little girl close as Zsuzsi covered Éva's body with a coat. I emptied my little suitcase and placed the dead infant inside, the only coffin we had.

'By the time we arrived at Auschwitz, two days later, more than half the people in the truck were dead, standing stiffly, shoulder to shoulder. The truck door was rolled back and a woman guard screamed at us, *Alles raus! Alles raus!*

Schnell!"* Lashing at us with her leather whip, she ripped the coffin suitcase from my hand and hurled it onto a mound of discarded luggage.[7] We were exhausted, almost paralysed, Zsuzsi beside me on the Juderampe, my mother holding on to the little girl's hand. I remember her small pale face, eyes wide open but seeing nothing. At least, I hope so . . . people were weeping, sinking to the ground, overwhelmed by the moment of arrival, the possibility of air, blessed air. Then we saw figures in striped uniforms brutally pulling from the wagons those people too weak to get out by themselves, dumping the dead in piles along the tracks. As we were driven along the ramp, truncheon blows rained down on us from every side. A stout woman in striped clothes lunged at one of the young girls from our wagon who was clutching a small boy. Tearing the boy from his mother, she ran over to another group, pushing the screaming child into the arms of an old woman. We didn't understand what was happening – that became clear later.

'And then – I was sure I was going mad, I heard music. Above the chaos of the milling, half-crazed passengers, beyond the wailing and cries of despair, came the sound of *Ländler*, waltz music. Over by the sheds there was a ragged group in striped uniforms, a violinist, a cellist, someone on a clarinet – and they were playing slow waltzes by Strauss. The menacing banality of that music![8] Officers were strutting up and down, people being ordered this way and that. As they approached, my mother hissed at me, "Cover your

*   Everyone out – quick!

hair with a scarf, don't let them see how beautiful you are."
And those were the last words she said to me. There was a
bright light shining in our faces. I remember the officer, very
handsome, with his baton, lining us up in orderly rows. Later
I was told his name – Dr Mengele. Zsuzsi and I were ordered
to the right, my mother and the little girl to the left. And in
that moment, before I could say a word, they were lost in
the crowd.'

There is a long silence. I sit pinned to my seat, watching
Mother cradling her head in her hands. Finally, she looks
up, her face drained of colour. 'I can't say any more – quite
enough for one evening, don't you think?' She pushes back
her chair and walks slowly from the room.

CHAPTER 12

September 1973

It was decided that I should join the sixth form of the local grammar school. I remember hesitating at the door of the common room, steeling myself to walk in and smile at a sea of alien faces, when all I wanted to do was cut and run. Mother rattled through a pep talk over breakfast: 'You have to do this, nobody knows anything about you, what you have been through. It will be fine.' Flashing a bright smile over her coffee cup, she added blithely: 'You can be whatever you want to be.' An echo of my father's mantra, but in her case pragmatic, the voice of bitter experience.

That first week I discovered, to my surprise, that some of the boys were welcoming. A couple of them gave me a guided tour and my nausea slowly subsided. It seemed, to my relief, that I had successfully slipped under the radar.

May 1974

At the end of the spring term, the music master arranged for me to join a string quartet. We met to rehearse one lunchtime and back home, hoping to impress Mother, I told her about the other three musicians. One was the son of an academic at Durham University, the viola player's father was a surgeon and the cellist's mother a prominent psychotherapist. Cutting through my chatter, Mother was aghast: 'But these names, they're all Jews! Weren't there any other boys you could have teamed up with, for God's sake? What happens when you give a concert at school – you expect us to turn up and applaud?' 'Does everything always have to be on your terms, Mother?' I knew the answer to that, and so did she, but I was on a roll now. 'There's nothing quite like an anti-Semitic Jew it seems, is there, Mother?' Pushing back from the kitchen table, quivering with carefully calibrated indignation and wounded hauteur: 'Don't be absurd, you know my reasoning, I refuse to be pigeonholed, exposed, not any more, and especially not by my own son.' Our volley of taunts gathered pace: 'OK, I may have screwed things up at my last school, but what right have you to control my every move, to ransack my desk, burn my letters, pluck me out of one life and into another, just because that's what happened to you? What is this anyway, some kind of weird payback?' Mother buries her face in her hands. 'What right? What right have YOU to talk to me like this? That is unfair, and unjustified. How dare you suggest I am anything other than supportive? What you fail to realise is that history does repeat itself. That is what I dread. You have no conception of how the world turns. How could you? And, in a way, I'm grateful for that. But believe me, if I wish to duck below the parapet, there are good reasons, God knows!' It looked as though I was about to be dismissed, but then she pinned me to a chair. 'Listen to what I have to say, then tell me if my efforts to conceal my identity, and yours, come to that, are misplaced or not.'

'Our first morning in Auschwitz. A place of complete desolation – not a blade of grass, no birdsong, nothing. I was in one of the BIIc Barracks, a huge hut with about five hundred other women. I was sitting outside – there was thick violet-coloured smoke belching from a chimney and this cloying, sickly smell. Beside me was a young doctor, Dr Klein, a Slovak. I asked her about the smoke – were they perhaps burning our clothes, our luggage? "No, my dear," she says, "not clothes – that's the smell of burning flesh." '[1]

Mother paused for a moment, fists clenched, staring out over the garden. 'Anyway, that first morning, I looked at this plume of purple smoke and thought, that is my mother, my grandmother, aunts, uncles and cousins. But I felt absolutely nothing, I simply registered the fact with absolutely no emotion. I realised that emotion, from one day to the next, had become a luxury – I must simply function from day to day, like a zombie, in order to survive. Like a fire curtain in a theatre – as it descends it cuts off one part of the building from another, head from heart. I was looking at this appalling smoke pouring from that chimney and there was no sensation, no tears, as if my body had shut down in order to save my sanity. I remember thinking – they have taken my family but they will not take my soul. I am going to fight, I am going to survive this somehow – I will not let them turn me into ashes.'[2]

'We had to sleep on the bare floors, there were no bunks, we could barely stretch out our limbs at all. The roll-calls were hellish – often before dawn, standing in the cold and dark. A woman beside you might faint, or die, but you were not permitted to move a muscle. It could take up to two hours. If you moved they beat you – the women guards were especially brutal, so eager to crack their leather whips with the heavy rubber tips to inflict maximum pain.

'Otherwise, we had nothing to do, which worried me terribly. I knew that the only way to stay alive in this godforsaken place was to prove that we could be useful. We heard that they needed people for the Planierung Commando, to help level the ground as preparation for the erection of new huts, so Zsuzsi and I volunteered. We were organised in gangs of four, dragging a heavy concrete roller back and forth over the rough earth – backbreaking work. German political prisoners were in charge of erecting the huts and one of them, a handsome chap called Bernhard, took us under his wing, told us we had to get out as soon as we could. It was imperative to be selected for a labour transport – otherwise the only way out was up those chimneys. So he started to smuggle food to us – half a loaf of bread every day to fatten us up. Every day, it was a godsend, just so we would pass the selection. I still had some fat on me, but Zsuzsi was too thin, and we wanted to stick together.

'Every morning we had to carry out the bodies of those who had died the night before, dragging them out in the same sheets they used to bring us the pitiful supply of black bread each day. Apart from the bread, we had small amounts of dried turnip and an abominable so-called soup – tepid watery liquid, with long, inedible strings of God knows what, no one wanted to know what it was, maybe some kind of thistle.[3] This muck was brought out in dirty troughs, one trough for five women. They gave us small enamel bowls but they always had a fetid, sickening smell – everyone suffered from dysentery and some women who couldn't reach the latrines during the night used these bowls instead. As you can imagine, I preferred to use my cupped hands to get at the soup. There was no water to wash with and very little to drink – each hut had a water tap but the water was often contaminated by sewage. We were only allowed to go to the latrines at certain times and when we did the SS men stood around jeering at us as we lined up by the wooden boxes – all in the open, no privacy at all.

'The gypsies were in a separate section of the camp – their task was to dig irrigation ditches and the foundations for huts to house new arrivals. They had food to barter with, so we would gather at the high barbed-wire fence when we could, offering what we had been given by the political prisoners – a clove of garlic, some aspirin tablets, a few cigarettes. One time they gave us a tin of sauerkraut, can you imagine? Such luxury – but we had nothing to open it with so we hid it until we could find a tin opener.

'Then one night we were awoken by pitiful cries and shrieks from their huts, the sound of lorries arriving, dogs barking, complete confusion. It was about two o'clock in the morning, and we watched through a crack in the wall as they were herded into the lorries. The gypsies knew what was happening, so did we. After that, how could we possibly touch the sauerkraut?

'Do you see now what I am trying to tell you? Survival was a complete lottery, based on seemingly arbitrary decisions over which I had no control. At any moment someone might point the finger in my direction, and that would be that. Now do you understand why I choose to hide? Do you? That instinct never leaves you. Never.'

CHAPTER 13

On my eighteenth birthday the curtains concealing our Jewish heritage were briefly ripped apart and then just as decisively closed again – Mother's emphatic instruction 'You may not tell a soul' proof of her deep-rooted fear of detection. Her mission to become more English than the English was all-consuming. I remember once finding her standing in front of the bathroom mirror, perfecting a parting flourish to insert at the end of a phone call – a tinkling 'Bye-bye!', breathless with implied urgency – so many, many things to do!

One of Mother's first purchases when my parents moved to a larger house was a telephone table in mock-Regency style, complete with a plush velvet seat. Here she would perch for daily phone calls with neighbours and friends, rattling off her carefully rehearsed interjections. After the usual flurry of farewells, she would walk back into the kitchen, patting her golden hair into place, as if to congratulate herself on her performance. But in her heart, it was a sham, she knew it, they all knew it. 'Central European,' they murmured behind her back – her memorised rendition of the required social niceties too eager, too insistent. Impossible to disguise the chink in her meticulously polished armour – that hint of a melodious accent betraying each grammatically impeccable phrase. The inescapable, destroying truth – a sabotage of her own making.

Spring 1981

Home – but not home – for a weekend that already, as I stepped through the front door, stretched out in its suffocating tedium. Mother was, as ever, on the phone. 'Coffee, darling?' – the words mimed theatrically as her hand cupped the receiver. With a gesture towards the kitchen, she resumed her conversation, attentively cementing an alliance with one of the neighbours ('Imperative to keep these people onside at all times'). I took advantage of her phone call to pour the old breakfast coffee down the sink and start again (an act of true bravery on my part – Mother regarded a fresh pot of coffee mid-morning as rank extravagance) while listening with half an ear to the ritual of her well-worn conversation: lazy charwomen, the tea rota for the local hospice patients ('But those people, my dear, the smell!'), the latest hair dye ('Vanessa really does have the magic touch, you know . . . ') and, relishing her role as Lady Bountiful, offering a trifle for the forthcoming charity fundraiser (made with stale biscuits and several dollops of resentment).

In an effort to contain the chaos of her inner world, Mother made it her mission to ensure that everything around her was without blemish, hoovered and burnished to museum-like perfection. She lived in permanent dread that someone might inadvertently forget to replace a glass on one of the carefully positioned porcelain coasters, the potential threat to her polished surfaces reducing her to a state of nervous exhaustion. This, in addition to her rigorously maintained personal appearance, kept her – and everyone within her orbit – on high alert. Relaxing was not an option.

Awaiting her guests, she would pass from room to room, making last-minute adjustments to her obsessively curated *mise en scène*, moving an ashtray on the coffee table until it was just so, smiling as she straightened the carriage clock on the mantelpiece (a tacit battle with Pearl the cleaning lady who always, after dusting, positioned it on the diagonal), plumping an errant cushion into the required shape. She would pause for a final check, scanning the colour-coded leather-bound books, a large volume of Kertész photographs prominently displayed on a coffee table (always, as I remember, open at the same page – an aerial shot of intersecting tramlines in the snow) and a Chichester Theatre programme of *Uncle Vanya* (presumably a useful talking point – 'My dear, Olivier was simply sensational!').

I don't think anyone in her circle of friends had the heart, or the courage, to tell Mother that she was widely referred to as the Duchess or – far more damaging – that, given the family name, there was a generally accepted assumption that the family was indeed Jewish, albeit in denial. Her friends would arrive to take coffee served in delicate Herend cups, gingerly balancing embroidered napkins and dainty plates laden with Mother's *meggyes piskóta* (a light vanilla-laden sponge cake studded with sour cherries), dreading a spillage or the reckless casting of a single crumb onto the immaculate carpets. The ordeal over, did she catch their barely stifled sighs of relief as they scuttled down the front path, racking their collective brains as to how they might possibly compete with her central European delicacies and minutely calibrated hospitality?

During the late sixties and early seventies, Mother's star was in the ascendant. She was attractive, vivacious, a stylish dresser and an excellent cook. I have her recipe books in my kitchen – chicken liver pâté laced with brandy, a rich *paprikás csirke* (paprika chicken) always accompanied by *galuska* (small dumplings) and a sweet-and-sour cucumber salad, a creamy boeuf bourguignon, apple strudel, poppy seed cake, *palacsinta* (light pancakes filled with melted dark chocolate or apricot jam and finely chopped hazelnuts) and *gesztenyepüré* – sweet chestnut paste, mixed with stiffened cream, espresso coffee and rum, pressed through a large stainless-steel mincer clamped to the kitchen table, creating thick strands of sweet, musky vermicelli. Best of all was an artery-blocking dessert called *színes rizs* (coloured rice), a family favourite – cooled pudding rice into which was folded candied fruit that had been soaked in brandy overnight. Piled into cut-glass bowls, each serving would be smothered with vanilla-infused whipped cream and presented at the table studded with jewel-like pieces of candied angelica. Her dinner parties were legendary.

When I visited, we would usually gravitate towards the kitchen. We discussed food, and every minute detail of its preparation, with a fierce intensity, but for someone so addicted to precision in all things, Mother could be infuriatingly vague: 'So how much flour?' 'Oh, you know, just enough . . . ' This laissez-faire approach, verging on the lavish, was particularly evident in her preparation for public-facing occasions, never stinting on generous quantities of butter, cream and liberal additions of alcohol.

Away from public gaze, however, she was obsessively parsimonious, hard-wired by the privations of the camps and post-war rationing.

15 January 1965

I am eight years old, getting ready for an Associated Board piano exam. It is, coincidentally, the anniversary of the date my parents first met and Father has presented Mother with a beautiful and no doubt costly Victorian bracelet, two intertwining bands of gold studded with cabochon rubies, sapphires and emeralds. Overnight the temperature has fallen – there is a delicate frost lacing the trees in the garden. Before we leave, Mother pulls two plump baked potatoes out of the oven. 'Put one in each pocket of your jacket. While you're waiting to go into the exam, hold the potatoes tightly – they will keep your fingers warm.

'But I want them back afterwards, do you hear? No point in wasting good potatoes.'

Summer 1985

Mother arrives for lunch at my flat, triumphant after an arduous morning at Harrods. She shows off a new crocodile handbag and matching gloves, along with several Dior silk scarves. 'Terrible confession, darling, but I also treated myself to a delicious snack in the Food Hall AND a glass of champagne!' She perches, giggling, on a stool in the kitchen, watching me assemble a fruit salad. As I start lopping the ends off strawberries, she lets out a horrified squawk: 'My God, you're throwing away the best part – you cannot do that, you cannot!' – scrabbling through the waste bin to retrieve the scrag ends. 'You will never understand. In the camp, freezing cold and racked with hunger, we would lie in our bunks at night, exchanging our favourite recipes which we all knew by heart. I used to dream about poppy seed loaves, fresh out of the oven. Once I remember finding a heap of discarded tulip bulbs in the camp. God knows why they were there, but I was so starving I fell on them, gnawing my way through a whole pile. Of course, they made me horribly sick and I retched everything back up, but the sheer joy of biting into something fresh, I can't tell you – it was absolutely worth the cramping stomach pains that gripped me for days afterwards.'

August 2016

On the topmost shelf of her fridge she stored food remnants that a scavenging dog would have refused. Small dishes stuffed with the limp, putrid remains of a week-old salad, scraps of cold meat thick with mould, a few scoops of cooked rice, desiccated and yellowing. She would make morning coffee in a large ceramic pot and afterwards run more boiling water through the already exhausted grounds, storing the bitter, dark brown liquid in old jam jars, kept in serried ranks at the back of the top shelf until these too started to bubble and turn blue.

As old age began to defeat her, she gradually relinquished her control over the kitchen, over the house in general. When she dozed in her chair, I took the opportunity to surreptitiously scour the cupboards, chucking away tins more than a decade out of date, emptying drawers stuffed with used paper napkins and cloths she had made from the usable parts of worn bedsheets, discovering plastic bags at the back of the scullery, under the stairs, in bedroom wardrobes, all filled with decaying packets of chocolate biscuits – pitiful evidence of the relentless siege mentality that haunted her always.

November 2016

One morning she hears me cracking eggs into a bowl and comes hobbling through into the kitchen, watching me in silence. I push the bowl to one side and wait. 'There was a little hunchbacked man, Sándor, who worked in the kitchen, helping to prepare the foul soup they gave us, mostly water with a few scraps of onion peel at the bottom.' She sinks onto a kitchen stool, staring out into the garden. 'Anyway, he took a liking to me and from time to time passed me scraps of vegetable he had saved. One day he beckoned me over, slipping an egg into my hands – can you imagine? By then I was in a sorry state, bleeding gums, bones jutting out, terribly weak. Frantic not to drop it, I scuttled away to find a quiet corner behind one of the huts, squatting in the mud to cradle this unbelievably precious thing, trying to resist the overwhelming temptation to consume it, just to prolong that life-giving moment. Then the klaxon for the Appel[1] sounded and I quickly cracked it open against a stone, throwing back my head to pour the gluey mess down my throat, almost gagging with pleasure. I remember running to the yard, standing together with the others in the biting cold, licking my lips guiltily, aware of the starving creatures all around me. So you see, even in that hell there were moments of kindness. That gift – I swear it saved my life. You don't forget that.'

That same little hunchbacked man by some miracle also managed to survive the camps, and in 1956 he arrived in England. How he tracked Mother down remains a mystery – possibly through mutual Hungarian friends. Early one April morning the phone rang. He was only in London for a few days, on his way to New York where he had family. Could he visit? Caught off guard, Mother found herself agreeing and the following afternoon at the appointed hour there was a polite knock at the front door. *'Gnädige Frau!'** – the small man smiled and bowed low. He was carrying an elaborately wrapped box which he formally presented, a gift for Mother.

She related this episode sometime during the late seventies – home from university, I was helping her clear out some cupboards. On a high shelf there was a dark green Harrods box which she asked me to bring down. Inside, sheathed in layers of yellowing tissue paper, was a beautifully tailored, honey-coloured suede jacket. I remembered her wearing it when I was a small child. I used to play with the suede-covered buttons, a row of three at each cuff, just within reach as I walked by her side. 'Such a generous gift. I remember how elegantly he was dressed, he wore a kind of strange opera cape which somehow disguised his hunched back. I gave him tea and *Kuchen* of course, but the occasion was so gauche! What on earth was I to say to this vulgar little man, endlessly fiddling with a large gold signet ring? I found myself regretting bitterly having agreed to meet him. I know, it's a terrible thing to admit. He asked to see you – you were just a month old, sleeping in your cot. I remember his wistful, tender smile as he looked at you and all I wanted was for him to go. All the fear and filth came flooding back – it was unbearable.'

Later, out of curiosity, I looked up the meaning of the name Sándor – it means defender or protector of man.

---

*   Gracious lady

CHAPTER 14

April 1977

My parents lived in a large house in a leafy suburb, the street lined with tall limes and chestnuts, planted at regular intervals along wide grass verges. Generously proportioned, the houses all dated from the period immediately after the First World War – solidly built, with steep gables and mature gardens. Living on such a sought-after street was enormously important for my parents, reassured to find that their neighbours were affluent without being ostentatious and – most importantly – that none of them was Jewish.

Mother set about creating a temple of domestic splendour. The rooms jostled with gleaming reproduction furniture, Persian carpets and paintings of variable quality, purchased enthusiastically by my father from local art dealers who saw him coming. To an extent, Mother had a better eye for colours and textures than many of her neighbours but, oblivious to the concept that less is more, liberally scattered shelves and mantelpieces with her Herend china, cut-glass decanters, carriage clocks and intricately embroidered cloths.

She was immensely proud to find herself the wife of a successful industrialist. Business was booming and my father was keen she should 'look the part'. A generous monthly allowance gave her the freedom to indulge herself in the trappings of her new-found status – elaborate outfits, expensive handbags and shoes, glacé kid gloves, silk scarves and expensive perfume. Calèche by Hermès was a particular favourite, heady with overtones of rose and sandalwood. She also had a weakness for hats and was a favoured customer at the best milliner in town. This establishment, located on the ground and first floors of an elegant eighteenth-century town house, was run by a Mrs Mulligan, always immaculately dressed and pleasingly deferential. The two women struck up a friendship and soon Mrs Mulligan had established herself as a regular member of Mother's monthly coffee mornings. This gave her a useful entrée to a gathering of well-heeled potential customers and Mrs Mulligan was not slow to work the room to her advantage. Mother, always susceptible to a limitless source of admiration, chose to indulge the lady's unashamed hunger for new business, no doubt exacting a hefty discount on her own purchases as a quid pro quo. As the years went by, Mrs Mulligan – relishing her acceptance into this rarefied circle – would arrive bearing an array of merchandise, to the wry amusement of the assembled ladies.

One such coffee morning fell during the Easter holidays. Home from university, I was on hand to take coats, usher the ladies into the drawing room, serve coffee and cake, ensure the glass coffee percolator was replenished and the wick of the methane burner periodically trimmed. So I was within earshot when Oonah Riddell, one of Mother's friends, turned brightly to Mrs Mulligan. 'My dear, I don't believe we have ever heard mention of your husband – what *is* his line of business exactly?' Mrs Mulligan, flushing, fiddled awkwardly with her slice of cake. 'As it happens, he specialises in marine chronometers.' She enunciated the words carefully, as if she anticipated the baffled glances this information would elicit from the women around her. 'To help establish a ship's bearings, you know?' There was a brief pause, before Mrs Riddell's pointed rejoinder: 'I see. So you are both, in your different ways, adept at navigation!' Bridling, Mrs Mulligan rushed on. 'He is also a most enthusiastic golfer, a member of the Bealham Golf Club. I believe the Bealham is widely regarded as the leading regional club.' But Mrs Riddell was on a roll now. 'Oh, my Geoffrey can't ABIDE golf! Tedious business, he says, chasing after a little white ball for hours and hours. I have to say, I rather agree, and I do think it rich the club still won't accept women members, don't you? In this day and age!'

Mother, sensing the need for distraction, moved quickly between the tables, offering more food in a loud, insistent voice. I was on the point of leaving the room when Mrs Mulligan, scrabbling to reclaim her audience, replied: 'Well, yes, I do agree that banning women may seem a little fusty' – she let slip a conspiratorial tinkle of laughter – 'but you have to admit it's a relief to know they are at least adamant about the Jews. I mean, can you imagine?'

A brief silence gripped the room, the ladies shifting slightly in their chairs, delving suddenly into their handbags for powder compacts and lipsticks. 'Well!' – Mrs Riddell quickly grabbing the tiller – 'That was without doubt the most delicious apple strudel I have ever tasted! A delightful morning, but we mustn't overstay our welcome, come along ladies!'

After she died, I asked Father what he would like me to do with the contents of Mother's many wardrobes – her fur coats, cocktail dresses, silk suits, boxes of handmade shoes, crocodile handbags, scarves and gloves. Everything was carefully ordered according to season – autumn and winter outfits, colour-coded, in one vast wardrobe, spring and summer in another. This was her armoury – now faded and shabby, armpits stained, raw silk suits with fraying hems and missing buttons – expensive outfits that she had not worn for more than thirty years, but could not relinquish, evidence of her moment in the sun.

Father, slumped in a chair, stared in silence. After a long while he levered himself upright. 'Leave it, don't touch anything. I can't bear it.'

As I closed all the wardrobe doors again, I realised that among all this finery we had not found a single hat.

CHAPTER 15

Summer 1979

I am in my early twenties, at my parents' house recovering from glandular fever. Most days I just sleep, so weak I can barely crawl from bed to bathroom and back again. Day after day of numbing greyness, until one morning my mother brings me a bowl of porridge. As I manoeuvre the spoon to my lips, I see her mouth mimicking my action, her lips moving in sync with mine, as if willing me to swallow. There is a strange urgency in her eyes, I want her to leave me alone, but I'm too feeble to ward off the clawing feeling of being held, owned. Her eyes are welling up, I push the bowl away . . .

'Watching you, something comes back to me, something I need to tell you . . .' She straightens my pillow, settles down at the end of my bed. 'Be patient, you'll see the connection all in good time. On Sundays in the camp the guards let us rest and, refusing to be defeated by the brutality all around us, we organised a weekly "salon". Incredible, when I think about it – there was a gym class, eurythmics, readings from French literature, recitations in Greek and Latin – we had in our barrack a bunch of teachers, eminent scholars from a renowned Hebrew high school in Kolozsvár.[1] In a way it was absurd – we didn't know if we would survive another day, but this was our way of reminding ourselves who we were. We managed to get my aunt Lili transferred to our hut – she had been a soloist at the Vienna Volksoper and sang arias from her starring roles. I remember one afternoon she performed Ulrica's aria from Verdi's *Un ballo in maschera*. How appropriate, no? An invocation to the King of Hades! All those women from every walk of life, huddled together in stunned silence, mesmerised by the drama of this music. And so, just for a few hours, it was possible to forget we were in Auschwitz at all. Poor Lili, she was completely broken – her career as a singer denied her, her marriage annulled. We begged her – we could bribe her a place on a transport taking prisoners to one of the *Arbeitslager*, providing labour for factories like the Buna Werke and IG Farben, but she quietly refused – 'Dear one, we must all accept our fate.' As far as she was concerned, her life was over. She had changed her name, her religion, all for nothing: she had no fighting spirit left.'[2]

I want to focus on Mother's narrative, but my mind drifts away at this point. I am ten years old, sitting in the morning assembly at my prep school. Morris Openshaw, the headmaster, announces that he is setting up an opera club. A snicker of derision ripples through the hall. I keep my head down, but later in the day I drop by the school office and sign up. A few weeks later a small group of us file nervously into Mr Openshaw's study. It is a large, handsome room – wood-panelled walls, deep-green carpet, a carved stone mantelpiece, logs crackling on an open fire, a pair of leather-covered arm-chairs. Shaded side lamps cast a gentle glow. Four speakers are positioned around the room and over by the bay window there is an impressive array of hi-fi equipment. Cushions have been arranged on the floor in a semicircle in front of the fire. Mr Openshaw has changed out of his formal school suit and is wearing a shabby cardigan with leather patches at the elbows. His tall angular frame seems somehow less for-midable in this setting, his pale grey eyes, which miss nothing in the classroom, are softer now. 'Come on, boys, don't be shy – settle down. Right-oh, we're going to kick off with a real corker of a piece – *A Masked Ball* by Giuseppe Verdi, one of the greatest of all operatic composers. I won't bore you with the plot, suffice to say it's a complicated tale of intrigue, deception, hidden identities and – inevitably, as with most dramatic opera – it ends with a tragic death. This is a brand-new recording featuring the magnificent Leontyne Price and Signor Carlo Bergonzi, two of the greatest operatic artists performing today.'

I am puzzled by the opening bars of the overture – I expected something dramatic, overwhelming, but instead the piece begins with muted plucked strings, two flutes introdu-cing a slow, sad tune, and then the whole string section edges in, menacing chords invading the room. I look at the bowed heads of the other boys, as the flickering shadows play across the walls of Mr Openshaw's study. We are the conspirators, meeting in a secret room of the royal palace, plotting the assassination of the king.

Lulled by the music, my eyes flit lazily around the room,

taking in a tall mahogany bookcase, a side table with a half-filled whisky decanter, a rowing oar placed high on one wall emblazoned with gilded lettering 'Merton College Eight, 1934'. Centrally positioned on the mantelpiece, a silver picture frame glitters with orange darts from the fire below – a black-and-white photograph of a handsome young man in RAF uniform, perhaps eighteen years old. I remember thinking he looked like a movie star, with his sleek black hair and perfectly modelled cheekbones. Curious, I keep returning to the photo even though I instinctively know I should not. Mr Openshaw sees me staring at the picture and I quickly turn away, but he moves swiftly to the turntable, lifts the arm and switches on the central light. The evening is at an end, the fire reduced to a feeble glow. As the boys begin to file out, I point to the photo. 'Who is that young man, sir?' There is a long pause. Mr Openshaw's eyes narrow slightly and now there is the familiar steel in his voice: 'Never you mind, off you go now.' The following week when we assemble in the study, I notice the photograph has been removed.

My eyes flicker open and I can see Mother looking at me intently. 'I am boring you perhaps?' 'Of course not, it's just that your story reminded me of something. Anyway, please go on.' 'OK . . . so there was a selection in early November. We were driven into a concrete hut, divided down the middle by a rope. People were being ordered to one side of the rope or the other – it seemed the younger ones were selected to the right to join labour transports, others to the left. Those on the wrong side of the rope tried to duck underneath but were beaten back by the guards. Zsuzsi was still painfully thin, so we were directed to the left. I swear Zsuzsi saved both our lives that day – she grabbed my arm, pulled me away from the rope to the wall where she had spotted a ledge leading to a ventilation shaft halfway up the wall. She told me afterwards that the ledge triggered a memory of the ceramic stove in our father's study at home. It had a shelf a few feet off the floor and as small girls we would jump up and cling to the curving sides of the stove to keep warm.

'Both our parents were dead by then. Thinking back now, to that moment in the selection shed, I wonder if they were guiding us in some way? Anyhow, Zsuzsi hauled herself up onto the ledge and pulled me up after her. We squeezed through the opening – others tried to follow us, we could hear their cries as they were dragged back. There was such a crush in the selection hut, the guards didn't notice we were missing. For years after, I had this nightmare that I didn't make it, that Zsuzsi was desperately trying to pull me up, but someone had me by the foot, dragging me down, back into that seething, vengeful mass. When we dropped onto the ground outside there was an Appel under way, so we quietly slipped among the ranks of prisoners. A girl whispered to me that they were to be transported to Ravensbrück.[3] When we arrived that evening there was no room for us, so we were made to stand all night on the Appelplatz in the bitter cold.

'The next morning, they moved us into our hut. Here we actually had bunks, arranged in three tiers, four women on each level, top to toe, so you always had two pairs of feet up against your face, but at least we weren't trying to sleep on the bare ground. Next they handed us five blankets – five blankets for five hundred women! Of course, immediately fights broke out, everyone scrabbling to get a piece of blanket. One of the women was the wife of a doctor from Eger. Suddenly she turned on me, pulling and scratching with her beautifully varnished nails, screaming at me that her husband was the personal physician to the Archbishop of Eger! Ludicrous, pitiful behaviour – so desperate to get a blanket.

'Each day they handed out small hunks of bread – one morning the women in the neighbouring hut came screeching over to us, trying to grab the bread. I noticed they still had their hair and none of them was thin. Among them there was a quiet one, she smiled at me and we started talking. Her name was Ági, she was actually a Gentile, imprisoned for marrying a Jew. The Germans, always so preoccupied with social niceties, didn't know where to place her. They didn't want to put her in a hut with the Jews, so they put her with the prostitutes – less degrading, you see.' Mother laughs savagely.

'In December the plumbing often froze, the toilets clogged to the brim. I had to wait until around eight o'clock in the evening just to find a place to wash in the washroom, less crowded than it was in the mornings. For me, washing every night was an act of defiance, a ritual that reminded me I was still alive. It was also an opportunity to check through the heap of corpses to see if any of the dead had shoes worth stealing.'[4]

Mother's voice has dropped to a low monotone, her eyes fixed on the bowl of porridge in front of me. 'I remember mostly the incessant, gnawing hunger. One time, the kitchen staff tipped us off that they were cooking potatoes and there would be potato peel left on the garbage heaps. We knew that the SS guards would be drinking so some of us sneaked out to dig out the peel from the frozen garbage, just using our bare fingernails. My God it was worth it – sitting on the floor of our hut gulping down half-frozen potato peel: we thought it was the height of luxury!

'Ravensbrück was like stepping into bedlam. You have to remember that by now it was the last few months of the war. We could literally smell the beginning of the end, the sense of panic – *Kapos** pushing wheelbarrows filled with documents to be incinerated in the crematorium, covering their tracks. And with the Allies closing in, Himmler[5] was issuing ever more frantic orders to accelerate the extermination of prisoners. In the so-called hospital wing where women delivered their babies, they received dried milk for a few days, but then nothing, and those desperate mothers were forced to watch their starving infants shrivel into wizened monkeys and die, their tiny corpses thrown out into the corridor to rot along with the other dead. I remember a crazed woman wandering around the camp in those last days of mayhem, clutching her baby to her shrivelled breast, desperately bargaining for food – but the little thing was long dead, its face all blotched and grey.

'There were Jehovah's Witnesses in the camp as well – remarkable, principled people, persecuted by the Nazis for

---

* *Kapos* were camp prisoners selected by the SS to oversee other prisoners on labour details.

their political neutrality. They spoke back to the guards, would not be intimidated and often did their best to protect us, passing us scraps of food when they could, taking enormous risks of reprisal. I remember Zsuzsi saying, "the smaller their number, the greater their merit" and it is true – not enough has been said about these people. And I will always remember the kindness of the German political prisoners – there is no logic to any of this but thank God for the occasional scraps of humanity shown to us. In the camp I would repeat to myself a quote by the Roman playwright Terence, something my father taught me, shortly before he was taken away: "*Homo sum, humani nihil a me alienum puto* – I am human and nothing human is alien to me."

'At the time I thought my father, ever the idealist, interpreted those words as an appeal to our innate sense of common humanity, to our generosity of spirit: whatever our differences – race, religion, politics – we are nonetheless all human beings. But now I'm not so sure. He had a keen sense of the ironic. Perhaps he simply meant there was nothing in the miserable spectrum of human behaviour that could surprise him any more. In any event, he wasn't shown much generosity of spirit, poor man, but for me those moments of unexpected humanity were very precious, when everything else had been so brutally stripped away.

'In January '45 we were transported from Ravensbrück to the Reinickendorf camp, located inside the Argus factory compound.[6] Each morning we were woken at 5 a.m., when the *Offizierinnen* would give us our orders for the day. My job was to engrave numbers onto aeroplane parts, using an oxyacetylene welding torch, no protective visors of course, which is why my eyes are shot now. Anyway, by February '45 the women in the *Schlusskontrolle* – where they did the final quality checking of the components – reported back that our work was being rejected because the material was too poor to be used in the aeroplanes. Secretly, of course we were delighted! Then all production ceased due to a lack of engine parts and the factory was closed.

'We were all assigned new duties – I was sent to work in the clothing store. There was nothing there of any worth, just filthy rags. In a box I found 180 sanitary towels, for a barrack holding eight hundred women! As it happens, they were redundant anyway because of course we had long ago stopped menstruating. I was lucky – the *Unterscharführer**took a shine to me, he would come and chat to me. I guess he just wanted to be listened to, like any man. He would tell me what a difficult job he had. His orders were to extract as much labour as he could from the prisoners for the minimum cost, in terms of maintenance – it was such a difficult balance to achieve! I nodded sympathetically, because I knew I must, although inwardly boiling with rage. Another time I noticed he was looking anxious, distracted. I asked him what was wrong – apparently his son was missing on active service, he had received no news for three weeks. The boy was training to be a classical musician, so we started talking about music – imagine, the two of us, he in his position of complete

---

* The role of the *Unterscharführer* was to ensure order was maintained in the prison barracks.

authority and me a nonentity, less than that even, discussing our favourite Schubert songs! After that he was kind to me, occasionally left me food, and once a thin slice of bread and jam wrapped in a newspaper from the previous day containing rather more information about the progress of the war than he might have wished me to see. Or maybe not?

'From early March we were sent out to help dig trenches all around Berlin and remove wreckage from bomb sites – I guess a last attempt to defend the city from the Russian advance. Then on 18 March came the big showdown, one of the final major bombing raids on Berlin. And we didn't get a single hit. I have often wondered if they knew there were Jewish prisoners in those huts. But maybe it was just luck. Then on 1 April we were marched out of the camp. I remember the silence and a fine white dust floating gently down. We shuffled past shattered buildings, sewage seeping over the rubble, horses half incinerated, charred corpses hanging out of blackened window frames. There was some graffiti chalked on a wall – *"Berlin bleibt noch Deutsch!"* and *"Wir siegen doch!"* – "Berlin still remains German!", "We are still going to win!" and then it struck me, the war must be over, or nearly over, otherwise why these defiant messages scrawled hastily on the wall, the morning after the bombardment? Everyone thought I was delirious with hunger, but I sensed it was true. I felt it. People in the streets turned their heads away when they saw us. To them we were the final insult, that we of all people should remain alive amid all this carnage.[7]

'I had to leave Zsuzsi, lying in the *Krankenrevier*. A few

days earlier she was out with a group of women piling earth and leaves to camouflage mines the Germans were laying for the Russians. An SS guard beat her with a spade and now she was so weak she could barely crawl on all fours. I managed to smuggle a message to her, but I had no idea if I would ever see her again.

'It was a bitterly cold spring and by then our striped uniforms were in rags. I had rough wooden clogs which hurt like hell as we marched, slithering along in the snow and ice, but at least they insulated my feet against the biting cold. Everyone was on the move, the roads teaming with civilians trying to escape the Russian advance, women with babies strapped to their backs, old people slumped on makeshift handcarts hauled by half-starved horses, everyone heading west towards the Elbe, hoping to reach the Allied zone on the far bank of the river. German soldiers were heading in the same direction, desperate to surrender to the Americans rather than be caught by the Russians. But even now, in the chaos of defeat, they still had the energy to jeer at us, jabbing us with their rifle butts as they marched past, cursing us, filthy Jews.

'Many of us could barely walk – the guards moved up and down the column, finishing off those that gave up and fell by the roadside. Sára, a girl who had worked in another section of the factory constructing altimeters for anti-aircraft missiles, was walking with us. One night in the camp, she'd told me she'd figured out how to skew the equipment so the missiles would fall short of their targets. She was so proud of this, her small act of revenge. That afternoon I could see she was weakening, so I suggested we walk together, her arm slung over my shoulders, but after an hour I just couldn't support her, I had no strength left. She slipped down onto the bank of snow at the edge of the road. I tried to pull her up again, but it was hopeless. Her eyes stared up past me – I could see she was dying. One of the guards came running towards us, thrusting me aside. The crack of a single gunshot and she was gone, a thin stream of blood trickling from her temple over the snow. I felt nothing, I just knew I must survive, somehow. But as I walked on, I remembered her story about the altimeters and smiled . . .

'One evening we were corralled into a barn for the night. It was peaceful in there – I remember thinking to myself, this is a good place to die, straw on the ground, a few cattle gazing calmly at us as we sank to the floor. I spotted a couple of girls huddling close to one of the animals against the far wall, heard them whispering to each other in Hungarian and crawled over to join them. Gradually the group of prisoners fell silent, everyone slept. A few hours later, one of the girls shook me awake, her hand over my mouth. She pointed to a small aperture set into the wall. Silently we edged our way to the opening and crawled outside. It was freezing and still pitch-dark. We had no idea where to hide, but nearby we found a house and behind it an orchard with a broken-down garden shed. It was open so we dragged ourselves inside, pulled the door shut, lay down together and slept. As grey morning light filtered inside the shed, I woke to the sounds of the guards shouting. Through a crack in the wall I watched the prisoners stumbling out of the barn back onto the road. Slowly the guards' shouts grew fainter, and after a few minutes the place was silent again. We lay there, wondering what to do next. I guess we must have drifted off to sleep again. The next thing we knew there was a thump on the door. We sat bolt upright, terrified of discovery. The door was nudged open and a child's ball rolled inside, followed shortly after by a small boy. He didn't say a word, just backed out, terrified at the sight of us – three skeletal figures cowering in the dark. We heard him running towards the house. We were sure we would be discovered – it was over, our feeble attempt to escape. But a few minutes later the boy's mother came to the shed, took one look at us and silently placed a finger to her lips. Instinctively we knew we could trust her, her calm eyes registering the striped clothing, she knew . . . She whispered to us to stay where we were, she would come back when it was dark – the people in the next house were Nazis.

'As good as her word, she reappeared later that evening and led us through the orchard into the house, took our striped rags and burned them in the kitchen range. Somehow, she found us three sets of clothes, produced a can of hot water and towels so we could wash and then, dear God, she sat us down at the table and gave us bowls of warm porridge. I remember taking the bowl from her and all I could do was weep, hugging the bowl to my chest, unable to believe this gift was really for me, just for me. For the first time in months my belly actually felt full. I mean really full. Do you know, that woman sat up that night in a kitchen chair so that the three of us could sleep in her bed? I remember the strange touch of smooth cotton sheets, the bolster cradling my head, the warmth of the other two girls beside me, and then nothing . . . '

Propped up against the pillows, I try to take in the enormity of Mother's narrative, but my eyes are blank. Fogged by my fatigue, my mind cannot find the required words of comfort – they fall away, like shifting sand. I am failing her, again. She receives my silence as indifference, takes the bowl and leaves. We don't revisit this narrative for several years. On the few occasions when I make some reference, she flinches as though I had hit her, unprovoked and without warning.

CHAPTER 16

November 1975

Mother's initial revelation of her Jewish identity to me as I turned eighteen seemed to unlock something within her. Over the months and years that followed, she would return to her past obsessively, filling in gaps, answering questions. It was as though her sense of moral obligation to tell me something about my Jewish heritage had become a compulsion. Yet, at the same time, I had been sworn to secrecy. It seemed an impossible, grotesque demand. I urgently needed to explore my sense of being Jewish. Could it only be framed in relation to the trauma that had gone before? Was a non-observant Jew still a Jew? And if so, in what way? And yet, how could I ever publicly acknowledge my heritage, given my parents' entrenched determination to keep the past firmly hidden from prying eyes?

My school life was now over. The next challenge was to figure out how best to fill the nine months that stretched ahead before I went up to Cambridge. In theory I now had at least one foot in the real world, and the whiff of potential freedom was intoxicating. One of my school friends was planning a year-long Interrail trip, another had a job logging in Canada, a few were heading off to teach in various prep schools, but my closest friend Peter, also Jewish, had been talking for some time about applying to work on a kibbutz in Israel. This struck a chord – the idea of doing productive manual work on the land after months of exams was exciting, but more importantly this was an opportunity to explore what it might mean to be Jewish. Or Jew-ish.

My plan got short shrift at the breakfast table. 'This you will not do! How can you even think of such a thing?' Mother stood before me in quivering indignation. 'After everything we have done to blend in, to be . . . to be invisible . . . ' Her face mottled with anger, she spat out the word. The idea of Mother blending in struck me as implausible, but I bit my lip. Father lowered his paper briefly, looked at me with glacial eyes. 'This is not happening. This discussion is at an end. *Punkt und fertig.*'*

There was a stand-off for a few days, but I knew I had lost. The very suggestion that their son should spend his gap year in Israel was to them unthinkable, unforgivable, a monstrous slap in the face, betrayal of the worst kind. Once again, public perception was all-consuming: my suggestion, innocent enough, profoundly threatened their illusion of anonymity. I had raised ghosts: fear of the pointed finger, fear of the past.

It was a humiliating defeat – I had failed miserably to stand my ground. Worse still, the consolation prize seemed overwhelmingly infantilising. Father took matters in hand

---

*   Over and out.

and enrolled me on a French language and literature course at the Sorbonne: six months in Paris, all paid. In the weeks following his decision, I convinced myself that I could travel to Israel at some point in the future, without telling my parents if need be. In the meantime, England felt dreary, in decline – miners' strikes, electricity blackouts and rising inflation blighting the final phase of the Wilson government. I had to admit I was excited to turn my back on it all.

6 January 1976

Snow was falling softly against a leaden sky as my train pulled into the Gare du Nord. I headed down to the fourteenth arrondissement to dump my bags in my lodgings. The Collège Franco-Britannique was a grim-looking mock-Tudor pile with long corridors of brown linoleum, my ground-floor room sparsely furnished, with peeling magnolia paint. A grimy laurel bush close to the window blocked out most of the light. Dispirited, I set off to explore the city. By the time I walked into the main courtyard of the Louvre, the light was starting to fade, the snow turning to sleet, the dark stone walls austere and unwelcoming. There was only an hour before closing time, but I bought a ticket and wandered the corridors until I found what I was looking for – Michelangelo's *Slaves*.

At grammar school, Wednesday afternoons were scheduled for revision – I had a table at the far end of the library, in an alcove tucked between the art history bookstacks. I was supposed to be writing an essay about Henry VIII's foreign policy but turned instead to scan the books around me, pulling down at random a volume of Michelangelo sculptures. The cover illustration showed a detail of the *Rebellious Slave*, the textured, raw muscularity captured minutely in the sepia photograph. I began, furtively, to turn the pages. An anxious, spotty teenager transfixed by image after image of male beauty. 'You may not tell a soul.' Mother's diktat had added resonance now – this is who you are, face it.

I must have drifted off to sleep, slumped on a bench in front of the two sculptures. A bell in a distant gallery began to chime, announcing that the museum was about to close. I felt a hand on my shoulder and looked up to see a young attendant, gently shaking me. '*Nous fermons – allez!*' Dazed, I began to scrabble for my coat. '*Alors, suivez moi.*' He led me through various galleries, but just before we arrived at the top of the main staircase, he gestured to a corridor. '*Par ici, c'est plus vite.*' Checking that no one else was around, he stroked my cheek, then swiftly unlocked a side door leading into an unlit storage room. Turning, he took my hand, drew me inside: '*Viens, beau mec.*'

A few weeks later, a fellow student invited me to tea with friends of her parents. Marc and Renée lived in a shabby apartment off the rue du Montparnasse. A wavering voice crackled through the door buzzer: '*Au troisième.*' The building had been elegant once, with a grand staircase curving up from the cavernous entrance hall, but there was a fine layer of dust coating the wrought-iron balustrade and many of the marble steps were cracked. Wisps of faded paper curled from the walls here and there, like torn rolls of parchment. The noise of the busy street receded as we ascended each looping flight of stairs. Renée stood in the doorway, a frail stooped figure framed by the massive double doors. A tentative, apologetic smile danced briefly across her lined face: '*Bienvenu – entrez, je vous en prie!*' Her grey hair was held in a loose chignon, a flimsy shawl fluttering around her thin shoulders as she ushered us into a large room. Tall windows were swathed in net curtains hung with tendrils of dust – the pale afternoon light struggled to penetrate the room but at one end I could make out a makeshift dais covered in a patchwork of threadbare Turkish carpets, surmounted by a dead Christmas tree. Faded strands of tinsel and pale cut-glass ornaments clung to its brittle branches, most of which had long ago shed their needles.

Marc shuffled in from the kitchen, bearing a tray. He noted my bewildered gaze and smiled sheepishly, like a small boy caught in the act. 'We have always loved Christmas, you see. We were so sad dismantling everything each year, so eventually we adopted a laissez-faire approach. Why bother? So now it is Christmas all year round.' He handed round tiny bowls of lapsang souchong tea. I noticed that both his thumbs were badly disfigured, and yet he handled the tea bowls with great delicacy. He turned to my friend for news of her family and I sat in a corner, letting the conversation swill gently around me, drifting into a confused daydream about this strange, ethereal pair. Suddenly I became aware that Marc was talking to me: 'So, Simon, we gather you are keen to leave your lodgings at the Cité Universitaire? We have a maid's room here – it is very small, but you would be welcome.'

Intrigued by this couple, their fragile other-worldliness and touched by their spontaneous invitation, their evident warmth, I accepted. It was a strange little room, tucked tight under the curve of the main staircase, so at night I lay in my camp bed looking up at the underside of three of the marble steps above. There was a tiny porthole window giving out onto an internal courtyard below. In the adjoining cupboard was a toilet pan and a low basin originally intended for the *femme de ménage* to swill out her mops. The monthly rent was minimal and included morning coffee and a tartine which I ate with Marc and Renée in their kitchen.

Over breakfast they helped me with my coursework, looked through my essays, suggested additional reading. They took me to the Théâtre de la Huchette to see Eugène Ionesco's absurdist plays, *La Leçon* and *La Cantatrice chauve*, compiled a list of places I must visit – the Rodin Museum, the tapestries in the Musée de Cluny, the Institut Néerlandais and Delacroix's studio on the rue de Furstemberg. Marc, as a retired architect, used his connections to arrange a visit to the Maison de Verre, an astonishing house completed in the early 1930s, a collaboration between interior designer Pierre Chareau, Dutch architect Bernard Bijvoet and craftsman/ metalworker Louis Dalbet.

One morning they asked me about my family, curious about my name. I explained that my parents were Hungarian. I hesitated, aware that I was on the brink of betraying the family secret, but felt strangely at ease sitting in this kitchen, with coffee bubbling on the stove and Marc slicing a baguette fresh from the bakery. After all, she would never know. I took a deep breath.

'My mother is a Holocaust survivor.' There was a silence around the breakfast table and then Renée turned to me. 'You did not realise perhaps, we too are Jewish.' I blurted out: 'But the Christmas tree?' Marc smiled. 'She said Jew-ish, *non?*' Renée patted my hand: '*Tiens*, Simon, you are on safe ground here.' And so I began, sharing with them Mother's story, the ghetto, the privation of the camps, the death march and finally her escape across the Elbe.

In turn, they told their story. Part of the Resistance network set up by Major Francis Suttill, they ran messages, smuggled guns and ammunition, helped set up safe houses for English agents. 'We lived in constant danger of arrest,' Marc said. 'Living with fear is a terrible thing – your mother will know this, of course. Inevitably, there was a leak in the network, whether deliberate betrayal or simply carelessness, a lapse of judgement, who knows? Anyway, one evening we got a tip-off that the SS were on our tail. I was still burning documents the next morning when they broke down the door. Renée managed to slip down the servants' stairway and escape, but I was caught, interrogated and tortured.' Marc held up his mangled thumbs. '*Et voilà* . . . when they realised they couldn't extract the information they wanted, I was dispatched to Drancy. From there, a few weeks later, I was put on a train.'

By then the purpose of these transports was well known – to remain on the trains meant certain death. Marc noticed that the bars across the grating were badly rusted, so with a few others he set to work, eventually prising a couple loose. 'I was the only one who squeezed through and jumped, the others didn't dare, poor souls. Tumbling down the railway embankment, I twisted one knee but managed to hobble across the fields to a barn, where a local priest found me. He brought me food and bandages – pure luck, he could have been a collaborator.' By early August '44 Marc had made his way back into Paris, travelling at night, just in time to join the Resistance as they scrambled to erect barricades during those last few days before liberation. They turned trucks on their sides, cut down trees, dug trenches, anything to hinder the Germans. 'When I disappeared, it was too dangerous for Renée to continue her work, so she went into hiding, moving from one place to the next. For a long time she lived in a wooden crate beneath a pile of coal in a basement. I tried to find her, but no one could tell me what had happened to her. Then one evening I heard a footstep on the stairs, and there she was.' He paused, taking Renée's hand in his. '*Mon ange* . . . it was a miracle, to find each other again just as Paris was liberated.' The morning was long gone, we were still at the table, the coffee by now cold. '*Allez!* I know where we must take you now.'

Later that day we stood at the very tip of the Île de la Cité, the vast flying buttresses of Notre-Dame looming above us, an icy wind churning the slate-grey waters of the Seine. The Mémorial des Martyrs de la Déportation commemorates the 200,000 people deported to Nazi concentration camps. The architecture is fittingly stark, claustrophobic.

Arranged in neat diminishing rows, 200,000 minuscule light bulbs illuminate the narrow chamber containing the tomb of an unknown deportee killed at Neustadt and two urns filled with ashes collected from other camps. We were the only people there. The wind howled at the open entrance, the endless rows of tiny lights flickering feebly in the gloom.

Prompted by Marc and Renée, I explored Montmartre, sketched tourists in the Place du Tertre (a useful way of earning some extra money), took trips to Fontainebleau and Versailles. One evening I bought a ticket for a performance of *The Marriage of Figaro* at the Palais Garnier, the star attraction being Kiri Te Kanawa who was singing the role of the Countess. The concierge – a diminutive harpy with a purple rinse – looked askance at my shabby clothes but let me pass. The cloying opulence of the building was overwhelming – elegant Parisians glided up the ceremonial stairway, a seething mass of mink coats and serious jewels. I was acutely conscious of my dishevelled jacket and jeans and skulked in the shadows of the Grand Foyer, jostled by haughty waiters carrying trays of cocktails. But my embarrassment slipped away as I took my seat in the uppermost gallery of the auditorium, which gave me a prime view of the astonishing ceiling by Chagall. Against a backdrop of vermilion, emerald, canary yellow and cerulean blue, Chagall mapped a lyrical, mystical evocation of the arts, but when the work was unveiled in 1964 it was almost universally reviled – declared a sacrilege, a scar on the face of the Garnier. The final insult was that the commission should have been given to a foreigner – even worse, to a Jew.

'You will adore Paris – the Seine, the tree-lined boulevards, the grandeur of it all.' I could see why the relentless order of the city would appeal to Mother – perhaps it reminded her of the more opulent areas of pre-war Budapest – but the uniformity of pale grey stone, the matching roof heights, even the iron grilles encircling the base of every tree – all suggested a tightly maintained control that felt at times stultifying to me. So discovering the Centre Pompidou was a revelation – an industrial-sized disruptor, clearly designed to shock the city out of its smug self-satisfaction. I had never seen a building that so spectacularly broke all the rules – the transparent tubular escalator snaking up the front of the building, the brilliantly coloured service ducts and the exoskeleton of vertical columns braced by what looked like colossal dinosaur bones. I loved its explosion of pure anarchy – the bravery of the building seemed to me to celebrate the possibility of standing apart, of flying in the face of received opinion.

A college friend mentioned that a teacher at the local high school was looking for English conversation lessons. Would I be interested? I arranged to meet Manon the following evening at a neighbourhood bar. A tall, striking woman in her early thirties strode across to my table, throwing back a mane of rippling blonde hair as she sat down opposite me. I could tell she was born to be a teacher – compelling, direct, no-nonsense. 'So, we will meet every Saturday afternoon, half an hour in French, half an hour in English. My apartment is in the Gambetta-Ménilmontant district, near the Père Lachaise cemetery – you will find it easily. Anyway, if you haven't visited the cemetery, you must – Colette, Piaf, Chopin, your Oscar Wilde, Proust, oh and Jim Morrison: quite a party, *non*?' I offered a glass of wine, which was met with a matter-of-fact refusal. 'I don't drink. Not any more. I'll see you on Saturday.' She gathered her coat and bag, stretched out her hand. I notice that the last section of her forefinger was missing, but her grip was nonetheless firm.

Manon lived on the rue Boyer. The top-floor apartment, underneath the eaves, was neatly arranged. Above the sofa was a large poster of Catherine Deneuve in *Belle du Jour*, and a smaller one of Che Guevara over the sink. Sitting at Manon's kitchen table, we read together a passage from Camus' *L'Étranger*. I tried not to, but my eye kept being drawn to the stump of her forefinger as she turned the pages. 'The result of a car accident. I had been drinking. Which is why I don't now.' The first of many such confidences over our shared lessons. During the English-conversation segments of our time together, perhaps because she felt somehow at one remove from her personal narrative, she told me about her work, the challenges she found trying to teach teenage boys – 'but don't worry, I don't mean you' – the married doctor with whom she had been having a prolonged affair – 'an arrogant bastard but good in bed' – the head teacher who once tried to get her sacked because she wouldn't sleep with him. All this delivered in a brusque, almost dispassionate staccato. After a few sessions I began to wonder why she even wanted English-conversation classes, given her evidently fluent grasp of the language. As the weeks passed, I also noticed that she seemed to be paying greater attention to the way she dressed – tighter jeans, jaunty cowboy boots and on one occasion a shirt revealing an ample cleavage. She paid me compliments too – noting a newly acquired bomber jacket, or the fact that my curly hair was now shoulder-length. 'Don't cut it, I love it like that.' I sensed what was happening, of course, but even though I knew I must eventually disappoint her, I was curious to see how this might play out. Then one Saturday Manon ramped things up a notch. 'I have invited some friends for the weekend to my parents' house in Fontainebleau – maybe you would like to come along too?'

We drove out of Paris in Manon's little Fiat, stopping at a service station for coffee and croissants. She insisted on paying – '*C'est à moi*' – placing her hand lightly on mine as I went through the motions of reaching for my wallet. We lingered at the table, Manon laughing as she corrected my stumbling French; at one point she reached over, brushing away a crumb of croissant from the corner of my mouth. As we got back in the car, I realised this wasn't a game any longer – I glanced across at Manon, driving very fast now, a knowing smile playing across her lips. I was her latest catch, her English Jew boy with the curly hair and soft brown eyes. So when was I going to tell her? And what would happen when we got to Fontainebleau? I had to fess up, now. 'Manon, please slow down, can you? There's something I need to tell you.' She glanced at my stricken face and laughed, stamping on the accelerator as she roared past a lumbering tractor. 'What are you trying to say, that you're a virgin? Don't worry, *mon p'tit*, my friend Delphine will be very intrigued and Annette has a thing for young boys – you'll be fine!' I said nothing, pinned to my seat with a feeling of sick terror.

We turned into a leafy suburban street. The house was not what I had expected – crisp and catalogue-fresh, with a scrupulously manicured garden. There were two cars already parked in the driveway. Delphine, mid-forties I guessed, was lounging by the pool. Wrapped in a batik sarong, she was carefully applying metallic burgundy nail polish to her toes, pausing to give me a cool once-over while air-kissing Manon. Annette, more corpulent, was busy in the kitchen – she looked as though she had already done some enthusiastic sampling while preparing our cocktails, giving me a hefty pinch on the bum by way of greeting. Manon gestured me to sit beside her at the edge of the pool. 'I forgot to remind you to bring swimming shorts – ah well, *tant pis*, we don't mind, eh, girls?' The three of them laughed raucously.

I knew I had to extricate myself from this mess, masquerading as something I was not. Making an excuse that I'd left something in the car, I slipped out of the front door and raced down the street to the railway station. A train back to Paris was just about to leave – flinging myself inside, I huddled in a corner, shamefaced and exhausted. As the train set off, I began to breathe again.

Among various posters tacked to a noticeboard in the Sorbonne was a flyer from the Accueil des Étrangers, a Christian organisation offering foreign students the opportunity to meet with French families. I was dubious, but a free meal was a free meal, so I signed up. A few weeks later I received a formal invitation: '*M. and Mme Blanchard would be delighted if Monsieur Weisz would join them for dinner.'* The apartment was in an imposing nineteenth-century block near Les Invalides. Hunting for a florist made me late, so I took the lift – an elaborate wood-panelled affair with an array of discreetly glowing buttons. Arriving at the first-floor landing, I caught a brief glimpse of the entire family lined up in readiness, from Monsieur all the way down to the maid, with numerous formally dressed children in between, but in my confusion pressed the wrong button and found myself descending once more to the entrance foyer. It was an awkward beginning to a stiff, awkward evening. Mme Blanchard was glacial, with bouffant hair and a Dior dress. As she introduced me to one of her many children, I noted the flicker of her pale grey eyes making a quick, efficient appraisal – scuffed shoes, rumpled jacket. I remembered thinking that Mother and Madame would get along just fine. The only other guest was Pierre, the family solicitor. As we moved into dinner, he clasped my shoulder and bent slightly to whisper, *'Bonne chance, mon brave . . . '* I was placed on one side of Madame, Pierre on the other.

No doubt prompted by my surname, Madame B. cut straight to the chase, with an icy smile of interrogation. 'So, Simon, tell me about your family, your parents.' I knew where this was going. The whole table was quiet, waiting for me to respond. This betrayal of our family secret seemed legitimate – I smiled back. *'En effet, madame, nous sommes juifs.'* Madame's expression flickered for a nanosecond – she patted her bouffant hair as if a slight breeze had momentarily displaced its perfect symmetry, *'Ah . . . intéressant . . .',* before turning pointedly to talk with Pierre. The chatter around the table resumed, but at a more muted pitch, it seemed to me. I spent most of the meal watching nervously to see which cutlery to pick up, which glass to use – and then disaster struck. The maid hovered behind me with a large silver tray on which a charlotte russe perched precariously. She offered me two serving spoons and I managed to secure a slice but realised, too late, that I had misjudged the distance between the tray and the table edge. In my panic I flung the wobbling portion towards my plate and missed completely, depositing most of the sugary glob onto Madame's exquisite dress. For a split second the pale grey eyes stared in horror at the gelatinous ruin, and then Madame leapt to her feet with an audible hiss of rage and ran from the room, the maid scuttling behind her. Silence gripped the room, all of us glued to our chairs as if in freeze-frame. At last, Madame re-entered in a new outfit, took her seat beside me, waving away my stuttered apologies with a glassy '*Il n'y a pas de quoi!*' The evening did not recover – I remembered Mother's mantra regarding social visits: 'Never fail to be polite and never outstay your welcome,' something she had learned through bitter experience. Well, this time I had really blown it. Pierre drove me home, chuckling at my embarrassment. Back in Montparnasse, I found Marc tidying the kitchen. '*Alors, comment c'était?*' I recounted my double faux pas and he smiled. 'I am sure Madame can afford the dry-cleaning bill. As for the rest, what did you expect?'

The end-of-term exams were done. I visited my favourite market stall on the rue Mouffetard one last time, walked through the arcades of the Palais Royal to a farewell meal with friends at Bouillon Chartier, and then one July morning Marc and Renée accompanied me to the Gare du Nord. Marc bought me a tartine, thrusting it into my haversack with a smile, and then they stood together, waving as the train pulled out. I watched them turn, two frail figures threading their way cautiously through the crowd.

Just before I was due to start at Cambridge, a letter arrived from one of my Sorbonne friends. Early one morning, returning from the market laden with bags, it seems Marc stumbled on the cracked marble steps leading to their apartment, falling backwards down the elegant curving stairway, over and over, down into the entrance lobby below. A neighbour found him sprawled among the wreckage of shopping bags, but it was too late. I wrote to Renée, now in a nursing home, but received no reply.

I am writing this fifty years later, in gratitude, remembering their friendship – Renée reaching out to touch my hand as we sat together in the kitchen: '*Tiens*, Simon, you are on safe ground here.'

CHAPTER 17

October 1976

My gap year now behind me, Mother and Father are driving me to Cambridge for the start of my first term. Sitting behind them, half asleep, I catch drifts of their pointedly animated conversation – '. . . let's hope he buckles down now, after Paris . . . such an opportunity . . . new challenges . . . doors opening . . . chosen few . . .' Burrowing into the plush leather seat, I try to stifle my resentment, press-ganged by Father into studying history, a subject not of my choosing. My disappointment increases when we arrive at St John's – I discover that my bid for rooms in the sixteenth-century First Court has been unsuccessful. Instead, I have been allocated a room in the Cripps Building, a Brutalist extension at the other end of the college grounds.[1] My parents leave me to unpack, with instructions to meet them later for dinner: '7 p.m. – on the dot!' The door closes behind them and I scan the room – anonymous, with a nod to Scandinavian design: solid block floor, one wall covered in hessian and a vast south-facing window offering an uninterrupted view out over the Backs. It could not be further from the historical setting I had imagined. Feeling completely disengaged, I flop onto the bed and fall asleep. It is dusk when I set out towards the hotel along King's Parade, passing the Senate House and King's College Chapel. I can register the beauty of the place but am overwhelmed by the sense that I am a fraud – that I have landed here under false pretences, that I have no right to be here.

Mother and Father leave after breakfast, Father's parting shot, 'Remember, you can be anything you want to be!', delivered with a conspiratorial wink. The old mantra, meaningless given his relentless control, feels like a stiletto between the ribs. The morning continues in a similar vein. I have a meeting with my tutor – a small, pudgy man, with a smile that chills. 'Ah, Weisz, come in.' Enthroned in a high-backed Victorian chair, he gestures me to a low sofa on the opposite side of the study while he riffles through some papers. 'I have been reviewing your entrance papers. Can't for the life of me comprehend why we awarded you an exhibition, if I'm honest. Borderline at best. Ah well . . . I dare say we should give you the benefit of the doubt, hmmm? Your first essay will be on the economic impact of the Black Death.' He hands me a long reading list and I am dismissed.

The History Faculty building on the Sedgwick Site, designed by James Stirling, is a stark affair – two vast retaining walls of bilious red brick set at right angles to each other support a cascading glazed atrium, freezing in the winter months, blisteringly hot during the spring and summer. Impossibly narrow corridors give congested access to the lecture rooms, which are cramped and stuffy. I steer clear of the miserable place as much as I can, preferring the plush calm of the University Library Reading Room, the added attraction being home-made cheese scones in the basement refectory. My essays are routinely botched, eleventh-hour affairs, marked down accordingly, then stuffed into the bottom drawer of my desk.

One evening during that first autumn term I wander into chapel for choral evensong and weigh up my options. I could throw in the towel and leave, but I know I'm too much of a coward to walk away. Perhaps I can carve out a different kind of identity for myself. Sitting in the gloom, I hear Mother's insistent voice piercing the waves of sound washing over me – 'Don't you realise how lucky you are? Let me remind you that some of us were not so fortunate . . . I would have given anything to have had this opportunity – how dare you think of abandoning it so casually? Toe the line, put in the work, do what is expected of you!' I glance along the pews – a scattering of bowed heads lulled by the cloying cadences of a Stanford anthem – ignoring Mother's imagined rebuke, I slip out of a side door into the night air.

The following week I audition for the part of the Duke in Middleton's *The Revenger's Tragedy*, a grizzly piece of Jacobean Grand Guignol, and two weeks later join the university orchestra, rehearsing Britten's *Cantata Academica* for performances with Peter Pears as tenor soloist. Later that term, friends invite me to lead a small group of musicians in a production of Kurt Weill's *Mahagonny* in the Corn Exchange, directed by an undergraduate called Nick

Hytner. Some string players in the orchestra ask if I would like to play in a quartet and soon we are meeting every week, exploring music by Brahms, Schubert, Dvořák, and demolishing bags of Chelsea buns from Fitzbillies. I draw cartoons for the student newspaper, design a couple of book jackets for Cambridge University Press, learn how to punt, host elaborate dinner parties that I can't afford and – most importantly – start hopping in and out of numerous beds.

This last activity depends on the tacit collusion of the college bedder who can usually be persuaded, courtesy of a fat tip, to turn a blind eye. I am not so fortunate. Mrs Bramble is as prickly as her name suggests, with a beady eye and a knack of banging on the outer door of my set at inconvenient moments. 'I know what's going on in there!' she hollers, standing on the landing with her mop and bucket, arms akimbo, glaring blue fire as the guest of the moment disappears down the staircase two at a time. Eventually, I receive a summons from my tutor. There has been a complaint. Am I aware I could be sent down? I pluck up the courage to enquire whether we would be having this conversation if the other party had been female. The mottled face puckers slightly. 'Weisz, I suggest you leave it there. Let this be a final warning.' Incensed, I deliberately slam the outer door of his set as I clatter down the oak staircase and out into First Court. Suddenly the austere beauty of the college has taken on a menacing aspect.

I recently came upon a box of letters from Father, and

one, written to me while at Cambridge, was clearly framed as a template for success – setting out attainments and enthusiasms that I would do well to emulate. He mentions with cheery bluster a recent order of vintage hock from the Wine Society and his admiration (as an émigré) for eminent English eccentrics, ending by urging me to join a London club. He also inserts a steely reminder that I should buckle down and work hard – his insistence on academic success ever-present. Re-reading it now, I am also struck by his inclusion of a love sonnet by Philip Sidney – I didn't register this at the time, but now I wonder if this was some kind of veiled acceptance of my sexuality. Possibly, but the parody that follows feels double-edged, a poor attempt to mask his disappointment.

Simon,

I am deep in wine lists. All are agreed that the '76 Hock vintage was the best this century. I am also buying a significant stock of Hungarian wine – it seems all my erstwhile patriotism (?) is turning liquid.

I am also reading a delightful biography of the four Knox brothers. They represent the England I have always admired: brilliant, eccentric, learned and witty. Eddie was the editor of *Punch* and wrote charming light verse; Dilly was a gifted mathematician and Greek scholar, and was employed by the Admiralty, code-breaking intelligence in both World Wars; Ronnie wrote detective

stories, translated the Bible and was an accomplished wit
and journalist; and Wilfred was an Anglo-Catholic priest
and teacher.

I had dinner last week at the Oxford & Cambridge
Club – elegant, good cuisine and an excellent library,
membership restricted to distinguished members of
those hallowed seats of learning. I strongly suggest you
apply: I would love to dine with you there on a winter's
evening in full glory!

I assume, by the way, that your studies are progressing
well and that you will be sensibly shelving all extracurricular activities for the time being, as you prepare for your
end of year exams?

For no reason whatsoever, I have dredged up from
the ragbag of my memory a parody of a Philip Sidney
sonnet. The original, or part of it, goes as follows:

> My true-love hath my heart and I have his,
> By just exchange one for the other given:
> I hold his dear, and mine he cannot miss;
> There never was a bargain better driven . . .
> My true love hath my heart and I have his.[2]

The parody is the lament of a man who has lost his shirt:

> The laundry hath my shirt and I have its
> By strange exchange one for another given.

I hold it dear, and mine they cannot miss;
Was there ever a better bargain driven?
The laundry hath my shirt and I have its.

I think I now rate an MA (at least!) Cantab in Eng. Lit, don't you?

Best, Pa

CHAPTER 18

Summer 1977

The end of my first year at university. I have not distinguished myself in my end-of-year exams, so by way of tacit reprimand my parents have arranged a summer vacation job for me at a country inn. It is run by two women, Kath and Sylvia, both excellent chefs who have built a reputation in the area for no-nonsense food sourced from local producers. Kath is in her sixties, spare of frame, cropped white hair, steely blue eyes and a strong jaw. Sylvia is fleshier, with small black eyes, flaring nostrils that suggest a peppery temperament.

Kath is in her office when I arrive. She peers at me over frameless half-moon spectacles. 'No time to train you, I'm afraid, just keep a clear head if you can. And don't mix up the orders, whatever else you do. Off you go, Sylvia will fix you up with an apron.' Her distracted air confirms what I had already suspected: my parents are valued customers, the two women have been coerced into taking me on.

It's a Sunday lunchtime, guests are starting to arrive. Sylvia propels me to the front bar, giving me a strange, sideways look. 'Just be charming – I'm sure you can manage that, can't you? Check people off the list, set them up with drinks. Come on, chop-chop!' She runs her stubby fingers through a mop of curly rust-coloured hair and stomps off to the kitchen.

Three hours later and lunch is over. The last guest – a ruddy-faced gent in an old hacking jacket – seems keen to linger, calling for another coffee and a port. Sylvia pulls me to one side. 'Watch that one, he's a bit of a groper. Take him the bill and make it clear we're closing up.' True enough, he proves tricky to dislodge, clumsily clasping my hand in his fleshy paw as he passes me a twenty-pound note. I watch him lumbering out to his beaten-up old Jaguar, driving away with a cheery wave.

Beyond the kitchen is a stone-flagged courtyard. Kath and Sylvia are sitting on a bench, Sylvia's arm draped round Kath's shoulders. Kath glances up at me. 'Not a bad start – thirty-two covers and no mess-ups.' Sylvia offers me a cigarette with a conspiratorial wink. 'We were rather dreading this I have to say – but you've done well.'

After a few weeks I am competently running front of house. One evening we have a block booking from the local hunt. 'Button your lip,' Sylvia says just before the guests arrive. 'I suspect these buggers are going to seriously challenge your pinko leftist leanings. Now get out there and strut your stuff. If you think you've got problems, try prepping beef Wellington for thirty.' More ferocious tousling of the red mop as she kicks open the kitchen door and disappears.

The dining room is crammed with raucous voices and a swell of entitlement – none of the guests appear to register that Sylvia has turned out one of the great classics of English cooking. At the end of the evening, surveying the wreckage strewn across the kitchen table, she downs a large shot of whisky and rams a cigarette in her mouth. 'Leave this mess, let's go for a stretch along the river before we tackle all this.' I don't say much, wary of her simmering anger. 'It's not so much this foul bunch I'm angry with.' She flings herself down on the grass, takes a deep drag of her cigarette. 'I'm getting threatening letters from my husband. My soon-to-be ex-husband, that is.' I stare down at my feet, not knowing what to say. 'He writes that he's burned all my clothes. I had some lovely things – all gone.' She begins to weep, cradling her head in her arms. 'And worse, far worse – he won't let me see my son. He's about your age, just finishing school. And his father has turned my boy against me. It's so fucking unfair.' I stare down into the water, mystified that she should choose to confide in me but too gauche to curb my curiosity. 'But why is he doing this?'

She laughs savagely. 'It's obvious surely? I chose Kath, I left him for Kath. And this is his revenge.' She turns towards me, I can smell the tobacco on her breath. 'You would never do something so cruel, I know you wouldn't – you're such a dear boy.' Too late, I sense the intent of her cloying words – in the darkness I feel her fingers pawing at my open shirt. I freeze, roll away from her, cover my revulsion by fumbling for a cigarette. 'I'm sorry –' panting now, gulping back her shame – 'please don't tell Kath, will you promise me? And I'm sorry too for telling you all this, really I am.' I leap to my feet and walk away, fighting off a suffocating wave of nausea.

Kath is in her office, totting up the takings. Silently, I help clear up the tables and swab down the bar, then let myself out and walk up the hill in the moonlight. Kath and Sylvia's house is a rambling stone construction with deep mullioned windows and low eaves, set behind a high wall. Herbaceous borders line a flagged path leading to a solid front door, always left unlatched. From the square hallway, an oak staircase leads up to a long galleried corridor which winds and twists through various sections of the house. My room at the far end of the corridor is sparsely furnished – a ship's bed on one side and a vast lacquered Chinese cabinet on the other.

Sylvia's story has stripped me of sleep. I sit cross-legged on the bare floor, staring at the cabinet's faded beauty – ghostly traces of delicate pavilions, fountains and flowering branches, and two courtly figures, their arms entwined, thrown into momentary relief in a sliver of shifting moonlight. I think of Kath and Sylvia, their arms casually linked – the prospect of ever being able to express affection so openly for another man seems impossibly remote. Or maybe not? Fatigue and fear smother my initial euphoria as I recall Sylvia's grief, the husband's fury, the burnt clothes – and then tonight's blundering, furtive betrayal.

A few days later, I head down to the inn to collect my walking boots. It's my day off and I'm planning a day's hiking over the fells. Kath is talking to someone at the bar – I don't want to intrude but she calls me over. 'Simon, my friend Li could use some help – you're free today, aren't you?' Turning to greet me is a wiry figure in baggy overalls, dark eyes below a thatch of black hair flecked with grey. 'Hullo! You will be my assistant, yes?' We set off in Li's old van. He drives very slowly, clicking his tongue as he shifts gears, muttering words of encouragement – I am unsure whether to himself or the van – as he negotiates each bend in the road, uncertain of what he might encounter. On the outskirts of a village, his craggy face brightens as he turns the van through broken-down gates and into a farmyard. A lopsided notice nailed to the wall welcomes visitors to the LYC Museum.[1]

'Come! I show you!' He takes me along a corridor lined with his abstract poems. Each poem consists of capitalised words arranged in a square format, creating diagonal gullies of white space criss-crossing the grid. I find my eye drawn to the intersecting spaces, then to the ambiguity of the words, then back again. One begins:

```
TELL ME           WHAT       DO          YOU        WANT
TELL ME WHAT       DO         YOU    WANT        REALLY
TELL ME WHAT DO    YOU WANT      MY        DEAR  FRIEND
```

And another:

```
WHOLE             I                   RECEIVE
WHOLE       I           GIVE       AWAY
```

I want to stay and study them more carefully, but Li takes my hand. 'Come!' The corridor leads into a large, white-washed room, at one end a long trestle table piled with gilded paper discs, each inscribed with an assemblage of letters. Li dances from one foot to the other. 'You know poem by Mr Blake "The world in a grain of sand"? So, this is my world, my "cosmic point". You see, the dot is the beginning, then it becomes a circle, it gathers a world within itself. In same way, time is constantly circling, never linear. My life has been like this, fleeing from China, finding my people in Taiwan, Bologna and then London. But always searching for that cosmic point. And it is here, now, in this unlikely place . . . so you see, the dot becomes a disc, then it multiplies. That is my wish for this exhibition. Now we work, yes?'

The day's task is to attach the discs to fine nylon threads and then suspend them from the ceiling. Li has measured out a precise grid – my job is to steady the rickety stepladder and pass him the next disc. After a couple of hours we take a break. Li makes tea in an old iron pot, pouring the smoky brew into tiny cups. We survey the effect – the discs move slowly in a light breeze from the open windows. As they turn on their threads, I try to catch the rotating words but Li laughs. 'No, no – these are not like notices. No! We create a puzzle, a little mysterious: you understand?' I am not sure I do, but I like that he has said 'we', proud that I have helped create this strange assemblage.

By late afternoon, the installation is complete – the entire room shimmers with gilded discs. I see now that Li has subtly altered the lengths of every thread, so the overall effect appears to be haphazard, organic.

There is one disc left on the table. Li passes it to me

with a slight bow. 'This one for you!' It carries the words 'HA – HOO – HUG'. In my embarrassment I stutter my thanks. 'But, Li, what does it mean?' 'Ha ha – it means whatever you want it to mean! The important thing is to find your own way. Here, take it!' He wraps it carefully in tissue paper and I tuck it into my rucksack. It is a fine evening and I decide to walk back. We shake hands and I set off along the lane. Just before dipping out of view, I turn back – Li is standing by the gate, both arms stretched high above his head in a strange salute. I still have the disc, my enigmatic talisman, the first thing to be packed and then unpacked with every move.

One evening Kath and I are sitting in her kitchen. It is almost midnight, we are both dog-tired. Kath looks drawn and pale, leaning hunched against the warmth of the Aga. 'Have I ever mentioned my son, Dominic?' After the collapse of her marriage, Kath and her small boy moved onto a longboat near Oxford. Kath worked as a teacher, Dominic attended a local school – a bright child, affectionate, popular. But as he grew older, he seemed to withdraw, became increasingly hostile and was often violent with his mother. 'Shortly after he turned sixteen, he just vanished. My golden boy . . .' She throws a shovel of coal into the Aga grate, then turns to me. 'Do you know Constance's speech from *King John*? Part of it goes like this:

> '"Grief fills the room up of my absent child,
> Lies in his bed, walks up and down with me,
> Puts on his pretty looks, repeats his words,

Remembers me of all his gracious parts,
Stuffs out his vacant garments with his form;
Then, have I reason to be fond of grief?"

'Occasionally the police would find him, bring him back, usually high on heroin. He's been in and out of rehab for years now. Last week he rang me. He's coming home. Of course, I long to see him again, and yet at the same time I dread it. Anyway, I felt you should be prepared. I'm sorry, it won't be easy.'

Our first encounter is on the upper landing, a tall figure in a black leather trench coat striding towards me, hands thrust in his pockets, head down, a mane of thick, unkempt hair falling to his shoulders. I stop, anticipating a brief exchange of some kind, but Dominic brushes past me with a low grunt. I watch his powerful figure crashing along the hallway, and as he turns the corner, I think I understand why he regards me as the enemy, something to be despised.

It is a particularly tiring evening shift, with a full dining room and a crowded bar. By the time I climb up the hill it's well after midnight. Picking my way along the upper landing I can see a shaft of light streaming across the corridor from Dominic's room. I try to step softly past his doorway but it seems he has been waiting for me. 'I want a word with you.' I hover in the doorway – from his sneering drawl, I can tell he's been drinking. 'Listen you, what's my meddling dyke of a mother been saying about me, hmm? Whatever it was, it's just a pack of lies. And I don't appreciate some snivelling Jew-boy spying on me, understood?' He is standing over me now, beads of sweat on his forehead, his pale blue eyes registering the fear in my face. Grabbing my arm, he spins me round. 'Why are you here anyway? What do you want with me, hmm?' But then he stops. Kath is standing in the corridor. 'Dominic, come downstairs now. The police are here.' Slowly he relaxes his hold on my arm, but as he turns to follow her, he hisses in my ear: 'You shopped me, didn't you, you little runt? I swear, I'll get you for this.' I slip into my room and lock the door. About an hour goes by, then I hear Kath's voice: 'Simon, they've gone. Come downstairs, I've made us some tea.'

She is standing by the kitchen table, hands me a mug, slumps into a chair. 'I found his stuff in the outhouse. He's been using again.' She peers intently out of the window, as if trying to make sense of the darkness outside. 'I wonder if I will ever really know where I went wrong, where his anger comes from. And why he has come back to haunt me now. After all this time . . . ' She turns to face me: 'I'm so sorry, you shouldn't have to witness all this, it's not right.'

I touch her lightly on the shoulder. 'Maybe he came back because he needs you – maybe he is trying to repair something. I think I'm going to get in the way of that, don't you?' I leave her nursing her tea and her sorrow. Climbing the stairs for the last time, I flick off the light in Dominic's room and curl up on my bed.

Early next morning, I pull my belongings out of the Chinese cabinet. In the bottom corner of the left-hand door there is a detail I hadn't noticed before – the wooden panel has cracked over time and the paint is faded but I can just make out the ghostly figure of a young fisherman, his outer robe tucked into his belt as he wades into the river, his arms outstretched high above his head, net circling, as he prepares to cast it out over the water.

Down in the kitchen I write a brief note, then close the front door behind me for the last time.

CHAPTER 19

Summer 1978

After my History Part I exams at the end of my second year, I received another summons, this time to a disciplinary board. I knew why – in my social-economic paper, unable to answer a single question, I had penned a four-page verse in rhyming couplets about the Great Famine of 1315–17. Six dusty-looking academics took great pleasure in grinding me to a pulp. 'Weisz, we are minded to send you down. Explain yourself!' I am not sure how I managed to persuade them to let me switch to the English Faculty for my final year, but they did, albeit grudgingly. 'No doubt your – ahem – creative talents will be put to better use in the English Faculty.'

I was acutely aware that I had narrowly avoided a very public disgrace. It was a blazing summer's day and, legs shaking, I wandered down to the banks of the Cam, haunted by Father's mantra: 'You can be whatever you want to be.' I knew that my exhibition to Cambridge had been a defining moment for my parents – a pivotal moment of arrival and cause for much celebration. As a result of the turmoil in wartime Europe, Mother's family had been almost completely annihilated, while Father's family had endured the trauma and cultural upheaval of forced emigration. My acceptance into this revered English institution offered the possibility of at least partial reparation for the losses they had suffered. They were delighted for me, certainly, but more importantly they found themselves, by association, ushered into the very heart of the English establishment. And now I had almost thrown it away. My overriding thought was that I had so nearly let them down.

Secretly, I had always regarded my arrival in Cambridge as little more than a lucky fluke, surely the result of administrative oversight. Trying to square my lack of self-belief with the relentless weight of parental expectations was a constant battle. Added to which I was mining a rich seam of resentment – Father had manoeuvred me into an area of study that wasn't of my choosing. As a result, sabotage was definitely somewhere in the mix – but now all sense of bravado had suddenly evaporated.

I downed several whiskies before dialling my parents' number. There was a stunned silence after I managed to blurt out that I had barely scraped a third. When I added that my request to switch faculty had been granted, there was an audible hiss of distaste from Father at the other end of the phone. 'Hardly a worthy return on our investment, is it? Let us hope you manage to redeem yourself in your final year.'

I chalked this up as some kind of victory, via the back door admittedly, but a victory nonetheless and spent the long vac happily cramming texts I would be studying the following autumn. In the spring term I pulled together a rather muddled dissertation on the novels of Patrick White and ended the year with a moderately acceptable degree.

July 1979

Graduation day – Mother and Father in their best bib and tucker, putting a brave face on their evident disappointment (Father having sailed through university with a first-class degree). Mother, rather plumper than she should be, is perspiring heavily underneath her broad-brimmed hat, her tailored silk two-piece already limp as we queue for more than an hour in blazing sunshine outside the Senate House. After the ceremony, we return to college for glasses of tepid Riesling and a stilted conversation with my tutor whose glazed eyes betray his profound lack of interest, despite – or perhaps because of – Mother's effusive and repeated thanks. Eventually we leave, Mother insisting on returning to the hotel so she can change clothes – I have booked a punt so we can spend the afternoon on the Cam. I stuff my hired gown into a carrier bag and wait below in the hotel lobby. An hour later Mother appears at the top of the stairs in a new outfit, complete with a long silk scarf which she has evidently decided is de rigueur for a punting expedition. She starts to descend the thickly carpeted stairs, bestowing on me a triumphant smile, and then disaster strikes. Somehow her heel gets caught in the trailing scarf and rather than clutching onto the banister she holds tightly to her large crocodile handbag. I watch in horror as

Mother, emitting a guttural cry of despair, begins to cartwheel slowly down an entire flight of stairs. By the time I reach her she is already sitting up, clearly somewhat concussed. Eyes bulging, she attempts, despite her dishevelled state, to reclaim her usual grande dame demeanour, but what emerges from her mouth – full volume – is a surprisingly unladylike Hungarian obscenity: '*Fostalicska!*' which roughly translates as 'Wheelbarrow of shit!' By now Father has appeared and we usher her, tottering on her crocodile heels, into the bar and ply her with brandy. After a second glass she begins to rummage in her handbag for a powder compact, signalling that the crisis is now over. I perch on a bar stool, remembering my eighteenth birthday when Mother had seized the moment to take centre stage. And here she is again, triumphantly repeating her party trick on my graduation day. Somehow we manage to bundle her into the punt and the rest of the afternoon passes without incident.

In the months leading up to the final exams I wrote letters to every publisher in London and shortly after graduation receive a letter offering me a position in the production department at Chapman & Hall. In my arrogance, I was hoping for a position, however lowly, in an editorial department, but it is my only offer and I am grateful just to get a toe in the door. Leaving Cambridge for the last time, I feel intense relief – my time at university is over, there are no more hoops to jump through, or so I believe.

I have a job in London, I am financially independent for the first time in my life, I am free.

August 1979

Chapman & Hall established its early reputation publishing the works of Dickens, Thackeray and Trollope, and one of its most illustrious managing directors was Arthur Waugh (father of Alec and Evelyn), but by the time I join in 1979 the list is predominantly scientific. Father is delighted, I am less so. The building is a dreary 1960s office block on Fetter Lane (recently demolished) with long gloomy corridors and stairways smelling of disinfectant. I share an office with Arnold, a man in his mid-forties who has been running the production department for more than twenty years. Arnold lives with his mother in Godalming – he has a relentlessly jolly demeanour which I suspect hides much sadness and, quite possibly, repression. 'Well, young man, what's new and exciting today?' he enquires breezily as he waddles over to his desk each morning, adjusting his comb-over as he sits down. The highpoint of his day is the arrival of Myrtle the tea lady at 4 p.m. Myrtle, who hails from Belfast, should have had a promising career in panto, if her disparaging glances at poor Arnold, fussing over whether to buy a Twix or a Penguin, are anything to go by. She takes a shine to me for some reason – leaning against the door and ignoring her customers further down the hallway, she would light a Silk Cut and launch into a detailed account of her bunions. 'My advice? Top yerself. Anythink rather than grow old.' Surely there is more to life than Arnold's despair or Myrtle's grim ailments? I resign at the end of my first month.

Another uncomfortable telephone call home. A sharp intake of breath from Father. 'So, what precisely do you plan to do now?' I have a plan but it is not something I am prepared to share with either parent. The following week I make an appointment at the local bus depot – the clerk at the admissions office looks sceptical, squinting up at me and scattering cigarette ash over my application form – 'A degree from Cambridge and you want to be a bus driver?' – but he is short of drivers so he signs me up. In the late seventies the great AEC Routemaster still ruled the road, a magnificent, beautifully engineered machine, elegant from every angle. The cab controls are rudimentary – a vast, almost horizontal steering wheel, a vertically positioned handbrake and a crimson indicator knob shaped like a mushroom to the right of the speedo. A pre-select gearbox and power steering mitigate the sheer scale of the beast, but it still takes some getting used to. Bernie, my instructor, claps me on the back as I clock off one Friday evening. 'Not bad, not bad – where are you off to tonight? Out with the girlfriend, eh?' I reckon telling Bernie I am off to Heaven wouldn't be the brightest move, so I mumble something non-committal and head out.

Heaven, recently opened under the arches at Charing Cross, is London's riposte to Studio 54 in New York. The autumn of 1979 is a strange time to hit London – Thatcher in power, unemployment soaring, the economy on the brink of a recession – the capital feels grey and rather shabby, so the glitz of Heaven offers welcome distraction. Arranged over several levels, bars and dance floors pump out deafening music, hot air swilling with booze and poppers, gyrating bodies squeezed into leather or smeared with glitter, or both, flashing in and out of the strobed ultraviolet lighting. It feels edgy, erotic and completely addictive. Heading to one of the bars, I soon find myself chatting to a six-foot blond from Stockholm wearing not very much. 'What do you do?' he screams at me over the din. 'I'm training to be a bus driver,' I squawk. 'Yeah, right!' he laughs back, flashing his perfect ultraviolet teeth as he drags me onto the dance floor.

When I get home the next morning there's a message on the answerphone from one of my university friends. She is quitting her editorial job – am I interested? Cowardice gets the better of me and so ends my glorious career as a London bus driver.

CHAPTER 20

In the early sixties Father bought Mother an old Ford. It was small, square and black, with red vinyl seats and a long quivering gearstick surmounted by an ivory-coloured knob. Mother, immensely proud of her new-found freedom, drove with an air of imperious authority, swerving out into traffic with a regal wave of entitlement. On one occasion, she drove for a considerable distance the wrong way down a one-way street, uttering colourful Hungarian expletives as cars swerved from her path. I hid in the footwell and prayed no one would notice me. When she was finally stopped, she stepped from the car and, ignoring the blaring horns of the halted traffic, berated the bemused police officer about the brutish behaviour of English drivers.

Compared to my father's plush Rover, the Ford was decidedly basic – three forward gears and erratic vacuum-powered windscreen wipers which operated frenetically as the car came to a halt but wheezily expired at speeds over 40 mph. One winter afternoon, while returning from a walk along Hadrian's Wall, it began to snow heavily and within minutes we found ourselves engulfed in a fierce blizzard. True to form, the wipers gave up completely. Unable to see ahead, Mother lost control and the car drifted sedately into a snowbank. After some time, we spotted lights edging slowly towards us. Mother grabbed her handbag, extracted her powder compact and lipstick. 'Don't laugh – not a word! Even *in extremis*, the lipstick should be just so.' Leaping from the car, she started frantically waving a large silk headscarf in the driving snow.

October 2017

The nursing home smells of pee and old cabbage. In the reception area two old men sit slumped in armchairs, their heads lolling forwards, eyes vacant. A nurse bustling past with a medication trolley flashes a businesslike smile. I find Mother sitting alone in the television lounge, marooned in her wheelchair on a sea of mauve carpet. Hands gripping the arms of her chair, she is staring intently at the television screen, which is turned off. 'Do you remember when we were stuck in the snow that time, and that kind farmer saved us? I remember climbing into his Land Rover, but what happened to my little car?' She pauses, pulling her shawl tightly around her hunched shoulders, batting away my efforts to help. 'Lord knows why that comes back to me now, here in this godforsaken place. Why does your father insist on keeping me here? I mean, just look at this frightful carpet, this room!' She is right, it is truly grim, one wall dominated by a vast painting of a prancing horse (I hope it doesn't remind her of the lost figurine), high armchairs upholstered in a swirling beige moquette, presumably to camouflage stains, the floor area left vacant, save for the offending carpet, to facilitate wheelchair access. And Mother, centre stage, but without an audience.

'Sitting in my car in that blizzard reminded me of our journey towards the Elbe. I couldn't talk to you about it then – you were too young. It was snowing, Emmi and Márta could barely walk, and then this car approached, picking its way past the carts, surrendering soldiers, people from the camps like us, stumbling along that icy road. We had scarves knotted around our heads – our hair was still very short then. I pulled my scarf off and waved it in front of the car. Turns out it was a German officer, but what had we to lose? Thank God we all spoke German – we pretended we were peasant girls fleeing from the Russians. He was rather handsome actually. I sat up in front beside him, the other two in the back. Can't remember what we chatted about – but I do remember his Mercedes, it had all kinds of white knobs on the dashboard and a radio which glowed softly. Of course, he had no idea who we really were . . .'

Mother extends a gnarled hand to take the glass of milk on the table beside her, sucking greedily on the straw. After a long silence: 'Why are you here?'

CHAPTER 21

In 1989 I was offered a scholarship to study opera at the Guildhall School of Music and from there auditioned successfully for Glyndebourne Opera Chorus. Confident onstage, I was selected for minor roles – the Customs Officer in *La bohème*, checking the paniers as the market women pass through the gates of Paris at the opening of Act III, and a drunk villager in *Peter Grimes*, bursting onto the stage in a soaked sou'wester to declaim 'There's a storm ooop the coost!' I was grateful for these small crumbs but longed for understudy work – the first step on the ladder for talented young singers – which didn't come my way. Undeterred, I managed to secure a respected agent, sang in oratorio, and was hired by some of the smaller opera companies to sing character roles, sometimes in exotic locations. Booked for an opera festival in Beirut, shortly after the cessation of the civil war, I rang home. Mother was in ecstasies, shrieking upstairs to Father: 'Come, come! Simon has been asked to sing in Bayreuth!' If only . . .

For a long while I chose to ignore the regular phone calls from my bank manager, but eventually I had to face up to the inevitable truth. I wasn't going to make it, however much I loved rollicking around onstage playing a variety of buffoons. I rang my agent who was – the final nail in the coffin – rather too quick to agree. We exchanged the usual pleasantries and I hung up. But half an hour later, he rang me back. 'Listen, I think I've got something for your grand finale.' I noted the caustic tone of voice but let him carry on. 'Someone's just dropped out at the last minute – can you step in to sing bass solo in *Messiah*?' I accepted eagerly. 'Good – it's a prestigious gig: performances at Birmingham Symphony Hall and the Barbican, and a recording – with the Vienna Boys' Choir.' I wonder what Aunt Lili would have made of that.

Summer 1961

I am five years old. It is a summer evening and a light breeze ruffles my bedroom curtains. I stare up at the shifting patterns on the ceiling above my bed and I think I can see Mother's face looking down at me, slipping in and out of focus with the moving folds of the curtain. She has no eyes and her mouth is stretched wide open and it scares me. I duck under my covers to hide but then pop one eye out again, just to check. She's back – there, I can see her, but now her mouth is wider than before. It looks like she's screaming . . . I scrunch up my eyes to block out the picture and drift off to sleep.

There were many nights when the screams were real. I would be shaken from sleep by a sound like whimpering, which grew and grew until her screams pierced the night. I remember my father's low, muffled voice through the adjoining wall, trying to calm her as she wailed, begging her to stop, and her ragged voice crying out, 'I can't, I can't!' Sitting up in bed, I would cry out for her and she would rush in, sweeping me up into her arms, her cheeks wet with tears as she comforted me.

There were other nights when she woke me, her light soprano voice floating up serenely from the dining room below. My parents both loved lieder, and there was one particular song cycle, Schumann's *Frauen-Liebe und Leben*, which they often revisited. I remember sitting at the top of the stairs, listening to the sombre despair of the final song 'Nun hast du mir den ersten Schmerz getan' (Now you have caused me my first pain) captured perfectly by Mother's instinctive, lilting phrasing.

February 2017

Not long before she died, we talked about the music in her life. 'It was Aunt Lili, Flóra's younger sister, who first encouraged me. Poor Lili, her career cut short, just as she started to win major roles at the Vienna Volksoper. All the Jewish singers and musicians received a letter from the opera house, citing the newly passed Nuremberg Laws and cancelling all further performances: *"Ihre Dienste werden nicht mehr benötigt"* – "Your services are no longer required." Her husband, Haymo Täuber, immediately requested a divorce, so anxious to safeguard his career as director of the Vienna

Boys' Choir. After the war he had the gall to write to Edit, the only surviving sister, insisting that it was Lili who had asked for a divorce – as if that might somehow exonerate him!

'Anyway, that's why she came to live with us. One evening, it must have been during the summer of 1937, we all clustered around the radio to listen to one of her last broadcasts put out by Radio Strasbourg: songs by Brahms and then Mahler's *Rückert Lieder*, with its plaintive dissonances, her rich alto voice rising above the texture of the orchestra. I remember, as the fourth poem began – *"Ich bin der Welt abhanden gekommen"* ("I am lost to the world") – she walked out onto the veranda, I don't think she could bear to listen. Other times, I would sit beside her at the piano while she played snatches of the music she loved. A phrase in the last song of *Frauen-Liebe und Leben* reminds me of Lili, sitting at the dining-room table, a cigarette held loosely between her long fingers, staring into space: *"Es blicket die Verlassne vor sich hin, / Die Welt ist leer."**

'That's how I remember her, wrapped in sadness. One night in the camp she came to sit with me, telling me stories about her time in Vienna. For a while she became quite animated, recalling her voice coach – a fearsome stick of a woman who drank schnapps and banged the piano with a cane – the conductors she worked with, the absurd backstage gossip. And then as she crept away, she said, quite simply: "Without music, why should I live?" She had the chance to

---

* *The deserted one stares ahead, / The world is void.*

leave with us but she refused and shortly after she contracted typhoid. She just wanted to die.'

We talked also of those other nights when we clung to each other. 'I'm so sorry, I desperately wanted to protect you from all that, but the nightmares – they just overwhelmed me. They still do . . .'

CHAPTER 22

Summer 1962

It is a hot August afternoon, the kind of heat that makes you screw up your eyes, so that when you peek through everything takes on a bluish haze. An occasional waft of fetid air shifts the weighted fronds of a laburnum tree – Mother is enthroned in front of this golden bower, draped over her sunlounger. She is wearing a flowered bathing suit, great splotches of colour sprawling over her breasts and belly. Her skin is already bronzed, shining with generously slathered sun oil. Angular sunglasses cover the upper part of her face – her lips, set in a triumphant smile, glint with freshly applied lip gloss, a gash of metallic pink. I am six years old, crouching at the foot of her lounger, making a daisy chain to offer up to the shrine. In the neighbouring garden, my friend Richard is staring down at us from the high branches of an old pear tree.

'Go and fetch me a large lilac leaf, darling' – the shrine has spoken. This is a summer ritual – a perfectly shaped leaf is required to cover Mother's nose to avoid sunburn. I trot to the lilac tree at the far corner of the garden, choose a leaf with care and return. 'Place it!' – I dislike this part, applying the inverted leaf so that it sticks to the oiled bridge of Mother's nose. She smiles luxuriantly, accepting this offering from the acolyte. The pear tree rustles, I look up, catch Richard's sidelong glance. Then he shimmies down the trunk and heads for his den at the back of their garden hut. I want to climb over the fence and join him, but I know I can't. I turn away, busying myself with my daisy chain.

Winter 1982

Twenty years later I am making a dutiful visit to the parental home – a long winter's afternoon stretches ahead. I am sprawled on the carpet in the drawing room, trying to ignore a presentation I have to finish for the coming week. Mother is in the breakfast room attacking a backlog of letters. Noticing that the bottom drawer of her bureau is, unusually, ajar, I take advantage of the steady staccato of her typewriter to quietly lift out a battered cardboard photo album, the cover decorated in geometric shapes of black and ochre. This is the only record of her early life and she does not encourage us to enquire – it is too painful, definitely off-limits. Once, when I was very young, she discovered me poring over these photographs. Wrenching the album from my hands, she clutched it to herself, spitting out: 'How dare you snoop about in my desk, this is private, do you hear me? Private!' From then on, she made sure the drawer was kept locked. She must have grieved that she was unable to talk about her family, point to the photos of her father, proudly standing in a long leather apron in his vineyard, tell me about her mother Flóra, always dressed in mourning after the death of her middle daughter Edit, or name the many cousins, aunts and uncles all locked away in those pages. But how could she? There would have been too many questions, questions she was not ready to answer.

The clattering of her typewriter stops suddenly and I freeze, like a shifty thief caught in the act. Then she continues and I greedily thumb through the stiff pages, each one a mosaic of stamp-sized black-and-white photographs, crinkle-edged in white. A family party in the summer of 1922 – four years before Mother's birth – at my great-grandmother's estate in Celldömölk, in western Hungary, near the Austrian border – my great-aunts, great-uncles and grandparents all dressed in their Sunday best, seated in wicker chairs beneath a lilac tree. In front of them a table set with glasses and a decanter of Tokaji, to the right a gaggle of children dressed in white. The group stares out at the photographer, perhaps a little bored by their indolent afternoon, secure in their well-dressed affluence, quite unaware of the catastrophe that awaits them: Ede (Eduárd), my grandfather, at ease in his wing collar and three-piece suit, one arm extended to hold the hand of Zsuzsi, his eldest daughter, will die as a slave labourer in Ukraine. My great-grandparents Franciska and Miksa, their daughters Margit (a poet and close friend of Thomas Mann), Sára, Flóra (my grandmother) and Lili – a rising star at the Volksoper in Vienna – all their stories incinerated in the ovens of Auschwitz. As I turn the heavy pages, a photograph slips to the floor. Three girls, one of them

Mother, are grouped in a studio portrait, their hair waved, smiling gently at one another. They are all wearing identically tailored frocks typical of the mid-1940s.

Stranger still, all three dresses are cut from the same boldly checked material. I know this photograph but have never asked about it. I walk into the breakfast room, hesitantly slip the photograph in front of her typewriter.

'Ahhh . . .' The keys fall silent, she pushes back her chair, stares ahead. 'After we escaped from the forced march, we headed towards the Elbe and the safety of the Allied Zone on the far side of the river. The riverbank swarmed with German soldiers, their rifles slung around their necks, waiting to surrender to the American Army, along with half-starved civilians fleeing the Russian advance. And us – three girls, Emmi, Márta and myself – without papers, without identity. Only Márta spoke English. There was a GI with a clipboard down by the water's edge, taking details of the surrendering soldiers, so she ran over to him, explained our situation, begged him to help. We later learned that it was expressly forbidden to take civilians over to the other side – only prisoners of war were allowed. The GI shrugged and turned away, but Márta grabbed his sleeve, gesturing to us lying exhausted on the grass. He seemed to relent, whispered in her ear, then continued to process the long line of soldiers shuffling onto the flotilla of boats.

'We hid in a thicket of reeds down by the water's edge and waited. As the day wore on, the riverbank gradually emptied of people, stragglers drifting off into the town – we were alone. We could hear the boom of guns in the distance, growing louder as darkness fell. It was hopeless – why should he come? There was a full moon – we lay shivering in the reeds, hoping no one would see us. Three Jewish girls, prompted by our Catholic convent schooling, whispering a Christian prayer over and over, *"Mi Atyánk, ki vagy a menny-ekben"* – "Our Father who art in Heaven . . ."

'At about three o'clock in the morning, during a lull between the street fighting in the town, we heard the sound of oars approaching. The GI's name was John Taylor. I tried to locate him after the war, without success. I wanted to thank him for rowing us across that river – we knew what the Russians would have done with us.

'They put us in a requisitioned house – the occupants were given twenty minutes to pack and leave. We watched, sitting in a US Army jeep as a squat well-fed woman and her two blond children filed down the path, scowling . . . We had a room each – I remember there was a toy Messer-schmitt hanging from the ceiling, circling over my bed as I slipped into a deep, numbing sleep. The GIs must have come by because when we woke the next morning the kitchen table was piled high with sugar, tea, milk and Hershey bars! We stayed there for a week or so, just eating, washing and sleeping – three stick figures shuffling past each other, slumped at the kitchen table, staring at the walls, barely exchanging a word.

'One morning they turned up with a jeep and we were taken over to the British Zone. The military HQ was in the old schloss in Hachenhausen – we drove into a wide cobbled courtyard and in one corner there was a group of British soldiers playing table tennis. The others had gone on ahead, but I stopped: I needed to lock this picture away somehow, four young boys at ease, just laughing together. I stood there, fists clenched, trying to remember my former life – the very idea of carefree laughter. But it was no good, I was just a starved girl wearing a stranger's coat. I felt mean-minded and spiteful, but above all very tired and very old.

'The interview took place in what must have been the great hall – empty except for a table at one end. A pale little man wearing glasses shuffled papers around on a desk, asked me questions – where I was born, my family, when we were taken away, where, and so on. His head was bent over the papers, and I could see his hair was thinning and he had carefully combed the sparse threads across the pale dome of his head. I couldn't find the words he wanted to hear, all I could think of was this man's terrible fear of ageing, his shame. And I wanted to reach out and touch his arm, just to say "you are here, it's enough to be alive, nothing else matters". We were interviewed separately – I guess they wanted to check if our stories matched.

'They didn't really know what to do with us, three girls without papers, but they were kind. We were allocated accommodation – a large villa in a quiet location, set behind high walls. Leading up to the front porch was a path lined with overarching lilac bushes. I trailed my fingers through the heavy purple blooms, burying my face in the heady perfume.

'The sergeant who dropped us off left some provisions in

the kitchen. And then, just as he was about to drive away, he turned back, flashing us a cheeky grin. "You know who stayed here last, doncha? You'll never guess – Herr Himmler!" He rammed the jeep into gear. "Cheerio!" We stood there in the hallway, staring at each other. Then Márta began to laugh, deep rasping shrieks, tears rolling down her face. Pretty soon we were all laughing uncontrollably, our hysteria filling the empty house, three ghouls linking arms, slowly circling over the polished wooden floor.'

'And the dresses, Mother?'

'Oh, that's simple, darling – there was a seamstress in the village, but she had no material. We searched each room, starting from the attics, working our way down through the house, but found nothing. Then I stepped into the main reception room – a handsome room with French windows overlooking the perfectly trimmed garden. And framing those windows, the most heavenly checked poplin curtains, Himmler's curtains . . .'

I place my hands on her shoulders. 'I know I would not have had the strength, the willpower, not at eighteen, probably never.' She turns to me, her grey eyes defiant: 'Yes you would. *In extremis*, you quickly learn how the world turns. You would be surprised what you are capable of.'[1]

CHAPTER 23

My childhood was framed by the tyranny of time. Until I was eighteen, I had no understanding of the frenetic urgency underpinning our family dynamic. I only knew that timing was all. Punctuality was adhered to with an almost religious fervour, the hour of every event, every arrangement, every appointment treated with reverence. Departure and arrival – words imbued with the strident echoes of the klaxon call, the staccato utterances of a railway station tannoy, the slamming of doors. The terror of the Appelplatz infiltrated every aspect of Mother's life, from the most mundane calendar jotting to her overarching need for control and order in all things. For Father too, rushing along the station platform to catch the train leaving Budapest in January 1940 was to remain an indelible memory. He invariably arrived for every flight at least two hours earlier than was necessary and, of course, I do precisely the same.

Under the imposing hall staircase stood a side table on which Mother kept a silver bell. Its tone – insistent and shrill – was unmissable. There was no corner of that large house where it could not be heard (Mother knew this, having tested it), so choosing not to respond was never an option. She would stand at the foot of the stairs, poised with a glassy smile, summoning me to meals, to practise the piano, to help with household chores. Testing her limited patience, I would wait for the second, more insistent and prolonged tinkling of the accursed bell, stomping resentfully downstairs to be greeted by an icy stare. Insubordination was not part of Mother's vocabulary and her cold fury would ripple through the house for days afterwards. As an angry teenager, I reacted by recoiling in sullen silence, numbed by this suffocating, military-style control. As an adult, her insistence on punctuality felt like a deliberate, infantilising humiliation.

Timekeeping was a religion for them both. My father installed clocks in every room, winding them all with great care every Saturday evening, without fail. The mahogany-cased mantel clock in the drawing room had a particularly penetrating, stentorian boom, sounding every quarter-hour. My perception was that time went backwards in that house, but the multiple chimes ricocheting from room to room confirmed that time was on the move, however slowly. When I turned twenty-one, I was duly presented with a heavy gold Schaffhausen watch, black Roman numerals engraved onto the gold face. I mumbled my thanks, knowing it to be an expensive gift, but I hated it for everything it represented – my parents' obsessive insistence on punctuality. Years later, I wore it when I was giving a concert and, changing out of my white tie and tails in the green room afterwards, forgot to pick it up when I left. I spent years afterwards fibbing that I had decided it was too expensive to wear around London and had stored it in a bank box. I don't think they believed me, suspecting I had sold it when funds were low.

May 1980

Mother's visceral fear of unpunctuality, combined with my father's highly regimented approach to every aspect of his life, means that their combined position is immovable, impregnable. On a weekend visit home, to mark my parents' thirtieth wedding anniversary, I commit the unpardonable sin of not appearing at the breakfast table at the allotted time. Mother raps sharply on my bedroom door and then barges in. 'It is almost seven thirty – we've been waiting for you downstairs. Your father has been busy preparing breakfast!' – eyes bulging with indignation, aghast at this intolerable display of insurrection. I bury my head underneath the duvet. 'Simon, look at me! Open your eyes and LOOK AT ME! Get dressed and come down immediately!' She bustles out of the room and I hear her footsteps stomping down the stairs. I hurriedly pull on some clothes, drag a comb through my hair, the errant child staring back at me from the mirror.

October 1985

I am invited to dine with the parents at their club, just off Berkeley Square. There is a legitimate reason, I can't now remember what, but I arrive half an hour late. They are waiting in the grand drawing room, empty gin and tonic glasses on the table between them. I can tell immediately there will be a showdown. My mother rises to her feet and proceeds to berate me, her voice loud and heavily accented. Ignoring the impact on the other guests, who turn away, suitably embarrassed by this very un-English behaviour, she booms out: 'How dare you turn up at this hour? – we thought you were dead!' Swathed in an expensive silk dress, bosom heaving, face livid, tears pour down her face and in her fury she swings her hefty crocodile handbag at my head. My father hisses in my ear: 'How could you do this to your mother, how could you?' then marches me with a stony face into the dining room, where I sit, seething and humiliated, loathing them both with every fibre of my body.

Shortly afterwards, I give a concert up in Glasgow and stay with my aunt Zsuzsi, long estranged from Mother. She asks about her sister and I relate the episode at the club. Zsuzsi thinks for a while. 'Darling, I'll tell you a story. In the spring of 1942 our father, your grandfather Ede, was in Budapest handling a case in the High Court. As you know, by the late 1930s Admiral Horthy,[1] an outspoken anti-Semite, was eating out of Hitler's hands, principally so he could reclaim territory annexed by the Treaty of Versailles at the end of the First World War. So Horthy caved into Nazi demands, limiting the number of Jews in the professions, government, commerce to a crippling 20 per cent, then further reducing it to just 5 per cent by 1940. It was catastrophic legislation – can you imagine, over a quarter of a million Jews lost their jobs as a result. And then a subsequent law prohibited Jews from marrying non-Jews. Now my father was a proud Hungarian, he simply could not stand by and see his country "sold to the Devil" as he called it, so he spoke out, using his position in court to denounce Horthy's policies. I was already in England by this time, but Father insisted I returned to Hungary. I have his letter still, urging me to come home, that the family should stick together in these difficult times. Unbelievable, given what was to happen. But how could he have imagined the horrors still to come? And so, dutiful daughter that I was, I booked my passage home. I stopped in Paris for a couple of days – my God, the feeling of sheer liberation in that beautiful city. I swear, I could have done cartwheels down the Champs-Élysées! Of course, Father's outraged diatribe in court was a form of professional suicide. The story was picked up by the papers and very shortly after he returned to Eger there came the inevitable knock on the door. He was bundled out of his office straight into a truck and driven away. That evening we waited and waited. We couldn't get through to the office – we were frantic, knowing how exposed he was. We never saw him again. He was transported to the Russian front, the rest you know. So, dear boy, maybe this gives you some understanding of your mother's outburst? You see, that kind of terror – however irrational you may think it now – it never leaves you.'

It was only when they were well into their eighties that my parents reluctantly agreed that, at least when I was visiting, breakfast might perhaps be rescheduled from 7 a.m. to 8 a.m. They would descend in the stairlift, immaculately dressed, and totter inch by inch along the hallway, their arrival accompanied by the uncertain clanking of their Zimmer frames. Sinking into their chairs in the breakfast room, they would exchange conspiratorial winks like naughty schoolchildren, shamefully late for class, while I skittered about in the kitchen, making sure their coffee was at just the right temperature, croissants warmed, freshly squeezed orange juice correctly chilled. I can see them now, cheerful faces upturned, as I carried in their breakfast trays. And I can hear their gleeful chorus: 'Aha! *Alles hat seine Ordnung!*'*

* Everything has its order, or place.

CHAPTER 24

October 2012

On a visit home, Mother asks me to take down several large boxes from the top of a wardrobe and open them. Inside are carefully folded tablecloths, linen sheets and napkins, all neatly embroidered with Mother's initials 'IH'. 'This was my trousseau. You should use these when I'm gone – promise me you won't throw them out? Zsuzsi sent them out to England after the war – they are very precious to me.'

I seize my chance. 'So, tell me, Mother, what happened between you two? After everything you went through together, you barely saw each other after the war, seldom spoke. Why?' Mother swings round to me, eyes flashing with fury. 'She betrayed me – my own sister! As if the torture of that horrendous year wasn't enough. OK, I'll tell you. She was insanely jealous of me – after our sister's death, my parents' focus was very much on me, their last child, often sickly in my first years. I was the pretty and vivacious one,[1] and yes, it's true, my father's favourite. Oh, he admired Zsuzsi's intellect of course, she was definitely the bluestocking in the family, his sparring partner around the dinner table, but watching me being scooped up in his arms must have been wounding, I admit that. I was too young to understand the hurt he caused her and, of course, I just loved the attention! Anyway, after the war, she wrote to me while I was still in Germany, begging me to come home, to take up my place at medical school and train to be a doctor. Home! God Almighty, that was no longer my home – I remembered that last journey down to the train station, our neighbour spitting in my face as we walked by . . . So I refused, horrified at the prospect of her over-attentive, obsessive protection. I wanted to taste freedom in England, real freedom, on my own terms. I have no doubt she felt rejected, that I could turn my back on her, after all we had been through, but I knew instinctively that to return was to shrivel up and die, all over again.

'When I finally arrived in Kent, I couldn't believe my luck. The Denchworths – Aunt Mildred and her stepdaughters Dot and Edna – all music teachers and in their quiet way remarkable, had some connection with my parents before the war, I can't remember what exactly. Anyway, they took me in as one of their own, enrolled me in college to learn English and train as a secretary. They lived in a rambling old house, rather threadbare, with a big garden where they grew their own vegetables, invariably overcooked to death, but never mind, they were so very kind to me, just when I needed it most. Longfield Hill was a charming little village in its way. I had the feeling nothing ever changed there – weekly meetings of the Women's Institute, a local choir, jam-making, a circle of friends who were welcoming. As if the war was just a bad dream – this was a new beginning for me.

'And then one evening after supper they sat me down and told me about my sister's letters, reassuring me that of course they didn't believe a word of what she had written, but felt I should know. It seems Zsuzsi had written to every single contact we had in England – relatives and friends – deliberately vicious letters filled with lies, warning them not to accept me, not to have anything to do with me, that I was "damaged goods", that I had not behaved well during the war. Yet another annihilation – this time by my own sister! Jézus Mária, can you imagine?

'I was appalled, incensed, that she should try to ruin my life, as if I hadn't already been through hell and back. That she would go to such lengths to get me back? It was unfathomable. I could not forgive her, not then, not now. By the late 1950s she too was living in England and begged me to visit, so I relented. It was a disastrous weekend, filled with her recriminations – *her* recriminations, I ask you! Years later, when she had a stroke, she wanted to see me. I could not. She tried to poison my life. You asked me once why I didn't go to her funeral. Now you know.'

Silently, we replace the linen, pack the boxes away. I have them still, stashed at the back of a cupboard. Long after Mother's death, they remain unopened, each yellowing fold of fabric interleaved with the bitterness of memory, hidden truths and lingering, uneasy questions.

CHAPTER 25

Spring 1946

Zsuzsi was not the only one to try and control Mother's destiny. While under the protection of the British military HQ in Gandersheim, Mother met István Király, a handsome officer of Hungarian extraction attached to the Canadian Intelligence Service as part of the Allied Control Council, whose remit was to gather information in preparation for the Nuremberg Trials. István was clever, debonair and witty, and within a few weeks of meeting he had asked Mother to marry him, but she had other ideas. In her old age she once reminisced about the affair. 'He was enchanting and so good-looking, but always insanely jealous. I was barely twenty, and he was forty-one – I wasn't ready, after everything I had just gone through, to offer the kind of commitment he was pressuring me to make. From one moment to the next he would suddenly fly into a tantrum. In the end I realised I had to get away.' She soon discovered this was not as simple as it seemed.

By early 1947 both Emmi and Márta, the two girls with whom Mother had escaped from the death march, had already secured their identification papers and were making plans to emigrate to England. But for some reason, Mother's paperwork had not yet been processed. She turned to István, but his response was evasive – he would look into the matter, but she had to understand he was under huge pressure to complete his intelligence work. As the weeks passed, Mother grew frustrated and set about charming one of the officers at the British military HQ who rashly agreed to drive her, without the correct paperwork, over the border to Brussels, where her application was currently being reviewed by the Inter-Allied Reparation Agency. An interview was arranged with Lewis Gielgud, the coordinating officer at the IARA, and elder brother of the actor John Gielgud. Mother was hopeful that her application would be straightforward, but Gielgud was suspicious and interrogated her as to how she had travelled to Belgium without the requisite paperwork.

Unaware that a stenographer was typing up the interview behind a screen, Mother confessed that a British officer had driven her across the border illegally. She was immediately imprisoned pending further investigation. 'Can you imagine, darling, after everything I had been through, there I was banged up in a cell with all the local prostitutes!' Surprisingly, her face softened. 'Do you know, they were actually very sweet to me, those girls. God knows what they had just been through themselves.' Somehow, she managed to get word to István, who commandeered a staff car and drove straight to Brussels where he pulled strings to get her released. On the drive back into Germany, he confessed that several months earlier he had written to the IARA, requesting they delay Mother's application – buying time in case he could still persuade her to marry him. 'We had an almighty row, I can tell you. I made it damned clear I wanted to go to England and finally he agreed.'

Within a few weeks Mother was back in Brussels – legally this time, courtesy of a travel permit dated 29 March 1947, specifying that 'Ildikó Heimler has permission to travel on the Nord Express to Brussels on 1 April 1947'.

I found Mother's diary for 1947 in her bureau after her death.

Wednesday 9 April 1947

Brussels – Ostende – Dover. A new life.

Monday 9 June 1947

Walk – wandering on the beach – swimming –
rowing – beautiful weather – dreamlike dusk.
Everyone is charming.

Saturday 14 June 1947

It is three years today that I last saw Mother. Such a
lethargic, apathetic mood – I don't even recognise
myself. I wish I could die. The future seems so bleak.

Saturday 21 June 1947

Children's concert with various ancient relatives of
the Denchworths. I think I'm in serious danger of
a nervous breakdown. Slammed my finger in the
car door. Bloody and bruised and painful. Surely
no one could label my depression as neurosis, after
everything I have been through?

Monday 18 August 1947

Drove a tractor at the Harvest Festival. I am swelling
with pride! Huge hike up to the highest peak of the
Beacon. Wonderful view. Drank cider at the pub
afterwards.

Friday 22 August 1947

Boredom, depression, the dreaded daily routine . . .
I feel like a bird in a cage. I would like to smash it
down with fury!

Sunday 14 September 1947

Singing in choir. Chaos in my head greater than ever.
Telephone call with István in the evening.

[István wrote to her regularly – increasingly forlorn letters,
begging her to reconsider. 'My Angel, I haven't received any
news from you, for at least a week . . . it seems like I have
to switch on the BBC to get any news! I so badly need to
know how things are going for you. I wonder what illustrious
Englishmen you are meeting on a daily basis! I hope I can be
very proud of you.' The reproachful words of a jealous lover,
seemingly unable to accept that the affair was over, that he had
lost her. In September he travelled to England, possibly in a last-
ditch attempt to persuade her.]

Monday 15 September 1947

István visits. I feel in every bone in my body that we
are not made for each other.

Thursday 18 September 1947

To the Hungarian Club in London – with István. I tell him no.

Tuesday 28 October 1947

To London to meet István. Dinner at Queen's Brasserie, Leicester Sq, then a drink at the Piccadilly Hotel. Long talk, moderate serenity. *Requiescat in pace!*

Wednesday 29 October 1947

István leaves for Canada this morning. I doubt we will ever see each other again.

I suspect it was not just the age difference, or indeed his jealous streak, that prompted Mother to reject István's offer of marriage. She had set her heart on England and the anonymity it appeared to offer her: the opportunity to start over, to erase the past, to bury her Jewish identity and throw away the key to the vault. With István, assiduously gathering evidence of wartime atrocities against the Jews, denial would not have been an option. Three years later, safely settled in England, she saw in my father a willing accomplice in her complex game of repression.

CHAPTER 26

April 1961

Mother is in her mid-thirties. She is at her most beautiful, her features vibrant, and for a brief period relatively trim of figure. Her hair, which naturally falls into tight kinks on the crown of her head, has been straightened that morning at the hairdresser's into a gleaming golden helmet, each wave immaculately sprayed into place. I am sitting with my knees pulled tight up against my chin. Perched at the top of the stairs, I have a hidden vantage point down into the hallway. A large stained-glass window halfway up the stairs throws dappled blotches of colour onto the wall below. Dropping her scarf and handbag onto a chair, she moves into this pool of iridescence and pauses, transfixed by the effect, her hand caressing her stomach spattered with crimson, turquoise and gold. Slowly she turns to explore the shifting colours as they fall about her, discs of light gliding dizzily across her patent leather shoes.

I shift in my hiding place, witness to something I don't understand, knowing I must not be caught. I try to retreat into the shadows of the stairway, but my awkward movement catches her eye. Her face, viewed from above, turns fleshy, heavy, the animated eyes suddenly clouded. Without a word she passes out of sight towards the kitchen at the end of the hall. Ashamed, I retreat to my room. There is a deep silence in the house. I sit hunched on the floor near my bed.

And then I hear the sound of splintering glass, smashing china, and my mother's groans as one object after another is hurled to the floor.

After a long while I tiptoe downstairs, push open the kitchen door. My mother is on her knees gazing at the ruin splayed out across the floor, bleeding hands clamped to her ears, her hair wild, a curling strand plastered to her forehead. I step towards her. She shakes her head. 'Don't come near me, go and fetch a broom. It was an accident, a stupid accident . . . ' In silence we sweep away the chaos together, everything tidied away and carried to the bins in the side alleyway. My mother goes to the fridge and pours me a glass of milk. 'I was remembering something bad, a long time ago. Drink your milk . . . and don't say a word of this to your father, do you understand?'

We moved a year later to a new house with plain windows casting their empty gaze out onto the street. I waited twenty years before she could bring herself to explain.

January 1981

'That episode in the hallway? Yes . . . those beautiful coloured lights.' She smiles. 'Dr Herta Oberheuser. She was assistant to Professor Karl Gebhardt,[1] Himmler's personal physician. They performed experiments on the prisoners at Ravensbrück. There were selections, you know? They conducted "research" into bone and muscle transplantation. We heard about these grotesque procedures and I read about them later – even at the time their methods were debunked, nothing more than gratuitous sadism. Oh, and to add to their games, they deliberately infected wounds with wood shavings, iron filings, ground glass and with bacteria – streptococcus and tetanus. The resulting infection was treated with sulfanilamide and other drugs to see how effective they were. Charming, no? Most of the so-called "patients" died later of gangrene poisoning. There was a roll-call on the Appelplatz, and I was selected. They rounded up a bunch of us young girls, all of us terrified. As we shuffled forward towards the doctors in their white coats, one of them muttered to his colleague: "Such a beautiful specimen." I was shaking with nerves, but suddenly a nurse came up to me. I discovered later her name was Sylvia Salvesen.[2] Anyway, she whispered to me, "Leave now, you don't apply." Without another word, she turned me round and pushed me towards the door. I had no idea what she meant, in what way did I not "apply"? I stumbled outside – it was a blindingly bright day and the sun was shining directly onto a piece of thick glass embedded in the barbed-wire fencing. It must have acted as a prism – as I walked forward, the ground just for that brief moment was splashed with discs of sharp multicoloured light. I felt I was about to faint. I froze, watching the coloured lights lap across my wooden clogs. In that moment I sensed my mother, very close to me, like some kind of benediction. Then I pulled myself together and walked quickly away.'

March 1981

I spot an advertisement in the jobs section of the *Guardian* – a distinguished art history publication is looking for an editorial assistant. I am aware of the magazine, having flicked through copies on display in the university library, and decide to apply. It seems a long shot, given that I am not an art history graduate, so I'm surprised to be selected for interview. I head to the London Library and ask the librarian if I might look through some recent copies. My eye is drawn to the name of the editorial assistant, Sally Salvesen. The interview goes well and two weeks later I receive a letter offering me the job.

I mention Sally's name to Mother when I ring to give her the news. Could there be a connection? It is arranged that Sally and I should overlap for a couple of weeks to ease me into the role and one afternoon, as we are poring over galley proofs, she confirms that her husband is indeed related to Sylvia, the woman who saved Mother's life.

CHAPTER 27

Summer 1961

We are travelling along the Süd Autobahn towards the Wörthersee in Austria. Suddenly, the traffic slows almost to a halt, our car inching past the littered debris of a major accident. Father barks out: 'Simon, don't look,' but I do, my nose pressed to the window. The back seat of a car lies stranded on the tarmac, the fabric streaked with red, shattered glass glinting in the sunshine. Over at the side of the road, paramedics are busy placing blankets over two small bodies. Nearby, a young couple are standing by a crumpled, overturned car. The man, just a few feet away, has his back to us, his arms clasped around his wife. She is staring directly at me, howling the words *'Es darf nicht! Es darf nicht!'*, her broken voice fading into the distance as our car slowly pulls away. Mother turns to me, dabbing her eyes with a handkerchief. 'Everything's going to be fine, you'll see.' 'Mama, what does *Es darf nicht* mean?' 'It means, it can't be true, darling. Now please don't think about it any more.' 'But it *is* true Mama, I saw it.'

Our guest house looks welcoming, its sombre wooden facade splashed with scarlet geraniums arranged in long window boxes – a picture-postcard holiday destination.

Guests are being served schnitzel and *Petersilienkartoffeln* (parsley potatoes) on a veranda overlooking the gardens that stretch down to the water's edge. We go on boating trips, Father buys me a walking stick for mountain excursions, we sip *Himbeersaft* (raspberry juice) at the local inn, sitting at a trestle table under the shade of a vast plane tree. Snapshots from an uneventful family holiday.

Some friends join us from Vienna and one evening we all drive into Klagenfurt for ice cream. Father leads us through the revolving doors of the Hotel Sandwirth, famous for its *Konditorei*. I am holding Mother's hand as we cross the marble floor of the lobby. Just at that moment, the mahogany doors of the hotel lift glide open and a distinguished-looking elderly man with silver hair and Tyrolean jacket steps out. He pauses, adjusts his cravat, walks past us and out into the bustling street. Suddenly Mother's body tenses, she lets go of my hand, her eyes fixed on the retreating figure of the silver-haired gentleman and then she crumples to the floor. Father rushes over, lifts her up and I hear her whisper to him, 'Say nothing, nothing at all.' Then the moment passes and a few minutes later we are all seated in the café and the waiter brings our ice creams.

Summer 2015

We are sitting in the garden at home and I remind her of that evening forty years ago. 'Ah yes. Dr Fritz Fischer.[1] Quite a man, that one. He was surgical assistant to Karl Gebhardt, and conducted so-called medical experiments on numerous Ravensbrück prisoners. He left the camp in 1943 so our paths didn't cross, as it were, but I followed his post-war "career" carefully. As you would expect, he was tried at Nuremberg in 1947 and convicted of war crimes and crimes against humanity. But despite being handed down a sentence of life imprisonment, he served only seven years. And to cap it all he was allowed to continue practising medicine, evidently drawing a very comfortable salary and holidaying in luxurious hotels.' She pulls her shawl closer around her shoulders. 'So you see, you never really escape.'

The doorbell rings and Mother shuffles indoors, navigating the polished parquet floor with her frame. I hear a brief murmur of voices and then the heavy front door slams shut. Mother re-emerges along the garden path. 'It was nobody important, just some darkie trying to sell me dusters.'

She notes my look of discomfort and shrugs. 'Darling, I am pushing ninety, so don't teach me your political correctness now, please!'

Even in her frailty, I can't let this pass. 'How can you sit there and ask for my compassion and then show someone the door with such casual bigotry? How is that even possible?'

Her voice shakes with fury. 'How can you sit there and make such a comparison? You know nothing, do you hear me, nothing!'

CHAPTER 28

July 1980

With the help of a bequest from my grandfather, I buy a flat in Camden Town, my first home. After a month spent painting walls and sanding floorboards, I decide I have earned a night off and head over to the Queen's Head pub in Chelsea, one of the less daunting gay pubs in London. It is a warm evening and the pavement is crowded with groups of men chatting and laughing. I clutch a glass of wine, wishing I had the guts to walk up to someone. Instead, I am hovering on the fringes, debating whether to leave, when someone claps me on the back. 'Hey, that glass looks a bit sad – can I get you a refresh?' Small, stockily built, tousled blond hair, a cheeky smile. 'Wait there, don't move!' He darts away into the crowd, emerging a few minutes later with two new glasses. 'Hullo you. I'm Sebastian.' He pulls off his wire-framed glasses and rubs them on the corner of his shirt tail, blue eyes blinking with mischief. We perch on the wall opposite the pub, and he points out a young lad chatting up a portly older gent. 'That's Ricky, we had a thing a few months ago. Terrible flirt that one!' I dig him in the ribs. 'Hmmm . . . takes one to know one!' He giggles. And so it begins.

Sebastian works in a tiny bookshop off Piccadilly that is a mecca for art historians and dealers – the owner, Adele, is a Jewish refugee from Vienna. Diminutive and tyrannical, she wears her hair swept up in the Edwardian style, anchored at the back with a tortoiseshell clasp. Cannily locating her business between Sotheby's and Christie's, she had developed a famously comprehensive network of international contacts. The shop is a narrow sliver of space on two floors, connected by a slender spiral stairway, the walls crammed with books and museum catalogues from all over the world. In the basement a clutch of bright young things beaver away at small desks slotted between the bookstacks. There is a small galley kitchen at the back with coffee on the stove and a workbench where books are packed into cartons ready for shipment. It feels like a meticulously regimented beehive, humming with energy.

On Saturday mornings, the atmosphere is more relaxed – Adele's mother holds sway, enthroned in a special chair by the entrance. She is in her nineties, immaculately coiffed, beady-eyed, dispensing *Vanillekipferl* – delicious crescent-shaped Viennese cookies – and expecting in exchange salacious gossip from customers and staff alike: love affairs, fakes, thefts, fraud – all are welcome and devoured with glee. She takes a shine to me, and one morning gestures me to sit beside her. 'So yung man, vat is your story, hmmm?' We talk, I tell her about my parents, Father's childhood in Budapest, Mother's experiences in the war. She dabs her eyes with a lace-edged handkerchief, then slips the remaining *Kipferl* into my satchel.

One evening, walking through Hyde Park together after a concert at the Albert Hall, I ask Sebastian to move in. A phone call home is now unavoidable.

'Mother, I have met someone.'

'That's wonderful, darling, who is she, what does she do? Where did you meet her?'

'Him, Mother. Him. His name is Sebastian.'

A brief silence, as Mother computes. 'I see, so – tell me about . . . him.'

At the end of the call, one last try: 'Are you sure about this, asking him to move into the flat?'

'I'm sure – will you tell Father?'

She sounds dubious but concedes. 'As you wish.'

When I phone home a few weeks later, Mother avoids any mention of Sebastian. Undeterred, I begin my PR campaign. 'He is incredibly knowledgeable about music. And, most important, he loves cooking. Yesterday when I got home, the flat was filled with the smell of newly baked bread.' A pause down the line – come on, Mother, surely that earns him a few approval points? 'That all sounds very nice, dear. Nevertheless, regarding your visit next week: I assume you will be coming alone?'

When I arrive, I am summoned to Father's study. They have clearly agreed on the line of questioning that follows: 'This flatmate of yours . . . Sebastian . . . I hope he's paying his way – what rent are you charging him?' I refuse to rise to the bait and change the subject.

A month later Mother and Father announce that they are coming to London. An invitation is issued – we are both to join them for dinner at their club. 'It's clear they want to inspect you but the place is a morgue, full of retired colonels. And the food is beyond awful.' Sebastian grins. 'Fine. Invite them here instead – an ideal opportunity to begin my charm offensive, don't you think?' He spends the following week thumbing through Elizabeth David recipes, making lists, lugging home bags of vegetables, a block of Parmesan from Lina Stores, duck breasts from the French butcher on Brewer Street and – triumphantly – a bottle of Tokaji.

They arrive in full regalia – Mother in a silk cocktail dress clutching the obligatory crocodile handbag, Father in a formal suit. Sebastian, who has already downed a couple of gin and tonics to strengthen his nerve, kisses them breezily on both cheeks (Mother thrown off balance, literally, Father clearly horrified) and bustles them through to the kitchen. I hand round chilled glasses of Puszta (a traditional Hungarian cocktail – equal parts dry Tokaji and apricot brandy, with a twist of lemon peel), hastily refilling their glasses as Sebastian regales them with stories of a recent trip to Budapest. A golden globe of shimmering soufflé appears on the table – Mother's 'grande dame' routine miraculously evaporates and Father, ditching his jacket, tucks in with gusto. This is followed by the duck breasts, perfectly pink, accompanied by dauphinoise potatoes and a bottle of Patricius Furmint, Father's favourite white wine. Mother, clutching her third glass, becomes almost coquettish – beguiled by Sebastian's shameless name-dropping as he describes a performance of Bartók's *Bluebeard* at the Met in New York, when he happened to sit right behind Jackie Onassis. A chocolate mousse laced with rum completes his winning streak. As we bundle them into a taxi and wave them off, Sebastian mutters in my ear: 'Game, set and match, my deario.' And he is right. After this, he can do no wrong.

It is a remarkable turnaround. They not only accept Sebastian, but over time become demonstrably fond of him. A phone call from Mother towards the end of the year: 'It's not what we hoped for you, you must know that . . . you make yourselves intensely vulnerable by choosing to live like this. After everything I went through – God knows, I wouldn't wish this on you.' A sigh of resignation. 'But I have to admit, he's a dear boy, very charming.' And in truth, he plays the part of the devoted son-in-law to perfection. He flirts with Mother, listens attentively to Father (neatly side-stepping his entrenched right-wing politics), remembers their birthdays and sends them carefully chosen postcards from our travels.

4 July 1984

Father marks Sebastian's thirtieth birthday with a case of wine. 'Do you know, I actually think they're rather dear,' which makes me laugh. 'You're so bloody shallow, you really are!' But I can see he is genuinely touched by this gesture. So am I.

Looking back, I am not so sure. It was easy for Father to navigate his way through life by reaching for his chequebook. At the beginning of each month he would hand Mother her allowance. He could as easily have slipped a cheque into an envelope and placed it on her dressing table, but instead he would wait until we were gathered for breakfast, then draw the chequebook from his suit pocket and slowly write out a cheque in front of us, so that we were witnesses to his largesse. With calculated solemnity, the omnipotent provider would then place the cheque face down on Mother's breakfast plate. Taking her cue, Mother would duly murmur her thanks and tuck it swiftly into her dressing-gown pocket. Even as a small child I sensed there was something demeaning about this ritual of Father's, a calculated reminder that in controlling the purse strings he controlled everything.

If my relations with Mother and Father had to some degree stabilised, in part due to Sebastian's benign influence, my sense of place in the world – of belonging – was starting to feel deeply threatened. The Aids crisis was gathering pace and suddenly we had friends who were falling alarmingly sick. Misinformation around the then-mysterious illness was rife, and the associated stigma and shame ran deep. One afternoon we were walking through Islington, hand in hand. Coming towards us was a lame old woman dragging her shopping trolley slowly along the pavement. When she saw us, her bloodshot eyes suddenly flickered with fury and she spun round, appealing to the passers-by in a raucous voice: 'Look at 'em – fucking perverts! You're disgusting, that's what. Fucking PERVERTS!' Her shrieks followed us down the road.

A call from Mother: 'We are so worried about this dreadful disease. It's all over the news now – I know it doesn't

affect you, of course, but still. Do be careful, won't you?'
I made the required reassuring noises, noting the implicit
question in her 'of course', but in truth we were profoundly
affected by an increasingly toxic atmosphere of fear and prejudice that surrounded us – the culprits, the bearers of a new
plague, degenerates to be targeted and belittled: outsiders,
unwelcome, a threat.

Summer 1987

A week of music with friends at the Schubertiade Festival
in the Vorarlberg. We find we have one morning with no
concerts scheduled and drive up into the hills. Sebastian's
guidebook recommends a particular *Wirtshaus* nestled
in the square of a ridiculously picturesque village, the
streets lined with wooden houses all festooned with geraniums. After a lunch of beer, pumpernickel and wurst, we
follow a lane winding up towards a small wood, mostly
sweet chestnuts as I remember. And there, to our surprise,
we come upon a Jewish cemetery behind a high stone wall.
The gates are badly rusted but I manage to push them
open and we step inside. A scene of complete devastation confronts us, the ground littered with piles of shattered masonry. We stand in silence, gazing at the ruin all
around – each gravestone smashed and freshly daubed with
red graffiti: *'Juden raus!'*

Returning to England, I decide to say nothing of this to
Mother. Describing that desperate place would only fuel her

fears of further reprisal. I remember her words, cautioning my teenage self: 'You have no conception of how the world turns.'[1]

Autumn 1989

Sebastian receives a solicitor's letter informing him that he is the beneficiary of a generous bequest. It is a serious sum – for the first time in his life he is suddenly financially independent. Over breakfast a couple of weeks later: 'There's something I have to tell you' – a slight catch in the voice – 'I've decided to chuck in my job, I'm moving to Florence.' I sit very still, trying to absorb this information – in his giddy excitement, he seems unaware of what this might mean for us. Or maybe he does. He signs up for a language course, takes out a lease on a tiny flat near the Cappella Brancacci, and books his flight.

Over the weeks that follow, we circle around each other cautiously, saying little, a new awkwardness between us that has never been evident before. And yet I wonder: had I – perhaps unconsciously – replicated Father's infantilising treatment of Mother? Sebastian was usually broke, so when we went out together, or booked a holiday or tickets for a play, it was always me who picked up the tab. At the time, I never gave it a second thought, but looking back I suspect that, like Father, I rather enjoyed the role of provider and the control that came with it. Now, I concede, Sebastian can finally break free, be his own man.

I telephone Mother. 'I don't believe it. After all you have done for him – you gave him a home for God's sake!' 'Mother, we've had eight good years together. Please don't demonise him – he was restless, unsure of what he wanted, confused. Maybe these things run their course?' A pause. 'Your father and I, we used to call him Peter Pan, did we ever tell you?' I let that barb hang in the air for a moment. 'Well, perhaps you were right. Anyway, it's over. He's leaving at the end of the week.' Another pause. 'Maybe it's for the best, no? This way, you have time to take stock, to decide what new path you might want to follow now.' The old hope, sur-facing again.

19 September 1989
Via di Camaldoli
Firenze

Dear heart,

I feel we have been hanging on to something which
is no longer real, which hasn't been real for a long
time. I have relied on the relationship to mask my lack
of direction, all responsibility for myself, all hope. In
truth, the legacy simply gave me the chance to opt
out completely, coward that I am. I should have done
something to stop the rot long ago, and I didn't. And
now I am losing you. I'm in a dark place, not knowing
where to go next.

S

Our letters continue, neither of us wanting to completely let go, but they assume a crafted, brittle tone. We set out to amuse one another, rather than connect. And then I receive this short note:

26 *June 1991*
Via di Camaldoli
Firenze

Dear heart,

I'm coming back to the UK. Shamingly, the money has run out. And I'm not at all well, haven't been for months.

S

Tucked into the envelope is another slip of paper on which he has copied out a short stanza by Salvatore Quasimodo:

Ognuno sta solo sul cuor della
terra trafitto da un raggio di sole:
*ed è subito sera.**

Back in London, Sebastian finds himself a job as a gardener and, through a charity, a small flat on the upper floor of a Victorian almshouse. Shortly after moving in, he calls me. 'Can you come round this evening? I've just had some news from the hospital and I really don't want to sit

---

* 'Everyone stands alone at the heart of the world, pierced by a ray of sunlight, and suddenly it is evening.'

here on my own.' When I arrive, he hands me a large glass of whisky – 'You're going to need this. Sit down – the tests are back, I have AIDS.' He gives me a brave, crooked smile. 'I knew something was wrong – I've felt lousy for weeks. One late-night encounter on the banks of the Arno and now my bloody life is hanging in the balance.' He sits across the table from me, cradling his head in his hands and weeps.

By the mid-1990s it is clear that Sebastian cannot fight the disease much longer. He displays all the classic symptoms – nausea, vomiting, persistent diarrhoea, fatigue, night sweats and alarming weight loss. Stoically, he has endured frequent hospital stays for blood transfusions, terrifying bouts of dementia, chemo sessions, consultations with his medical team to adjust the ever-increasing cocktail of medications, visits from social workers and occupational therapists. For weeks at a time, he is laid low with open sores and enlarged lymph nodes, immobilised by grotesquely swollen legs. I busy myself in his tiny kitchen, preparing food he cannot eat, massaging his feet, adjusting his pillows, my forced cheeriness masking despair as I watch his gradual collapse, too weak now to fight off the relentless cycle of infections.

December 1997

Encouraged by a brief period of remission, I book a three-day trip to Prague. Annie, a loyal and supportive friend, offers to come with us. We arrive in deep winter, the city swathed in thick snow. On our first evening, Sebastian insists we dine at an expensive restaurant on the Old Town Square. 'Let's go wild!' Annie and I exchange nervous glances as he proceeds to order far more food than we need, as well as an expensive bottle of wine and shots of slivovice. Our waiter, one eyebrow raised, bustles away and returns with many glasses, bowls of steaming *guláš* and plates laden with *vepřo knedlo zelo* – a traditional Czech dish of roasted pork with dumplings and a side of pickled cabbage. Annie and I check our wallets and realise we certainly don't have enough cash to pay for all this. At the end of the meal, Sebastian waves the waiter over, thumbs through his *Time Out* book for Prague and points to the phrase '*můžeme mýt nádobí?*' (can we wash the dishes?). Gesturing to our inadequate pile of Czech notes, he flashes him a wicked smile. Scowling, the waiter snatches the few notes from the table and asks us to leave.

Sebastian can only manage short walks in the biting wind and driving snow. On our last evening as the light begins to fail, the three of us stand together on the Charles Bridge, watching as the lamps are lit, the snow eddying around the blackened statues, skimming over the dark waters of the Vltava below. 'I'm glad we came . . .' He huddles against me to try and keep out the cold. 'Now, please take me back to the hotel.'

February 1998

Sebastian is shuffling around his room, hospital gown flapping loosely around his blotched, stick-like legs. There is a new lesion on his forearm that wasn't evident yesterday.

His eyes flicker towards me as I walk in, but he doesn't stop. 'Wait! I'm busy, sit there –' pointing at a chair heaped with soiled sheets from last night. I hesitate. 'I said sit, for Chrissakes!' He continues darting from bed to wardrobe to basin and back again, intently moving packets of his medication from one place to another. 'No, no – that's not right.' He wheels round to me. 'Where have you put them, where?' 'What are you looking for, lovely?' 'My keys, my fucking keys!' 'Why do you need them right now?' He throws me a pitying look. 'You know perfectly well, don't be more dumb than usual – I'm going out on a date. I've hooked up with this gorgeous dude . . . ' His eyes are flashing now, he lets out a lewd cackle. 'He's got a cock the size of the Empire State Building and he's mad about me. I've got to go, I've got to go!' And then he hurls himself at me. 'Why won't you let me go, why?' Eyes dilating, a fleck of spittle at the corner of his lips. 'Jealous, is that it?' He sneers at me, arms feebly flailing against my chest. I grab his shoulders, sharp blades of nothing – the flesh falling away, day by day. 'Come and lie down for a moment, lovely.' Suddenly, he collapses against me, exhausted; I lower him gently onto the bed, a bundle of dry kindling, and he sleeps.

March 1998

Sebastian's parents have come up from Devon to be near him. A quiet dignified couple, his father a Baptist minister. They have already lost their first child, killed in a cycling accident.

And now this. We spend alternate days at the Royal Free Hospital, sitting with him as he slips in and out of consciousness. In the brief periods when he is awake, he still manages to josh with the nursing staff, who are infinitely attentive and kind. He is no longer able to eat and very weak, but perks up when one of the male nurses, Brad, is on duty. 'He's my new date, aren't you, Brad?' A quip, the ghost of a flirtation, also a plea – reminding us that he is still here, still with us.

One evening, Brad takes me aside, holds my hand. 'Not long now.' He brings a camp bed into the room, and for the first time in many years, Sebastian and I lie side by side. For a long time neither of us speaks. I turn on my side to see if he's asleep but he's looking at me calmly. 'I fucked up – I had this wonderful thing, and I just threw it away.' I hold his withered hand and we sleep, fitfully. At four in the morning, I can hear Sebastian breathing gently and creep out of the room to take a quick shower. As I walk back down the corridor, Brad comes to meet me.

I ring Sebastian's parents and an hour later they arrive in a taxi. We walk hand in hand down the long corridor – Brad has tidied the room, laid a fresh sheet and placed a single annunciation lily over the still body. I step outside, and as I close the door behind me I hear their raw cries of grief breaking through the morning silence.

Back home I sit at the kitchen table exhausted, too tired even to weep. I make myself a coffee (using the little machine Sebastian brought me from Florence), steeling myself before calling my parents to break the news. I don't know what I imagined I might expect from them, but their gauche, stilted response offers no comfort – brittle platitudes masking their relief that, finally, all this unpleasantness is over. 'We will write to his parents, of course.' But as far as they are concerned, no further action is required. I ask, tentatively, if they plan to attend the funeral. Mother's riposte is categoric: 'We couldn't bear it, too awful. But, of course, we will be thinking of you.' Of course. The default reflex of denial. I replace the receiver and sit, angry and hurt, cradling my coffee, now cold. At least her sanitised response – entirely predictable – means I will be spared the prospect of Mother, centre stage, engaging in a public show of feigned grief.

A blustery, biting day. The church in Aldeburgh filled with friends and Sebastian's favourite music. Somehow, I manage to give the address, at the request of his parents, who sit, small and frail, in the front pew, gazing in disbelief at his coffin, covered in a carpet of wild flowers.

CHAPTER 29

July 2016

Towards the very end of Mother's life, we sit together one morning in the breakfast room, the two of us. I have cleared away the breakfast things and return to find her staring at the opposite wall.

'I want to make *meggyes piskóta*, one last time. Will you help me?' She drags herself to the kitchen stool where she perches precariously, issuing instructions. I grease a rectangular baking tin and line it with parchment paper.

'Nine tablespoons flour, nine tablespoons caster sugar, a little water.'

'How much water, Mother?'

'A little, don't fuss me! Now, separate six egg yolks in one bowl, whites in the other' – Mother is regaining energy by the minute. 'Now whip the egg whites, BUT DON'T OVERWHIP, most important – they should be floppy, not stiff. Do it! Now whip the yolks, sugar and vanilla essence and the water in the other bowl until creamy. Good! Next scatter over the lemon zest and now carefully fold in the egg whites. Then gently stir in the sifted flour and baking powder – SLOWLY!' The resulting cake dough is frothy and light. I pour it into the tin, Mother greedily licks the mixing bowl. 'It's good. I hope you're making notes, I won't be around when you next make it.'

I remonstrate, she waves me away. 'Don't get mushy, that's how it is. Next, we dot the cake with the pitted sour cherries and straight into the oven, so!'

In thirty-five minutes, the cake is ready. I cut a couple of slices, place them on her favourite Herend dishes, dredge them with icing sugar. Mother eyes my every move. 'It will always turn out very well if you do it this way, OK?'

We sit in silence opposite each other, munching sweet-and-sour cake, sipping coffee. After a few mouthfuls, the initial delight drains suddenly from her face.

'I have been thinking, remembering . . . so much to remember, too much really . . . ' Her eyes flicker towards me. 'Just humour me, can you? Most nights I lie awake, as if I were in a cinema watching episodes of my life flash by: our neighbour's spittle running down my cheek as they marched us down to the station, the women guards lashing out at us with their whips. But other memories too – our holiday house on Lake Balaton, the hammock under the apricot tree. Oh yes! Sitting very still on my father's lap on the veranda as he looped cherries over my ears. And Flóra, your grand-mother, washing my long hair in lemon juice to bring out the blonde highlights – so important to be blonde back then.' She pauses, shoots me a crooked smile.

'Last night I was remembering a summer ball at the Hotel Lővér in Sopron with György – did I ever tell you about him? God, he was so sweet – clear blue eyes and breath smelling of liquorice. I wonder what happened to him . . . What else? Standing in the dark in my mother's pantry, the night they came to take us away. Lying frozen in my bunk in the camp, too exhausted even to pick off the lice running up my legs. Falling asleep wrapped in clean white sheets in that house where Himmler stayed. And then a dinner dance at the Savoy – I was wearing an emerald-green gown and felt like a million dollars. Oh! And our holiday picnic high up on the Grossglockner Pass, do you remember?'

She stops, picks up her fork, then replaces it on the table. 'But most often I just have this image of the three of us, Emmi, Márta and myself, shuffling along that icy road out of Berlin, the soldiers beating us with their rifles. And later, lying in the reeds by the banks of the Elbe, waiting for the sound of the oars dipping through the water.'

Exhausted, frail and in pain, she has let down her guard. All her life she has learned to play a part, to duck and weave, constantly juggling with conflicting identities – Jew, non-Jew, Catholic, Hungarian, English, secretary, mother, daughter-in-law, trophy wife, the gracious hostess. She has acquired all the costumes, slipping them on and off with varying degrees of success, but in the end, the years of role-playing have taken their inevitable toll.

Reaching out a trembling hand to me across the table, her voice empty of all emotion, she says, very quietly: 'I don't know who I am. I never have.'

CHAPTER 30

September 2016

On the advice of the United Kingdom Holocaust Memorial Foundation, the Department for Communities and Local Government launched an international design competition for a National Memorial and Learning Centre to honour the victims and survivors of the Holocaust and Nazi persecution. The intention was that the memorial, adjacent to the Houses of Parliament, should reflect the country's committed opposition to prejudice and hatred, inspire reflection and compassion, and encourage present and future generations to respect and embrace difference.

I was working for an architectural practice at the time, and the decision was made to submit a proposal. The scheme had a simple but powerful poetry – the topography of the Victoria Gardens would be gently lifted to create a grassy mound, at the centre of which a crater-like space would contain a conical tower consisting of six million triangular stones.

In Jewish tradition, relatives paying respect to the deceased leave a stone on the grave, a simple act binding the generations together. The word for 'stone' in Hebrew (*eben*) can be seen as a contraction of *ab* (father) and *ben* (son) and so the word is a powerful construct, symbolising the continuity between generations.

My modest contribution involved helping the team to frame some of the written element of the submission, but it was undoubtedly the visual impact of the scheme that persuaded the jury to shortlist the proposal, along with nine others, from more than a hundred international entries.

One morning, the project director called me into her office. It had been decided – in order to fully comprehend the enormity of the catastrophic events which the scheme would memorialise – that the team would visit Auschwitz. Would I like to travel with them? Touched by this gesture, I expressed my thanks and asked for a little time to consider the idea.

I had never visited Auschwitz. I had never felt the need to confront the place – I felt I already knew every haunted stone. I had no wish to watch schoolchildren taking selfies, tourists jostling to view the mounds of shoes, spectacles, suitcases and hair, earnestly comparing the capacity of the ovens with those at other camps – ticking off the deadly statistics of the Nazi killing machine. The trip was scheduled for early December when the site would be at its most bleak – a fitting time, remembering Mother's description of standing for hours in the icy wind, while the guards conducted yet another deliberately protracted headcount.

In the end, I told the team I wouldn't go. Was it arrogance or cowardice? Possibly both, but on reflection, perhaps neither. I know that one day I will pay my respects to those silenced women – to my great-grandmother, my grandmother, my great-aunts, Éva and her little girl, to the Jews in their thousands who perished alongside them. But I will go alone to honour the memory of my lost relatives, and at a time of my own choosing.

There was little over a month to refine and develop our ideas. We felt it was critically important to present a sample display of the stones themselves, the granite to be sourced from the quarry at the former concentration camp at Mauthausen, notorious for the brutal 'steps of death' which claimed the lives of tens of thousands of prisoners. Since several of our team had lost family members in the Holocaust, it was agreed that the impact of our submission would be enhanced if the stones were engraved with the names of our murdered relatives.

I rang Mother, now ninety years old and frail, fearful of her reaction. There was a long pause and then, to my surprise, an emphatic response. 'I have kept quiet all my life' – a slight catch in the voice – 'but now I agree. God knows I have waited long enough. Our story should be told.' I could hear her weeping softly. 'I give you permission. Use our names. All of them.'

At the very end of her long life, still haunted by what she had endured, she was prepared, once again, to stand and be counted.

CHAPTER 31

March 2017

Mother is draped like a rag doll over her chair, mouth agape, eyes staring at the ceiling of her nursing-home room. She is barely eating so I have brought some freshly squeezed orange juice. I gently touch her arm, her eyes swivel to focus on me. With great effort she hauls herself into an upright position and sips the juice through a straw.

After a few minutes, she turns to me. 'You know, I remember a conversation my parents were having in their room. I'm sure I wasn't supposed to hear it, but I did. My father was very animated – "Flóra, we must leave for Palestine NOW!" He was a fervent Zionist, did I tell you? "We should buy an orange grove, become peasants, start over again." I must have been eight or so, I remember smiling to myself at the thought of Father, of all people, in his three-piece suit and his fob watch, as a peasant farmer with an orange grove. It seemed so unlikely – and yet at the same time it sounded so exotic![1] Of course, Flóra dismissed the idea out of hand – what about her elderly mother, her sisters? She could not think of leaving them behind.'

Her eyes dim, cloud over, exhausted again. 'If only she

had known . . . ' She takes another sip of the orange juice, then waves me away.

28 May 2017

I am sitting listening to her deep, rasping breath. Her remaining flesh is wasting away, most of her hair is gone, in a matter of weeks she has been reduced to a pitiful bag of bones sheathed in papery, jaundiced skin. During a previous stint in hospital, she turned to me, frightened: 'Darling, don't remember me like this, I beg of you . . . ' Even in those final years, it was her self-image, rather than her sense of self, that she wished so fiercely to protect.

Her room looks like a mortuary, the staff insisting that the harsh neon light should be kept on so that they can check on her. The bleak white light diminishes yet further, if that is possible, the shrunken form beneath the sheet. Someone has removed her perfect teeth, so skilfully fashioned long ago by the Knightsbridge dentist, and her collapsed lips, flapping with every desperate, defiant breath, are now unrecognisable. Having cheated death at nineteen, she is not ready, it seems, to capitulate at ninety-one. One flailing, shrivelled arm moves incessantly, first clawing at my hand, then arcing over to pluck at her face, her eyes staring intently at the ceiling, her cracked voice barking out a single word, over and over again: 'Hell! Hell! Hell!'

Despite increased doses of morphine, her distress is unabated. There is unfinished business.[2] There is fury at being dragged back to the one defining moment of her life. Still, even now. The nurse assures me that her heartbeat is strong. 'You go home, young man, and look after your father, I'll take good care of her.' It is almost midnight and I am desperately tired. I kiss her gently on the pitted ravine that once was her cheek. 'Goodnight, Mother, try and sleep. I'll be back soon. God bless,' and I close the door behind me.

They called me at six the next morning.

CHAPTER 32

September 2017

Mother's fellow escapee and close friend Emmi was the first person I called when Mother died. Her voice was faint, a wavering echo down the line. 'I know why you're calling me, I know . . .' A few weeks after Mother's funeral I flew out to California. We sat on Emmi's veranda one September afternoon, sipping green tea, both of us aware that this was probably our last meeting. She talked of her childhood in Pécs in south-western Hungary, the deportation in the summer of 1944 and meeting Mother on the forced march out of Berlin. Unlike Mother, she recalled their experiences together with a wry humour, somehow detached, undamaged if that is possible. 'Can you imagine, the three of us billeted in a house where Himmler had stayed, of all places?' Well into her nineties, bent and frail, she remained quietly philosophical about her wartime experience. 'Stuff happens, darling, what can I say? You either get over it, or you don't. Oh boy . . . There's not much to celebrate when you get to my age, but I worked out the other day that Hitler has been dead for over seventy years. Now that *does* give me some comfort!' She laughed gleefully.

I asked her about her long friendship with Mother. She thought for a while, drawing the rug closer around her knees, reached out to hold my hand and sighed. 'I remember sitting together in Himmler's kitchen – your mother would tell me stories about her early childhood. She was invited to a fancy-dress party when she was about seven – a friend of her mother's made her a special costume in the style of a white carnation, hat and all. There we were, sitting around the table in our thin rags, your mother describing in minute detail that elaborate outfit. A few years later, when she and your father married, I made sure he chose a large bunch of white carnations for her wedding bouquet. She gave me one when they drove away on honeymoon – do you know, I think I still have it somewhere, pressed inside a book.

'She used to boast about her childhood pranks. Apparently, one of her favourite games was to tie a five-pengő banknote to a fine silk thread and gently lower it from her bedroom window until it lay on the pavement below. When some poor unsuspecting passer-by bent down to pick it up, she would quickly jerk up the thread and the person below would be left looking like a fool, while she giggled from her window. I remember her telling me this with great relish – make of that what you will.

'I think she was terribly spoiled as a young girl – your grandparents had already lost one daughter and when she was eight she developed an ear infection which spread into the mastoid bone. Of course, there was no penicillin in those days. She was too ill to be taken to Budapest, so the director of the Eger hospital came to the house. Her mother disinfected the kitchen, the poor mite was strapped to the table and then the surgeon administered anaesthetic and set to work, cutting out a section of her skull behind the ear. It must have been agonising for your grandparents, standing by helplessly. But he saved her.

'It's not easy to sum up your mother. She could be a delight – warm-hearted and witty. She had many fine qualities, always fiercely loyal, which I found very touching. I remember being intensely jealous in those first few months in Germany after we escaped to safety – she had this knack of gathering around her a bevy of handsome, adoring young men. I think that really defined her in a way – in the end, she just wanted to be adored, it's that simple.'

When it was time for me to go, Emmi dragged herself painfully down the hallway on her Zimmer, determined to wave me off as I stepped into the taxi. 'Come back soon – promise?'

She died just a few months later. Shortly afterwards, I was going through some old files and a folded piece of yellowing paper floated down to the floor. Picking it up, I saw it was a letter from Emmi, written when she visited me in Cambridge in 1979.

Dearest Love,

I am so happy we met, even though time was much too short! I feel somehow very close to you, and it is not just because you are Ildikó's son. I do want you to know that if you should ever need us, now, later, or whenever – you can always count on us, in any way, at any time. Please don't forget that!

Best of luck for the Finals.

Love, Emmi

CHAPTER 33

October 2019

I am standing in the hallway of my parents' house, poised to dismantle the whole tired edifice, Mother's brave attempt to mask her enduring sense of loss. It will be my final act of sabotage and betrayal, disassembling everything that she had so carefully curated as a stage set for her life. I have often thought about this moment – enthusiastically sacking the temple, sweeping away the detritus of two long lives. But, confronted with the reality of the task, I relent, stickering a surprising number of items that I am unable to part with. I earmark a silver cigarette box, a Herend bowl, three matching pigskin suitcases that my parents bought for touring holidays in Europe and a huge monogrammed tablecloth with twelve napkins, carefully stored in the secret room in the house in Eger, in the hope of better times to come.

György, who looked after my grandfather's vineyards, was entrusted with constructing that secret room behind the ceramic stove in my grandfather's study. Flóra, Zsuzsi and my mother lugged everything they could inside – packing cases with most of the silver, my mother's trousseau, embroidered linens, the best of my grandmother's jewellery, the good porcelain, family photo albums and a couple of the better Persian carpets rolled up tight. They were careful to leave out enough china and silver so that no one should be suspicious. Then the false wall was papered over, and after it was done, they washed it with a solution of weak tea – when they had finished it was impossible to detect that anything had ever been altered. The three women were given two days to pack some things. The house was to be occupied by German officers, so they had to drag heavy mahogany bookcases, sideboards, a vast dining table, even my grand-father's great oak desk into a back room to create more space. I remember my mother telling me that Flóra insisted they scrub and polish every floor in the apartment, determined that the Germans should not have the satisfaction of saying that Hungarian Jews lived like pigs.

György by all accounts was devoted to my grandfather. They used to spend hours together discussing the vintage, examining the rows of grafted vines, considering the merits of a new spray against mildew. These two men – peasant and lawyer – had real respect for each other. György lived in a cottage in one of the vineyards. My mother used to go there sometimes after school – his wife, Frida, would bake her cookies. One morning, after my mother and her family had been taken away, two men from the Gendarmerie broke down the door, dragged György down into the wine cellar together with his wife and baby daughter and shot them all. Because they had worked for a Jewish family. This was routine of course.

I know I will never use that vast tablecloth, but I also

know I cannot consign it to the heap destined for the charity shop. I cook an indifferent meal, using up scraps from the fridge, and sit for the last time at the dining table, staring at the stiff expanse of white damask, carefully embroidered with my grandmother's initials.

After dinner, I head upstairs to Mother's bedroom. Soon the bed is heaped high with the contents of her many wardrobes – silk cocktail dresses, tailored linen suits, an emerald-green satin ballgown, complete with train, crocodile handbags and matching shoes, the softest kid gloves in pale colours, mohair and cashmere wraps, silk scarves, mink stoles – all tagged for the local charity shop.

I remember a visit home back in the 1980s. 'Come and look!' – the voice, oddly girlish, breathless. Mother, decked out in a complete Hungarian peasant costume, is performing a stately pirouette in front of her bedroom mirror. 'What do you think? You see, it still fits me!' It is quite obvious that squeezing into this outfit has been a heroic struggle, but I say nothing, smiling mutely as she paces up and down in triumph. Finally, the constraints of the tight bodice prove too much and she sinks into an armchair, panting heavily, one hand smoothing the full skirt and the apron embroidered with flowers. When she looks up I can see there are tears in her eyes. 'You see, my father so loved me to wear this costume . . .'

On a high shelf there's a battered cardboard box that falls to pieces as I pull it down. I lift out a crumpled skirt, bodice and an embroidered apron, adding them to the pile on the bed along with everything else. Downstairs, I set to work in the dining room, methodically going through the sideboard drawers, putting to one side the trays of silver cutlery that formed part of Mother's trousseau. Opening the drawer below, I find one of her most treasured possessions – a large and heavily embellished silver tray, edged with pie-crust flounces. Always referred to as the Murderer's Tray, it was a gift from a grateful client to Mother's father Ede, whose skilful performance in court had saved the defendant from the noose.

Mother gave luncheon parties for her women friends on the second Tuesday of every month. If these fell during a school holiday, I would scurry about in the background, assisting Pearl the housekeeper. Once the meal was over, Mother would reverently draw the great tray from its linen shroud, carefully setting out slender glasses filled with Tokaji for her guests, anticipating the excited murmur of approval – it was, after all, a rather exotic flourish in 1970s suburbia. On one such occasion, watching her prepare the tray, I saw her falter: 'I am picturing my father just now, it's how I always imagine him, this great jovial man, always the absolute life of the party, so erudite, so witty, hugely respected in his profession – and there he is, helpless, weak from lack of insulin, lying on a stretcher on a railway platform in the depths of winter, knowing he has only days to live . . . ' She grasped the edge of the sideboard, her shoulders tense with sadness. In the adjoining room we could hear the chatter of women's voices, their tinkling laughter. Slowly, she straightened up, dabbed her eyes and took hold of the heavy tray. Her armour now securely in place, she readied herself for the tilting yard and sailed into the drawing room. 'Now, ladies!'

The last person to see my grandfather alive was Bandi Meister. Transported to Kyiv to work as a forced labourer in one of the camps, he was savvy enough to persuade his camp Kommandant that he could use his expertise to identify antique icons being sold cheap on the black market. As a result, he was allowed to wear civilian clothes and roam the streets in search of these precious artworks, and it was on one of these expeditions that he happened to see a bedraggled procession of other forced labourers passing down one of the city's main streets. At the tail end of the line was a donkey and cart, laden with kitchen utensils, and straddling this sad transport was my grandfather, already terminally ill. The two men recognised each other and waved, but there was no opportunity to talk. The procession moved on up the street and disappeared.

I used to visit Bandi and Klára in Croydon and sometimes he would recount episodes from his wartime experiences. On one of his recces in Kyiv, he heard that the director of the Museum of Western and Oriental Art[1] was living in the building to protect its treasures as best he could. Bandi found the museum and rang the bell at the main entrance. After a while he heard footsteps and the great door was cautiously opened a crack. He explained that he was an art lover, that he was a prisoner at the nearby camp, could he possibly come in just for a few minutes? The director, Professor Sergei Gilyarov, took pity on him 'and there I was, in my miserable rags, looking at masterpieces by Greuze, Veronese, Ribera, Poussin, Van Dyck, Canaletto, Vermeer, also fifteenth-century Italian majolica and spectacular Sèvres and Meissen dinner services – can you imagine? It was unbelievable! Finally the professor unfurled an astonishing, flame-coloured bolt of pleated Fortuny silk. I nearly fainted with joy – just the sheer, shocking beauty of that colour, after months of grey misery, starvation and cruelty. It reminded me not so much of what we had lost, but – more importantly – of what might still be possible.'

In the drawing room I sift through family photo albums, slicing out images from our childhood that I can't part with, at least not yet. One album documents a family holiday in the Austrian Alps from the early sixties. On the Grossglockner Pass we stopped for a picnic – Mother, sporting elegant sunglasses and a headscarf, is dispensing chicken sandwiches and *Apfelsaft* (apple juice). To the outsider, the perfect family group. The holiday had been Father's idea – to revisit the same hotel on the Wörthersee where he had holidayed with his parents in the mid-1930s – an attempt, I see now, to reconnect with a lost life.

I think back to Father's death, a 'good death', lying quietly in the drawing room, overlooking the willow tree where Mother's ashes are buried, listening to Glenn Gould playing (and humming) Bach, drifting gently away. How different from Mother's end – her guttural cries of defiance and rage cutting through the antiseptic silence of that empty hospice corridor as I walked away.

I imagine myself walking around that secret room now, my fingers tracing the join where the new paper meets the old, peeling back the trickery to reveal the treasures packed tightly into that hidden space so that they cannot survive to haunt me. My aunt told me that when she returned to the town after she was liberated, she saw a woman walking down the street wearing her dead mother's fur coat. And why not? People were so sure no one would ever come home.[2]

Can one ever paper over the cracks? Perhaps it would have been better if everything had been ransacked, each last precious item looted and lost. Instead, sixty years later I stumble over the worn Persian rugs, lay the table with the china and silverware from that secret hiding place, point them out to guests, retell the story in minute detail, noting with satisfaction their sharp intakes of breath. Your narrative is mine now, Mother, I am word-perfect. After everyone has gone, I tell myself, 'You have to get rid of all this stuff, you cannot go on being shackled by the past.' But the next morning I open the silver polish, work the cream carefully between the sharp prongs of every fork and then return everything to its allotted place, safely protected between layers of soft dusters.

CHAPTER 34

20 July 2022

It is a sweltering summer's day and I am walking along Am Grossen Wannsee, a leafy avenue winding its way between opulent villas bordering the lake. Through the dense foliage I catch glimpses of heavy overhanging eaves, elaborate Tyrolean balconies, Gothic turrets and neoclassical pomp. No. 56–58, however, dispenses with any such frivolous architectural detail, relying instead on its palatial proportions to create impact.

It was here, on 20 January 1942, that Reinhard Heydrich, chief of the Reich Security Main Office (which included the Gestapo and the Security Service) and one of the prime movers behind the 'Kristallnacht' operation of 1938, gathered together high-ranking representatives of the Nazi Party, the SS, the Reich Chancelleries, the Ministry for the Occupied Eastern Territories, the Interior, Foreign and Justice Ministries, and Göring's Four Year Plan Agency – including Otto Hofmann, head of the *Rasse- und Siedlungshauptamt der SS, RuSHA* (SS Race and Settlement Main Office) and Lieutenant Colonel Adolf Eichmann, head of Referat IV B4 of the Gestapo – in order to propose and coordinate the

Endlösung, or Final Solution – in other words, the deportation and murder of the 11 million Jews whom Heydrich estimated lived in Europe, both within and beyond the territories under Nazi rule.

The Wannsee Conference lasted less than two hours. Known as the Wannsee Protocol, the minutes taken by Eichmann's secretary, Ingeburg Werlemann, were later carefully edited by Eichmann, in consultation with Heydrich, both at pains to ensure that the proceedings should not be recorded verbatim. Otto Thierack, president of the *Volksgerichtshof* (People's Court) and appointed Reich Minister of Justice the following August, formally approved the proposals, surrendering all jurisdiction of the Jews to the SS.

The grand salon where the conference was held overlooks the formal gardens and the waters of the lake beyond. The generously proportioned room is now arranged as an exhibition space. Displayed in a small vitrine is Heydrich's elegantly printed invitation:

> On 31 July 1941, the Reich Marshal of the Gross-deutsches Reich commissioned me, together with other pertinent central agencies involved, to carry out all necessary preparations in regard to organisational, practical and material measures requisite for the total solution of the Jewish question in Europe, and to submit to him in the near future a general outline thereof. I am enclosing with my letter a photocopy of this order.
>
> Considering the exceptional importance of these

measures, and in order to reach a common agreement on all aspects connected with this final solution among the central agencies concerned, I suggest that we make these problems a matter of joint discussion, especially because since 15 October 1941 Jews are already continuously being evacuated from the territory of the Reich, including the Protectorate of Bohemia and Moravia, to the East.

I therefore invite you to attend such a meeting, to be followed by a light lunch, on 20 January 1942 at noon, at the office of the International Criminal Police Commission, Berlin, Am Grossen Wannsee No. 56–58.

I step out onto the terrace – the sun sparkles on the lake, water lapping against the balustrade, the scent of lilac in the summer air. I hear the sound of chairs being pushed back across the parquet floor as fifteen men rise from the conference table, relieved that the tiresome business of the day has been concluded. Adjusting their immaculate uniforms, they begin to chat informally, slapping each other on the back, now in jovial mood as they saunter through to the adjoining anteroom to enjoy a light lunch washed down with glasses of Riesling.

I remember Mother showing me a photograph of my grandfather. 'Here he is, standing in front of one of the two vineyard houses we owned. The place looks like a real Austrian *Wirtshaus*, don't you think? Ah, he was always so delighted to dispense with his formal attire – look at his broad belly covered with that full-length leather apron. And that huge glass pipette he's holding – he would dip it carefully into the tall wooden barrels in order to test the wine, to check whether it was maturing correctly. And there's your grandmother, sitting at the table on the veranda. She's bending over some embroidery, do you see? And that's me beside her, shelling peas – I was telling her some wicked story about the nuns at my convent school. I made her giggle, but afterwards she told me off. God – I remember it all so clearly.'

It is the summer of 1942. In less than two years, all this would be swept away, obliterated at the stroke of a pen by the men seated around the conference table at No. 56–58 Am Grossen Wannsee.

21 July 2022

Leaving the Berlin Hauptbahnhof, the train passes through a gently undulating, well-ordered landscape dotted with neat villages. The station at Fürstenberg/Havel is generously decorated with hanging baskets of obligatory scarlet geraniums and in the cobbled square local matrons are sitting at café tables under the shade of lime trees, chatting over *Kaffee und Kuchen*. Behind the town church a discreetly placed signpost indicates the road to Ravensbrück – the white letters on a brown background identifying it as a heritage site.

I walk along the road skirting the Schwedtsee and pass the entrance to a holiday campsite bordering the lake, busy today with families arriving in motorhomes towing boats and dinghies. The road continues on to the nearby village of Himmelpfort (Heaven's Gate) where at Christmas the post office receives hundreds of thousands of letters written by children from all over the world who believe, given the name of the village, that St Nikolaus must live there. Every year, Deutsche Post hires extra staff to ensure that all the letters are answered.

But I am not heading to Himmelpfort. After only a few hundred metres, the road forks and a stark bronze sculpture, *Müttergruppe* by Fritz Cremer, marks the entrance to the Strasse der Nationen – a cobbled approach road winding through woods heavy with the scent of pine – built by the first prisoners in 1938. Ravensbrück was conceived as a *Muster-Lager*, or model concentration camp: to the right, beyond the trees, the seemingly untroubled waters of the lake; to the left a row of comfortable villas built for the families of the senior camp staff, now repurposed as an education centre. Just beyond is a large rectangular area cut into the forest, roughly the size of a football pitch. A small notice announces that this was the site of a supermarket erected in 1991, subsequently demolished. No further explanation is given – perhaps none is needed.

The handsome structure of the camp's central administrative building is designed in the neoclassical style, with broad stone steps leading up to an imposing colonnaded portico. Originally accommodating offices for camp Kommandant Fritz Suhren[1] and his SS staff, the building also housed a cinema and a refectory and is now a museum. Behind is a row of former garages and motor repair workshops. On one wall a carefully preserved notice in Gothic script exclaims: '*Rauchen und Tragen von offenem Licht verboten!*' (Smoking and naked flames are forbidden!).

I walk through an archway and before me is the Appelplatz, a vast empty expanse covered with black cinders, beyond it the central *allée*, the Lagerstrasse, planted in the early 1940s with fast-growing white poplars,[2] evidently an attempt to camouflage the site from prying eyes. Neat rectangles of fine grey gravel delineate the footprints of the demolished barrack huts, each of which held as many as 1,200 prisoners, four women allocated to every bunk.

At the far end of the site are the industrial workshops, over to my right the cell block where prisoners were routinely tortured. Immediately adjacent is the canteen for the female SS guards and next to that the sick bay, the *Krankenrevier*, where a group of Polish prisoners, known as the *Kaninchen* (rabbits), were used as human guinea pigs for experimental surgical operations involving the removal, often without anaesthetic, of bone and muscle, the resulting wounds contaminated with gangrene, tetanus and streptococcus; where syphilis germs were injected into prisoners' spinal cords; where women were sterilised by exposure to high levels of X-ray; where inmates who had contracted typhoid, diphtheria and tuberculosis were left to die; where pregnancies were crudely aborted and new-born babies strangled or drowned in front of their mothers.

Near the lake shore, part of the original perimeter wall has been repurposed as *Die Mauer der Nationen*, the Wall of Nations. In front of it a rose garden has been planted, beneath which are the remains of prisoners previously buried in mass graves across the campsite. There are two vertical markers – behind me the tall chimney of the crematorium, across the lake the spire of the town church.

It is impossible to estimate the death toll at Ravensbrück – information provided by the Ravensbrück Memorial Museum suggests a figure of 28,000 but it is probably far higher: few SS documents survive, so no one will ever know for certain. In the final days, prisoners' files were hurriedly burned in the crematorium or on bonfires, along with their bodies, the ashes thrown into the lake. The holidaymakers I watch criss-crossing the water in their dinghies and boats can have no idea what lies below and the local townspeople are unlikely to enlighten them.

The sun is high in the sky now and the heat thrown up from the arid ground of the Appelplatz is becoming unbearable. I stoop down and pick up a small piece of black cinder, tuck it into my pocket and walk away.

Epilogue

Summer 1992

The last performance in the old opera house at Glynde-bourne is a production of Tchaikovsky's *The Queen of Spades*. I am singing in the chorus and also have a silent role as a footman. In Act II, I escort the old Countess – formerly a celebrated beauty known as the 'Muscovite Venus' – as she returns from a masked ball. She totters slowly into her bed-chamber, a grotesque confection of feathers and brilliant jewels. Slumping exhausted into a chair, her maids begin to undress her. First, the powdered wig, embellished with ribbons and pearls, is removed, revealing the old crone's bare skull, a few wisps of white hair floating down to her shoulders. Next, her maids loosen her stays and remove the elaborate ball gown. The maids depart, leaving the Countess in her shift, staring longingly at a portrait of her youthful self. Alone in her chamber and aware that she faces imminent death, she sings a poignant lament.

In the weeks following the completion of this book, I have a recurring dream. Mother appears weeping, bitterly reproaching me for my final act of betrayal: 'How could you? How could you?'

Like the footman in *The Queen of Spades*, I am silent. There is nothing left to be said.

Appendix

Spring 2021

Two years after the house is sold, I am starting to go through boxes of Hungarian letters retrieved from my parents' attic. In one box I find several pages ripped from an exercise book – Edit Lengyelfi, a translator and researcher in Budapest, sends me the English text, confirming these are Mother's diary entries for the two years prior to June 1944. They are the jottings of a teenager, giddy accounts of a charmed life – her many admirers, a summer ball, visits to a fashionable spa accompanied by an unnamed count, holiday visits to her grandmother's country estate at Celldömölk on the Austrian border, American movies she has seen, books she is reading, new friendships formed. Ostensibly the carefree diary entries of a pretty girl from a well-to-do family, and yet an oblique reference in August 1942 to 'current circumstances' reveals her growing unease.

Strangely, there is no mention of her father's conscription in 1942 as a forced labourer, supporting the Hungarian Second Army in the occupied territories of the Soviet Union but an entry in late February 1943 notes her concern: 'We have had no news from Father these past five weeks.' The tone of the writing shifts markedly, increasingly aware of the family's vulnerability, of the pressing need to convert to Catholicism. Although life goes on – she describes her high school graduation and gives a detailed account of her birthday presents – there is a new sense of realism: 'I think that it is very unwise to be a fatalist now, to rely on hazardous fate – there are some serious things going on . . . It is foolish now to believe in any positive things in the future.'

Cycling past a lake on a summer's afternoon, she stops to make a garland of grass and wild flowers and throws it out onto the water. I wonder what that young girl thought as she watched the garland drift away. She never mentioned it and now I will never know. This and so many other untold stories.

A few lines from Father's favourite poem float by:

> One may not doubt that, somehow, Good
> Shall come of Water and of Mud;
> And, sure, the reverent eye must see
> A Purpose in Liquidity . . . [1]

Diary entries, 1942–44

Saturday 1 August 1942

At the end of Dezső's visit[2] he said goodbye in such a shy, slightly awkward way . . . I almost started to laugh – but he asked when he could see me again, and where we might meet. Aunt Malvin asked him: 'So, dear sir, what are you trying to say?'

Then – oh, glorious words – he said: 'I wanted to say that she is fascinating, dizzying, dangerously beautiful.'

Don't blame me, dear Diary, I don't write this because I'm self-confident, I am simply quoting someone else's words. Everyone is so sweet to me here. If I stayed here too long, I know I would be spoiled too much! And now I have to record what took place next: Dezső was sitting here in front of me and said: 'Your hands are so beautiful!' Deferentially he took my hand to his lips and slowly kissed it. 'You are as beautiful as a goddess.' Now that was probably an overstatement, but a very witty and entertaining overstatement!

Monday 3 August 1942, Celldömölk

I arrived here on Wednesday evening from Pápa where I saw a film everyone is talking about: *Duel for Nothing*.[3]

On Saturday, a cellist from Szombathely[4] was visiting here and played a programme of Mozart, Brahms, Wagner, Schubert, Schumann, Mahler and Bach – it was so beautiful. He left this morning. He is only 26 years old but so accomplished – it was such a delight to hear him play.

This afternoon Éva came and said a gentleman is looking for me. I asked his name. She said Pista[5] Lengyel, or something like that. Apparently, he is very handsome. She was right. He arrived at 3.30 p.m. and left at 5.30 p.m. He came just for my sake, for me – all the way from Szombathely: very flattering for my vanity! Grandmother has been teasing me – she says that I have charmed all the boys in Szombathely!

Tuesday 4 August 1942

Today I was in Alsóság, invited by Katona Erzsébet for lunch. They were very nice. On my way home by bike, I stopped by a lake and made a garland of wild flowers and grasses, and before setting off again I flung it out onto the water and watched it slowly float away in ever widening circles. And when I got back to Grandmother's, there waiting for me was a real, genuine love letter from Pista. This was a memorable day.

I am reading an interesting book by Richard Voss: *Villa Falconieri*.[6]

Sunday 9 August 1942

On Thursday I went to the cinema again, this time with Kato and György, to see an American movie, *Johnny Apollo*.[7] György invited me to go hunting this afternoon, but I don't think Grandmother will let me go.

Yesterday we had guests, Adrienne Brettfeld[8] and her mother. They are landowners – Adrienne's father is a baron! Yesterday Kató was in Sömjén.[9] She told me that Laci was pretty interested in me, even though he is known for being very choosy. I really wanted to go to Sömjén too, but Grandmother didn't let me go. I am very, very sad that I couldn't go. I will travel to Sopron[10] on Tuesday, and I will stay there for around a week. I hope I will have a marvellous time there. I received my fourth letter from Pista yesterday. On Wednesday I had lunch with the Katona family – they are certainly far from boring!

Saturday 15 August 1942, Sopron

I arrived here yesterday morning, travelling together with a very handsome young count.

In the evening we had guests, among them was the 24-year-old Gyorgy Kaál. I think I must have had some success since he has asked me to go dancing with him tomorrow afternoon at the Hotel Lővér.[11]

Today I met a very nice girl called Margit Schiller. In the morning we went together to the museum, and afterwards we went out to the Erzsébet Park. I like her a lot and I think she likes me too. It would be nice to have her as a good friend. Her father is Jewish, her mother a Catholic, but her parents have separated and she now lives with her father and her stepmother who is also Jewish. She is a Catholic herself.[12] Last night I was looking out the window and saw two soldiers. It took me a great deal of self-control to contain my laughter. They stood in front of the window and gazed at me for a full 20 minutes, then they saluted and left. They were very handsome, especially one of them.

Monday 17 August 1942

On Saturday we had a wonderful visit to Aunt Zseni. She lives in such a beautiful part of the country. I collected wild cyclamen – tiny purple flowers dotting the forest floor – they suit their surroundings so perfectly. My heart was filled with awe when I looked up at the enormous mountains forming a vast circle above us, they looked protective and intimidating at the same time. I will never forget them!

Yesterday morning we went to a very nice photo exhibition and in the afternoon I went dancing. There were some wealthy young men there, one of them, from Ózd, was called Bandi Gerő. He just called me on the telephone today from Bakta.[13] He says he is completely in love with me. He is very nice! He asked whether he could visit me. There is also another chap called Sacher, who is a very handsome, elegant, gentle boy. He has been studying medicine in Prague but has not finished his studies yet because of the current circumstances. He is also a very talented piano player, very musical, a student of Dohnányi.[14] He is also coming here together with Gerő. They wanted to come today, but some days ago one of their friends died in an accident, so they will be in mourning for a week, which means their visit has been cancelled, for the time being.

I will travel to Budapest next week, I have to go to the dentist. I have a beautiful new dress, I think I look rather good in it!

We are waiting for Father to return home in the next few days, but unfortunately it is still uncertain when he will come.[15] Heller, who was also in Kyiv, has already been home for a few days.

Sunday 28 February 1943, Eger

I was at the dentist in Budapest on 19 January, but fortunately I also had some fun. I went to two movies. I met Rudi once, and also Ervin Fenyves. I had lunch with the Kerekes family and also with the Rejtő family. I stayed at Böske's place. On the last evening, Pista Balogh took me to a ball. We had such fun, we stayed there until 1 o'clock in the morning! I met two very nice girls there: Zsuzsi Beck and Éva Juhász.

I invited guests to my birthday party and was given a lot of presents. From Lali a beautiful Rosenthal bonbonnière with flowers, filled with delicious chocolates. From Erzsi[16] a beautiful piece of Herendi porcelain.[17] From Vica, Lili, Zsuzsi, Éva T., Éva D. and Éva F. a Herendi porcelain figure and a photo album. From Ági a Herendi ashtray. From Orsi and Kati flowers. From Mother a beautiful piece of pink fabric from Madeira.

We have had no news from Father these past five weeks. All we have heard is very confused information, which is simply not enough, just empty promises. In his last letter to Mother, he wrote 'If this old crock of a man is somehow essential to Herr Hitler's war efforts, then surely the war cannot last much longer!' Brave words, dear Father, but we know otherwise. It is foolish now to believe in any positive things in the future.

Saturday 27 March 1943

Today we received a note from the camp priest informing us that Father died of a stroke on 2 March. I can't take this in, I can't believe it, I can't write about it. Dear Father, this cannot be true, can it?[18]

Friday 7 May 1943

Erzsi had her school graduation, we all worked hard and everything went well. They say it was the best ever.

Yesterday we received a letter from Zsuzsi, saying that Pista had called her on the phone and then visited her in Pest. 'He's very good-looking, intelligent, smart, he seems to be decent and well mannered.' And I have just received a long, sweet and nice letter from him in which he said that he would like to spend his next holiday with me. I wish it would happen! God please make it happen!

Wednesday 9 February 1944, Eger

Today I have started teaching two new students. I give them six lessons per week. They are in the third grade of the secondary school. I teach them Latin, I earn 60 pengő[19] per month. I'm extremely proud of it. This is my present to you, Father, on your birthday.

Pista is like an angel in his letters – he writes quite often. The only problem with him is that he loves me too much!

Recently I seem to be always very busy. At the school graduation I'd like to make my presentation on Mihály Babits.[20]

We are living in dangerous times. The air feels as though it were charged with high voltage – I feel it everywhere around us. We cannot know what will be the result of the current political situation but I sense that there will be irreparable consequences for us. Nowadays we are[21] thinking about converting to a different religion. I think that it is very unwise to be a fatalist now, to rely on hazardous fate – there are some serious things going on. We cannot be indifferent – everything is in the balance: 'to be or not to be'.

Tuesday 29 February 1944, Eger

Three days ago it was my 18th birthday, but I would have preferred to skip it. It was a painful and bitter birthday. The second one without a kiss from Father. So I had a really weepy birthday. I couldn't behave as I should have done – even though I received such a lot of nice things. I got a beautiful brown coat and dress. Poetry by Árpád Tóth[22] and Attila József[23] from Zsuzsi. From Vica, Lili, Zsuzsi B., Éva I. and Éva T. a very nice marble bookend.

My half-year certificate in school was not bad.

Yesterday the weather was really lovely. The kind of spring warmth which you can feel on your skin. It is thrilling and fills you with happiness. I feel as though I have a lot of love piled up in me, and I have no one to give it to.

I am not 70 years old, only 18 years. Spring is here, but my mood is very much up and down, I feel it in all of my nerves that I am missing something, someone.

I have a new hairstyle and people say I am looking good. Someone should come who could be happy for me. Oh God, I really would like to be loved by someone!

Tuesday 21 March 1944, Eger

19 March – Black Sunday.[24] Mother is with Grandmother in Celldömölk and I don't know when she will come home again. May God be with us!

Acknowledgements

Thanks are due first to my sister. Her story is very different from mine and so, at her request, she is not referenced in the text. Nonetheless, she has supported the writing process with many constructive suggestions.

My cousins, Piers and Michael, read drafts and made important suggestions regarding the book's scope and structure; Dr Esther Bonta in Sydney assisted with information regarding various family members.

My thanks to Philippa Donovan of Smart Quill Editorial, whose thoughtful input helped shape the initial manuscript; to Doug Young at PEW Literary, who believed in this book; and to Nigel Wilcockson and Hannah White-Steele at Hutchinson Heinemann who have edited the manuscript with such care, in the process markedly improving its structure and pace. In addition, freelance copy-editor Katherine Fry's forensic sweep through the final text has been invaluable. My thanks also to the judges – Dina Nayeri, Philippe Sands and Elif Shafak – who shortlisted the book for the inaugural Footnote X Counterpoints Writing Prize, launched in 2023, as well as to Vidisha Biswas of Footnote Press and Almir Koldzic of Counterpoints Arts. I am grateful for the support of many kind friends: Albrecht Ollendiek, who generously assisted with the translation of various German texts, and suggested an alternative turn of phrase or more detailed amplification where he felt these were required, and who presented me with a silver napkin ring engraved with the letter 'X'; Lucy and David Kynaston, who both set aside time to read the second draft of the book and offer detailed feedback; also Carol O'Brien, Christobel Kent, Jay Merrick and John Wakefield, whose incisive readings encouraged me to reconsider issues of balance and tone; Peter Lantos, survivor of Bergen-Belsen, former chair of the Institute of Psychiatry at King's College London and the author of a remarkable autobiography, *Parallel Lines,* who read an early draft and asked important questions; Anne Elliott Evans, Paul Glassner (son of Emmi, with whom Mother escaped from the death march from Berlin), Corinne Mellul and Jane Thorburn, who all gave constructive commentary; and Katina Noble, who listened to each section as I completed it, offering perceptive reflections.

In February 2022, on the eve of the Russian invasion of Ukraine, Dr Olena Zhivkova, deputy director of the Bohdan and Varvara Khanenko National Museum of Arts in Kyiv, provided important information regarding the works that would have been on display in the museum in early 1943. I am particularly grateful to her, given the gravity of the situation she was then facing.

My thanks, also, to Edit Lengyelfi, my Hungarian researcher in Budapest, who translated my mother's diary entries as well as many letters and official documents. Additional thanks to Dr Andrea Genest (director) and Sabine Röwer (museological services department) at the Ravensbrück Memorial Museum (Mahn- und Gedenkstätte Ravensbrück / Stiftung Brandenburgische Gedenkstätten). Dr Piotr Setkiewicz, Director of the Centre for Research at the Auschwitz-Birkenau Memorial and Museum and Dr Wanda Witek-Malicka, Assistant at the Centre for Research, Auschwitz-Birkenau Memorial and Museum both offered generous assistance. I am grateful to staff at Yad Vashem, the World Holocaust Remembrance Center in Jerusalem – Eszter Stern (archivist), Dany Melkonowicki (References and Information) and Dr Cornelia Shati-Geissler (director of the Deportation Research Project) – for their help in locating important documentation. My thanks to Eike Stegen at Haus der Wannsee-Konferenz for responding to various queries regarding key documents and to Dr Lindsey Davidson, Lecturer in Jewish Studies at the University of Bristol and Rabbi Rachel Benjamin, Rabbi Emerita of Mosaic Liberal Synagogue in North London, both of whom kindly assisted with Hebrew texts. Dr Rainer Schubert, Archivist at the Vienna Volksoper, provided helpful information regarding my great-aunt Lilian Reinau, a member of the Volksoper company during the 1930s.

I am very grateful to Bruce Haines, a Trustee of the Li Yuan-chia Foundation, who kindly allowed me to reproduce two of Li's poems in the book, and to Sally Salvesen for agreeing that I might reference her when describing the important encounter between my mother and Sylvia Salvesen at Ravensbrück.

Lastly, special thanks to my partner, who patiently listened to me as I began to sketch out the structure of this book, offering encouragement and then carefully reading and commenting on each section, as the work progressed.

Select Bibliography

Anglada, Maria Àngels, *The Auschwitz Violin*, Constable & Robinson, 2011.

Barlay, Nick, *Scattered Ghosts*, I. B. Tauris & Co., 2013.

Berest, Anne, *The Postcard*, Europa Editions, 2024.

Bettelheim, Bruno, *Surviving and Other Essays*, Thames & Hudson, 1979.

Bowlby, John, *A Secure Base: Clinical Applications of Attachment Theory*, Routledge, 1988.

Buber Agassi, Judith, *Jewish Women Prisoners of Ravensbrück*, Texas Tech University Press, 2014.

Cesarini, David, *Final Solution: The Fate of the Jews, 1933–49*, Pan Books, 2017.

Cesarini, David (ed.), *Genocide and Rescue: The Holocaust in Hungary 1944*, Berg, 1977.

Crankshaw, Edward, *Gestapo – Instrument of Tyranny*, Greenhill Books, 1990.

Crankshaw, Edward, *Maria Theresa*, Longmans, 1969.

De Gaulle Anthonioz, Geneviève, *God Remained Outside: An Echo of Ravensbrück*, Souvenir Press, 2000.

Drutman, Irving (ed.), *Janet Flanner's World – Uncollected Writings 1932–1975*, Martin Secker & Warburg, 1979.

Eger, Edith, *The Choice*, Rider/Ebury Press, 2018.

Eichler, Jeremy, *Time's Echo*, Faber & Faber, 2023.

Erikson, Eric H., *Childhood and Society*, W. W. Norton, 1993.

Frankl, Viktor E., *Man's Search For Meaning*, Rider/Ebury Publishing, 2004.

Freedland, Jonathan, *The Escape Artist*, John Murray, 2022.

Gay, Peter, *Freud: A Life for our Time*, Anchor/Doubleday, 1989.

Gilbert, Martin, *Second World War*, Weidenfeld & Nicolson, 1989.

Helm, Sarah, *If This Is a Woman*, Abacus/Little, Brown, 2016.

Hillesum, Etty, *An Interrupted Life – The Diaries and Letters of Etty Hillesum 1941–43*, Persephone Books, 2020.

Hoffman, Eva, *Lost in Translation*, Vintage Books, 1998.

Höss, Rudolf, *Autobiography (in KL Auschwitz)*, Auschwitz-Birkenau State Museum, 1998.

Jacobs, Michael, *The Presenting Past*, McGraw Hill/Open University Press, 2012.

Karpf, Anne, *The War After*, Faber & Faber, 2008.

Kawaguchi, Toshikazu, *Tales from the Cafe*, Picador/Pan Macmillan, 2020.

Kempowski, Walter, *Swan Song – A Collective Diary of the Last Days of the Third Reich*, W. W. Norton, 2015.

Kertész, Imre, *Fateless*, Vintage Books, 1975.

Lantos, Peter, *Parallel Lines – A Journey from Childhood to Belsen*, Arcadia Books, 2006.

Levi, Primo, *The Drowned and the Saved*, Michael Joseph, 1988.

Longerich, Peter, *Heinrich Himmler*, Oxford University Press, 2012.

MacGregor, Neil, *Germany: Memories of a Nation*, Allen Lane, 2014.

Miller, Alice, *The Drama of Being a Child*, Virago Press, 2008.

Moorhead, Caroline, *A Train in Winter*, Vintage/Random House, 2012.

Morrison, Jack G., *Ravensbrück: Everyday Life in a Women's Concentration Camp*, Markus Wiener Publishers, 2000.

Music, Graham, *Nurturing Children*, Routledge, 2019.

Rogers, Carl R., *On Becoming a Person*, Robinson, 2016.

Rothenstein, John, and Alley, Ronald, *Francis Bacon: Catalogue Raisonné and Documentation*, Thames & Hudson, 1964.

Rothschild, Erika, 'Eine Erinnerung: Ein Gespräch mit Erika Rothschild, die Auschwitz überlebt hat', *Badische Zeitung*, 21/22 January 1995.

Rozett, Robert, *Conscripted Slaves – Hungarian Jewish Forced Laborers on the Eastern Front during the Second World War*, Yad Vashem, 2013.

Saidel, Rochelle G., *The Jewish Women of Ravensbrück Concentration Camp*, University of Wisconsin Press, 2004.

Salvesen, Sylvia, *Forgive But Do Not Forget*, Hutchinson, 1958.

Sands, Philippe, *East West Street*, Weidenfeld & Nicolson, 2017.

Schwarz, Géraldine, *Those Who Forget*, Pushkin Press, 2020.

Shapiro, Dani, *Inheritance – A Memoir of Genealogy, Paternity and Love*, Daunt Books, 2019.

Stargardt, Nicholas, *The German War*, Vintage/Penguin Random House, 2015.

Stone, Dan, *The Holocaust – An Unfinished History*, Pelican Random House, 2023.

Stone, Norman, *World War Two – A Short History*, Penguin, 2014.

Szirtes, George, *The Photographer at Sixteen*, MacLehose Press, 2020.

West, Rebecca, *Black Lamb and Grey Falcon*, Canongate Books, 2020.

Wiesel, Elie, 'For Some Measure of Humility', *Sh'ma: A Journal of Jewish Responsibility*, 5 October 1931, 1975.

Williams, H. A., *Some Day I'll Find You*, Mitchell Beazley, 1982.

Wiskemann, Elizabeth, *Europe of the Dictators, 1919–1945*, Collins, 1966.

Yalom, Irvin D., *Love's Executioner*, Penguin Books, 2013.

Yalom, Irvin D., *Staring at the Sun*, Piatkus/Little, Brown, 2020.

Zsolt, Béla, *Nine Suitcases*, Jonathan Cape, 2004.

Notes

INTRODUCTION

1 When I turned eighteen, Mother decided I was old enough
   to be entrusted with accounts of her wartime experiences.
   Immediately following these conversations, I would make
   detailed notes, capturing as accurately as I could the tone and
   content of our exchanges. The information contained in these
   notebooks, collected over several decades, has been a key
   resource in the preparation of this book.

2 Dani Shapiro's remarkable memoir, *Inheritance*, describes the
   corrosive effect of family secrets. She grew up 'in a house
   where the air crackled with the unsaid'. Shapiro, *Inheritance*,
   p. 131.

3 Josef Rudolf Mengele, also known as the *Todesengel* (Angel
   of Death) was a German SS officer and physician. He was a
   member of the team of doctors at Auschwitz who selected
   victims to be killed in the gas chambers and was one of the
   doctors who administered the gas. He conducted genetic
   research on prisoners, focusing primarily on twins, with no
   regard for the health or safety of his victims. Assisted by a
   network of former SS members, Mengele fled to Argentina

in July 1949, eventually settling in Brazil. He eluded all extradition attempts and died in 1979.

4 Peter Gay's biography of Sigmund Freud offers a striking image of the unconscious as 'a maximum-security prison holding antisocial inmates languishing for years . . . harshly treated and heavily guarded . . . but barely kept under control and forever attempting to escape'. Gay, *Freud*, p. 128.

5 Rothenstein and Alley, *Francis Bacon*, p. 15.

6 Music, *Nurturing Children*, p. 118.

7 Bowlby, *A Secure Base*, p. 121.

CHAPTER 2

1 Churchill, in his speech to Zurich University on 19 September 1946, exactly captured the immediate post-war zeitgeist, namely the imperative to look forward rather than backwards: 'We must all turn our backs upon the horrors of the past and look to the future. We cannot afford to drag forward across the years to come hatreds and revenges which have sprung from the injuries of the past. If Europe is to be saved from infinite misery, and indeed from final doom, there must be this act of faith in the European family, this act of oblivion against all crimes and follies of the past.'

2 Bruno Bettelheim writes in his essay 'Eichmann: The System, The Victims' of our limited emotional response to mass tragedy: 'If one individual suffers, or a few, as in an airplane crash or a mine explosion . . . we feel for the victims

and their relatives . . . but let thirty thousand be killed by a volcano erupting . . . then we are not deeply moved . . . A few screams evoke in us deep anxiety and a desire to help. Hours of screaming without end lead us only to wish that the screamer would shut up.' Bettelheim, *Surviving and Other Essays*, pp. 259–60. After the war, survivors soon realised that there was no audience for the stories they felt compelled to share: the enormity of the horror was too much to grasp, and in most cases the established Jewish community – processing their guilt or relief that they had escaped the inferno – could offer no adequate emotional response. Mother's strategy was clear: better to keep silent. The last thing she wanted was to be labelled a victim. 'Often, as it turned out, the families did not really want to hear: the stories were too unbearable to listen to.' Moorhead, *A Train in Winter*, p. 308.

CHAPTER 4

1 In June 2023, I finally decided to apply for a Hungarian passport. I was duly summoned to the Hungarian Consulate and so began a Kafkaesque process involving endless application forms, all requiring almost identical information, and all of which had then to be translated by an approved translator. Two further visits to the Consulate were necessary, the first to present my completed dossier and later to have my photograph taken and my fingerprints recorded. Eighteen months later, my new passport eventually arrived, exactly sixty years after my first visit to Hungary. I am glad to have

it. After Hungary's profound betrayal of my mother and her family I regard it as a piece of poetic justice.

CHAPTER 5

1 After the First World War, a short-lived Hungarian Soviet Republic was established in March 1919. Béla Kun, who served as the Republic's Foreign Minister, had a Jewish father and in the eyes of many Hungarians was the embodiment of Judaeo-Bolshevism. The notion that Bolshevism was part of a Jewish plot to achieve hegemony was commonly held, due to the high visibility of communists of Jewish origin within the Kun government. The following year the Romanian Army overthrew the Bolshevik regime and on 1 March 1920 Admiral Miklós Horthy, leader of the right-wing Hungarian counter-revolutionaries, was installed as regent. The subsequent election of Gyula Gömbös as prime minister in 1932, one of the foremost representatives of the Hungarian radical right, coincided with the spectacular electoral victories of the Nazi Party in Germany. By aligning Hungary's foreign policy with that of Nazi Germany, Gömbös smoothed the way for the Third Reich's influence over key aspects of Hungarian domestic policy, specifically the implementation of increasingly harsh anti-Jewish legislation, which continued during the subsequent premierships of Kálmán Darányi and László Bardóssy.

2 Ward was born in 1585 in Mulwith, West Riding, the first child of Marmaduke and Ursula Wright Ward. From 1589 to 1594 she lived with and was educated in Latin by her maternal

grandmother, Ursula Wright, who had been imprisoned for fourteen years for the 'exhalation of the Catholic religion'. Mary left England at the age of twenty-one in order to enter a monastery of Poor Clares at Saint-Omer in northern France. She then moved to the Spanish Netherlands as a lay sister and in 1606 founded a new monastery of the Order specifically for English women at nearby Gravelines, funded in large part by her own dowry. Ward applied to the Holy See for permission to expand her institute and established schools in the Netherlands, Italy, Germany, Austria and throughout Central Europe, but by 1631 her views were held to be too radical and she was confined in a convent as a heretic on the instructions of the Pope. Undaunted, she issued coded letters written in lemon juice to trusted friends who continued to run her schools. In 1637, Mary returned to England, establishing several free schools in London for the poor, as well as nursing the sick and visiting prisoners. In 1642 she established a community school in Hutton Rudby, dying three years later at Heworth Manor during the English Civil War. She was buried in Osbaldwick Churchyard, and her tombstone reads: 'To love the poor, / persevere in the same, / live die and rise with them / was all the aim of / Mary Ward / who having lived 60 years and 8 days / died 20th January 1645.'

3 It seems that, despite Grandfather's hefty bribes, the process of changing the family's religious affiliation was, no doubt deliberately, protracted. Mother's amended birth certificate states that her conversion to Catholicism was not completed until 11 May 1944, ironically the same week that she, her

mother Flóra and sister Zsuzsi were herded into Eger's newly established ghetto.

CHAPTER 6

1 Rose Hill, so named because during the Ottoman occupation the Turks planted an abundance of rose gardens here. Dotted with remarkable art nouveau and Bauhaus-inspired villas, this has always been an exclusive neighbourhood in the Buda Hills, with views down to the Danube. Adolf Eichmann, who oversaw the transportation of Hungarian Jews to Auschwitz after the German invasion of Hungary in March 1944, lived on Rose Hill in a luxurious villa stolen from its Jewish owner.

CHAPTER 7

1 One of the most expensive cars in the world, it cost the equivalent of seven Rolls-Royces. Erich von Stroheim chauffeured a similar car for Gloria Swanson in the 1950 film *Sunset Boulevard*, directed by Billy Wilder.

CHAPTER 10

1 *A Conversation with Oscar Wilde* was commissioned by a committee including Sir Jeremy Isaacs, Dame Judi Dench, Sir Ian McKellen and Seamus Heaney. The work is inscribed with a quotation from *Lady Windermere's Fan*: 'We are all in the gutter, but some of us are looking at the stars.' The statue is

located behind St Martin-in-the-Fields Church, London, and was unveiled on 30 November 1998.

CHAPTER 11

1 Between 16 April and 9 July more than 14,000 Hungarian Jews were transported daily to Auschwitz, 75–80 per cent of them gassed immediately upon arrival.

2 'The decisive factor in the destruction of Hungarian Jewry was the whole-hearted cooperation of the [Döme] Sztójay government, which was appointed on March 22 1944, with the consent of Miklós Horthy, the regent of Hungary.' Randolph L. Braham, 'Hungary', in David Wyman (ed.), *The World Reacts to the Holocaust*, Johns Hopkins University Press, 1996, p. 205, cited in Stone, *The Holocaust*, p. 160.

3 12 June was also Anne Frank's fifteenth (and final) birthday.

4 Eger's Orthodox synagogue was designed by Lipót Baumhorn, one of Hungary's most noted architects whose portfolio included a Moorish-style synagogue in Esztergom, and the synagogue in Szeged, one of the largest in the Austro-Hungarian Empire. Commissioned by Dezső Kánitz of Nagyecser, a prominent member of Eger's then extensive Jewish community, its construction started in 1911 and the building was completed in August 1913 at a cost of 300,000 koronas. Chief Rabbi Dr Zoltán Rácz was deported to Auschwitz in 1944, along with his entire congregation. Only Rácz survived. During the war, the synagogue was used for storage by the Germans and was heavily damaged during their retreat. By November 1945 the Jewish congregation in

Eger had been reduced to a mere 150. The emigration that started before the war continued during the 1950s and the synagogue was demolished in 1963. Today a hotel occupies the site and the current census lists just three Jewish households remaining in Eger.

5 Six days earlier, on 6 June, Operation Overlord was launched, with Allied forces landing troops on the Normandy beaches in the largest amphibious assault in history. The successful Allied landing was a significant psychological blow, calling into question the German Army's ability to control Western Europe and encouraging renewed partisan activity against enemy occupation. From this point onwards, the balance of power on the continent, already weakened by Soviet offensives into Poland, began to tip decisively in favour of the Allies.

6 A passage in Neil MacGregor's book *Germany: Memories of a Nation* echoes this unanswerable question: '. . . how could it happen? How did the great humanizing traditions of German history – Dürer, Luther's bible, Bach, the Enlightenment, Goethe's Faust, the Bauhaus, and much, much more – fail to avert this total ethical collapse, which led to the murder of millions and to national disaster?' (p. 473).

7 Jewish personal effects represented big business for the Nazis – the concentration camps were highly profitable economic hubs. Discarded suitcases yielded watches, jewellery, precious stones, rolls of American dollars squeezed into toothpaste tubes, wedding rings – all crated up each month and driven under armed guard to the SS headquarters in Berlin to be deposited in a designated

account at the Reichsbank. As a final insult, the name of the fictitious account holder was Max Heiliger (meaning saintly). Jonathan Freedland, in his remarkable account of Auschwitz escapee Rudolf Vrba, offers the following statistic: 'Between 1942 and 1944 . . . the haul [including dental gold] from the archipelago of Nazi-operated death camps across Poland reached 326 million Reichsmarks: in the US currency of the early 2020s, that would be $2 billion.' Freedland, *The Escape Artist*, p. 87.

8 Erika Rothschild recalled being 'driven from the cattle cars and lined up . . . In addition, a band, consisting of the best inmate musicians, played, and depending on the origins of the transport, they performed Polish, Czech, or Hungarian folk music. The band played, the SS tormented, and there was no time to think . . . one person was driven into camp, the other to the crematorium.' 'Eine Erinnerung. Ein Gespräch mit Erika Rothschild, die Auschwitz überlebt hat', *Badische Zeitung*, 21/22 January 1995.

CHAPTER 12

1 'Hungarian Jews, when they arrived in Auschwitz in the spring and summer of 1944, found it hard to believe that the ash and smoke overwhelming their senses came from the incinerated bodies of their fellow Jews.' Rumours circulating in the ghettos about mass murder were dismissed as fantasy, understandably given 'the unprecedented enormity of the Nazi enterprise, which was so utterly opposed to normative human values.' Rozett, *Conscripted Slaves*, p. 31.

2 Mother's defiant resolve reminds me of a sentence from Primo Levi's *The Drowned and the Saved*: 'The aims of life are the best defence against death' (p. 120).

3 The lack of food left prisoners permanently famished, bloated and constantly needing to urinate – legs swollen, lips black from the cold, gums bleeding and bones protruding.

CHAPTER 13

1 The Appel marked the start of the working day in the camps, at 4.30 in the summer and 5.30 in the winter. The prisoners got up at the sound of a klaxon, washed and relieved themselves before drinking their 'coffee' or 'tea'. At the sound of a second gong, they ran outside to the roll-call square, where they lined up in rows of ten by block. The calls were supervised by German women guards, *Offizierinnen*, and Poles, *Blokowas*. The Poles, fearful of losing their jobs, terrorised the prisoners continuously, more zealously than the *Offizierinnen*. Mother described one particular occasion in the depths of winter, when the prisoners stood for more than two hours in a howling snowstorm while the guards counted and then recounted when the figures didn't tally with their records. Many prisoners simply collapsed where they stood but no one was allowed to help them. 'I just remember the searing pain in my feet, standing on that icy ground. There was a girl beside me, Mitzi, who was asthmatic. After an hour she started to cough so badly she could barely breathe. I wanted to reach out to her but of course that was forbidden. A guard shouted at her to stop and when she couldn't, he ran

at her, swinging his rifle butt viciously at her head. I heard her neck snap and she fell to the ground. I remember thinking "You're the lucky one, now at least it's over." '

CHAPTER 15

1 Mother uses the old Hungarian name for what became, following the Treaty of Trianon in 1920, the Romanian city of Cluj. Her father studied law at Kolozsvár, obtaining his degree there in 1905.

2 Shortly after succeeding to the Habsburg throne in 1780, Emperor Joseph II (1741–90) issued a cluster of sweeping reforms, among them Edicts of Toleration relating to his Hungarian Jewish subjects. His more liberal outlook was in sharp contrast to that of his mother, Maria Theresa, who said: 'I do not know a worse public plague than this nation; with their fraud, usury and money dealing they reduce people to beggary, practising all sort of evil transactions that an honest man abhors. Therefore, they are to be kept away from here and their numbers diminished as far as possible.' Crankshaw, *Maria Theresa*, p. 99. Following the Austro-Hungarian Compromise of 1867 which restored the territorial integrity of the Kingdom of Hungary, the ruling classes encouraged Jews to engage in business and industry and to assume regional names – Egri (from Eger), Tihanyi (from Tihany) and so on. This process of enthusiastic Magyarisation by the Jews continued after the close of the First World War and on into the late 1930s. In 1929 my great-aunt Lili changed her Jewish surname from Rosenberger to the Hungarian name

Remete (meaning hermit, from the Latin *eremita*) in order to assimilate more successfully within Hungarian society. She subsequently adopted the stage name of Reinau to safeguard her singing career in Vienna. However, neither her adoption of new names nor her subsequent conversion to Catholicism would save her from deportation to Auschwitz in 1944. She died there, aged thirty-seven.

3 Ravensbrück was the largest concentration camp for women in the German Reich. In the concentration camp system, Ravensbrück was second in size only to the women's camp in Auschwitz-Birkenau. It was located about eighty kilometres north of Berlin, and construction began in 1938. Prisoners came from over thirty countries, including Poland (36%), the Soviet Union (21%), the German Reich (18%, including Austria), Hungary (8%), France (6%), Czechoslovakia (3%), the Benelux countries (2%) and Yugoslavia (2%). On 3 November 1944 some 2,000 women prisoners (of whom 1,235 were Hungarian) were transported from Auschwitz to Ravensbrück.

4 'It was impossible to clean off the mud and excrement that clung to the women's feet – mud haunted their dreams . . . To lose shoes could also bring death – women found without shoes were often sent straight to the gas chambers, women being easier to replace than shoes.' Moorhead, *A Train in Winter*, pp. 194–5.

5 Heinrich Himmler (October 1900–23 May 1945) was a leading member of the Nazi Party and one of the main architects of the Holocaust. In 1925, he joined the SS, a small paramilitary arm of the Nazi Party that served as a

bodyguard unit for Adolf Hitler, rising through the ranks to become *Reichsführer-SS* by 1929. Under Himmler's leadership, the SS became one of the most powerful institutions within Nazi Germany. From 1943 onwards, he was both Chief of the *Kriminalpolizei* (Criminal Police) and Minister of the Interior, with oversight of all internal and external police and security forces, including the Gestapo. He also controlled the *Waffen-SS*, a branch of the SS that served in combat alongside the *Wehrmacht* (armed forces) in the Second World War. As the principal enforcer of the Nazis' racial policies, Himmler was responsible for operating concentration and extermination camps as well as forming the *Einsatzgruppen* death squads in German-occupied Europe. In this capacity, he played a central role in the genocide of an estimated 5.5–6 million Jews and the deaths of millions of other victims during the Holocaust.

6 On 20 November the women from the Auschwitz transport were split up – some sent on to Lippstadt, the Buchenwald labour camp, others to labour camps at Barth, Beendorf and Malchow. Mother was one of 800 Hungarian women sent from Ravensbrück to the Berlin-Reinickendorf subcamp of Sachsenhausen, located at the Argus Motorenwerke GmbH compound on Flottenstrasse, to the north-west of Berlin. This is where the AS 014 pulse jet for the V-1 flying bomb was developed. The women had to work in twelve-hour shifts, but towards the end of the war they were mostly engaged in digging defensive trenches around Berlin. Only 93 of those 800 Hungarian prisoners are known to have survived the war.

7 The renowned journalist Janet Flanner, in her 'Letter from
   Berlin' published in the *New Yorker*, 12 July 1947, reflects on the
   physical devastation of Germany in the immediate aftermath
   of the war, and the seeming incapacity of most Germans to
   comprehend the cause of their country's ruin: 'The Unter den
   Linden section of Berlin is like a coffin a mile long . . . this is
   the symbolic mile of Berlin that millions of Russians, British
   and American armed men fought against. There is still an
   awful majesty about it – spacious, wrecked and historical, with
   nothing left but its name, not even its own linden trees. The
   meaning of its devastation has not yet grown stale. It looks
   like what it was meant to be – the greatest, most humiliating example of punishment to fit the crime that the modern
   Germans have suffered. Most Germans regard it . . . not as
   punishment but as a sort of martyrdom . . . the new Germany
   is bitter against everyone else on earth . . . bursting with
   complaints of her hunger, lost homes and other sufferings, she
   considers without interest or compassion the pains and losses
   she has imposed on others, and she expects and takes, usually
   with carping rather than thanks, charity from those nations
   she tried to destroy.' Drutman, *Janet Flanner's World*, pp. 140–1.

CHAPTER 17

1 Completed in 1967, the Cripps Building was designed by
   Powell & Moya and is now Grade II* listed. It was hailed by
   Pevsner as 'a masterpiece by one of the best architectural part-
   nerships in the country' – so much for my youthful ignorance.
2 Sir Philip Sidney (1554–86) enjoyed a long-standing

relationship with Hubert Languet (1518–81), a French diplomat and professor of civil law at Padua.

CHAPTER 18

1 The LYC Museum & Art Gallery (1971–82), located in rural Cumbria, a short distance from the Northumbrian and Scottish borders, was the inspiration of Li Yuan-chia. As well as displaying works of international artists lent by private collectors, the museum showed Roman artefacts from the nearby archaeological site at Vindolanda alongside traditional Cumbrian crafts. The gallery hosted exhibitions by artists from all over the UK.

CHAPTER 22

1 In the Epilogue to Sarah Helm's *If This Is a Woman*, the author quotes from an interview with Jeannie Rousseau, a Frenchwoman who gathered vital information about German operations for the Allied intelligence. She was arrested in 1944 and deported to Ravensbrück, which she survived because 'You can refuse what is happening. Or go along with it. I was in the refusal camp.'

CHAPTER 23

1 Miklós Horthy (1868–1957) was a Hungarian admiral and statesman who became Regent of Hungary from 1 March 1920 to 15 October 1944.

CHAPTER 24

1 Mother's school report was carefully stored with other important family documents, along with the Persian rugs, silverware, porcelain, linens and jewellery in the secret room for the duration of the war. Dated 24 November 1937, it states tersely: 'Ildikó is lively, undisciplined and likes to chatter.' A subsequent report, dated 26 April 1938, says: 'Ildikó still chatters a great deal.'

CHAPTER 26

1 Professor Gebhardt was president of the German Red Cross, professor of orthopaedic surgery at Berlin University and former chief surgeon to the 1936 Olympics.

2 Sylvia Salvesen, wife of the court physician to the King of Norway, helped establish a group called the King's Messengers which secretly supported Norwegian resistance fighters. She was arrested in 1942 and sent to Ravensbrück where she worked as a nurse in the *Krankenrevier*. In 1958 she published a memoir of her imprisonment: *Forgive But Do Not Forget*.

CHAPTER 27

1 Dr Fritz Ernst Fischer (1912–2003) was appointed troop physician of the SS Division Leibstandarte Adolf Hitler in 1940, subsequently working as a surgical assistant to Karl Gebhardt, participating in medical experiments conducted on

inmates of the Ravensbrück concentration camp. After the war, he was tried in the Doctors' Trial in Nuremberg in 1947, convicted of war crimes and crimes against humanity, and condemned to life imprisonment. His sentence was reduced to fifteen years in 1951 but he was released in March 1954, having served only seven years. Fischer subsequently regained his licence to practise medicine and started a new career at the chemical company Boehringer in Ingelheim, where he stayed until his retirement.

CHAPTER 28

1 Following the end of the Second World War, Austria refused to address its national role in the Holocaust or to pay compensation to victims of Nazism. According to the founders of the Second Austrian Republic, the 1938 Anschluss had been an act of military aggression by the Third Reich – Austrian statehood had been interrupted and therefore the newly revived Austria of 1945 could not be considered responsible for Nazi war crimes. Former Nazis were reintroduced into social and political life, and for almost half a century the Austrian state denied the existence of any continuity between it and the political regime which existed in Austria from 1938 to 1945.

Kurt Waldheim was elected president of Austria in June 1986. While campaigning for that office, his participation in Nazi atrocities as an intelligence officer in the *Wehrmacht* came to light. On 23 March 1986 the World Jewish Congress revealed that the United Nations War Crimes Commission had concluded after the war that Waldheim was implicated

in Nazi mass murder and should be arrested. On 27 April
1987, the United States Justice Department's Office of Special
Investigations established a prima facie case that Waldheim
had participated in Nazi-sponsored persecution during the
Second World War. Nevertheless, in 1994, Pope John Paul II
awarded Waldheim a knighthood in the Order of Pius IX and
his wife a papal honor. He died aged eighty-eight on 14 June
2007 and was buried with full military honours in the Presi-
dential Vault in the Zentralfriedhof. It was only in 2021, on 9
November (the eighty-third anniversary of Kristallnacht), that
the Austrian government finally inaugurated a 'Shoah Wall
of Names Memorial' at the Ostarrichi Park in central Vienna.
This memorial is engraved with the names of the 64,440
Austrian Jews who were murdered during the Holocaust.

CHAPTER 31

1 My grandparents' discussion was undoubtedly prompted by
news of the assassination of King Alexander of Yugoslavia
together with Louis Barthou, French Minister of Foreign
Affairs, in Marseilles on 9 October 1934. Barthou had
attempted to create an Eastern Pact to include Germany, the
Soviet Union, Poland, Czechoslovakia and the Baltic states.
He invited King Alexander to France in order to sign a Franco-
Yugoslav agreement which would pressure Mussolini into
renouncing his claims against Yugoslavia, thereby potentially
forging an Italo-French alliance, his long-term aspiration being
to constrain Germany's increasingly aggressive foreign policy.
For my grandfather, Alexander's assassination marked the

inevitable ascendancy of Germany on the world stage. The League of Nations was notably cautious in response to the king's murder, no doubt anxious to avoid further destabilising already fragile international relations. As Rebecca West notes in *Black Lamb and Grey Falcon*, 'every totalitarian ruffian in Europe rejoiced to see one of their kind strike down a foreign king in peacetime and go scot-free, and all honest men lost heart' (p. 616). Grandfather could see the writing on the wall – it was, in his words, 'the death knell for European Jewry'.

2   Ilse Gostynski was a prisoner at the newly constructed concentration camp at Ravensbrück. Gostynski, a communist, was released in 1939 through English contacts and settled in England, where she married and had a daughter. Sarah Helm records an interview with the daughter in *If This Is a Woman*. Describing her mother's last days, she said: 'I see the shadow of her imprisonment falling across the end of her life – unfinished business.'

CHAPTER 33

1   Since renamed as the Bohdan and Varvara Khanenko Museum of Art, honouring the Jewish founders who gifted their art collection and magnificent house to the trusteeship of the Ukrainian Academy of Sciences. Bohdan Khanenko was a Ukrainian lawyer, sugar industrialist and art collector. He served as a judge in St Petersburg and Warsaw and in 1906 was elected to the State Council of Imperial Russia. His wife Varvara was the daughter of the sugar industrialist Nikolai Tereshchenko and a great supporter of local

crafts. I am indebted to the current deputy director of the museum, Dr Olena Zhivkova, who provided valuable information regarding the works of art on display in the museum at the time of Bandi's visit. Closed after the German invasion, the collection evacuated its most valuable items to the city of Ufa (Bashkotorstan). The museum reopened in January 1942, solely for the benefit of *Wehrmacht* officers, but after six months the remaining contents were packed up and dispatched to Germany. The museum is still trying to trace many of these lost items. Dr Zhivkova, writing to me in February 2022, with Russian troops massing on the borders of Ukraine, observed: 'How sad that we are now, once again, preparing an inventory for the evacuation of the collection, just in case the worst happens.'

2 Bruno Bettelheim, writing specifically of Jewish persecution in Germany, observed: 'Today . . . it is easily forgotten how many Germans – by no means only Nazis – derived tangible advantages from the persecution of the Jews. Many Jews owned businesses, held lucrative positions, owned nice homes. During the last year before the war, when Jews emigrated, they could take none of their possessions with them, and the same was true when they were first sent to the ghettos in Poland and later to the camps. Rather than see the Nazis acquire all their possessions . . . most Jews preferred to give their art objects, jewellery, valuable furniture and clothing to gentile acquaintances, either as presents or for safekeeping. The end result was nearly always the same: the Jews died in the camps and nobody was left to claim what had been left behind.' *Surviving and Other Essays*, p. 86.

CHAPTER 34

1 Fritz Suhren was a German SS officer and commandant of Ravensbrück from 1942. His policy was to exterminate the prisoners by allowing them the minimum amount of food and working them to death. Tried by a French military court, he was executed by firing squad on 12 June 1950 – on the sixth anniversary, to the day, of Mother's deportation from Eger to Auschwitz.

2 Researching this particular species of tree, I discovered that the wood is soft but close-grained and easy to carve. A famous example is Donatello's *Penitent Magdalene*, dated *c.*1440. Probably commissioned for the Baptistery of Florence, this extraordinary sculpture, depicting Mary Magdalene as a gaunt, emaciated figure, is now in the Museo dell'Opera del Duomo in Florence.

APPENDIX

1 'Heaven' by Rupert Brooke, 1913.

2 Dezső was one of Mother's young admirers.

3 *Párbaj semmiért* – a Hungarian film (1940), directed by Emil Martonffy, starring Gyula Csortos, Lili Berky and Alice Nagy, based on a novel by Sándor Hunyady.

4 Szombathely is the tenth largest city in Hungary, located near the border with Austria, where the Alpokalja (Lower Alps) mountains meet the Little Hungarian Plain. The oldest city in Hungary, it was the birthplace of St Martin of Tours.

5 Pista is a nickname for István (Stephen).

6 Richard Voss (1851–1918) was a prolific German dramatist and
   novelist.

7 *Johnny Apollo* (1940), starring Tyrone Power and Dorothy
   Lamour.

8 Adrienne Brettfeld was the daughter of Baron Egon Brettfeld
   of Kronenburg and Alice Péterfy. Adrienne later married
   Dr Peter Veghelyi (born Veigelsberg), a noted paediatrician.
   They collected important examples of twentieth-century art,
   including works by Joan Miró, Marc Chagall, Henry Moore
   and Aristide Maillol, later bequeathed to the Museum of Fine
   Arts in Budapest.

9 Sömjén or Kemenessömjén is a village five kilometres to the
   north of Celldömölk.

10 Sopron is a spa town near the Austrian border, just seventy
   kilometres from Vienna.

11 The old Hotel Lővér was torn down and replaced with a
   modern building in the early 1960s.

12 Hungarian racial laws passed between 1938 and 1941 reversed
   the equal citizenship status granted to Jews in Hungary
   in 1867. The first anti-Jewish law passed in 1938 limited
   the role of Jews in the Hungarian economy and professions to 20 per cent. Another, ratified by parliament in 1939,
   further reduced the role of Jews in Hungarian economic
   life to just 6 per cent. The wealthier segment of the Jewish
   population was largely unaffected – it was the lower middle
   classes, artisans, white-collar workers and most profes-
   sionals, including those working in the civil service, who
   suffered. Widening the gap between rich and poor, the law
   accelerated the impoverishment of the Jewish community

as a whole. A third anti-Jewish law passed in 1941 closely
followed the Nazi Nuremberg Laws in tone and racial
definition of the Jews, prohibiting marriage between
Jews and non-Jews and effectively sanctioning the seg-
regation of Jews as an inferior race – a keystone in the
process of excluding Jews from Hungarian society. Finally,
a bill adopted in 1942 abolished the status of Judaism as
a recognised religion in Hungary and banned Jews from
owning or purchasing land.

13 Baktalórántháza is a town in Szabolcs-Szatmár-Bereg county,
in the Northern Great Plain region of eastern Hungary.

14 Ernő Dohnányi (1877–1960) was a Hungarian composer,
pianist and conductor. In 1894 he started piano studies at the
Royal National Hungarian Academy of Music with István
Thomán, a former pupil of Liszt, and composition with Hans
von Koessler, a cousin of Max Reger and a former pupil of
Brahms. He was among the first to conduct and popularise
Bartók's music.

15 My grandfather was based at a forced labour camp at Shostka,
300 kilometres north-east of Kyiv. He was diabetic and for
a time was allowed to receive packets of insulin sent by my
grandmother. By late 1942 these packages were no longer
permitted and his health declined rapidly, due to lack of
medication and the gruelling work he was obliged to undertake.

16 A nickname for Erzsébet.

17 The Herend Porcelain Manufactory was founded in 1826
and still specialises in luxury hand-painted and gilded
porcelain. Queen Victoria ordered a dinner service for
Windsor Castle and other notable customers included

various members of the Habsburg Dynasty and Hungarian aristocracy.

18 My grandfather Ede (b. 9 February 1883, d. 2 March 1943).

19 The pengő was the currency of Hungary between 1927 and 1946, when it was replaced by the forint.

20 Mihály Babits (1883–1941) was a Hungarian poet, writer and translator. His lyric poetry was influenced by classical and English forms and he also translated Dante's *Divine Comedy*. After the Hungarian Revolution of 1919 he was briefly professor of Foreign Literature and Modern Hungarian Literature at the University of Budapest but was dismissed due to his pacifist views after the fall of the revolutionary government.

21 My grandmother Flóra (b. 29 September 1891, d. June 1944), my aunt Zsuzsi (b. 27 December 1918, d. 13 October 2005) and Mother (b. 26 February 1926, d. 29 May 2017).

22 Árpád Tóth (1886–1928) was a Hungarian poet, theatre critic and translator. His poetry explored themes of fleeting happiness. He translated works by Milton, Wilde, Shelley, Keats, Baudelaire, Flaubert, Gautier, Maupassant and Chekhov.

23 Attila József (1905–1937) was one of the most celebrated Hungarian poets of the twentieth century. Despite his humble origins, he studied French literature at the Franz Joseph University, but was expelled after publishing the revolutionary poem 'Tiszta szívvel' (With a Clear Heart). He travelled to Vienna in 1925 where he made a living selling newspapers and cleaning dormitories, and later studied at the Sorbonne in Paris. During this period he read the revolutionary works of

Hegel and Karl Marx. He returned to Hungary, studied at Pest University for a year and later became editor of the literary journal *Szép Szó* (Beautiful Word). A staunch supporter of the working class, József joined the illegal Communist Party of Hungary (KMP) in 1930. His 1931 work *Döntsd a tőkét* (Blow Down the Capital) was confiscated by the public prosecutor. His later essay 'Irodalom és Szocializmus' (Literature and Socialism) led to indictment. In 1936, he was expelled from the KMP due to his independence and interest in Freud. From early childhood, József began showing signs of mental illness and was treated for depression and schizophrenia. His early death at thirty-two, crushed by an oncoming train, is thought to have been suicide.

24 In early 1944 Prime Minister Miklós Kállay, with the knowledge and approval of Regent Miklós Horthy, had begun secret negotiations to secure peace with the Allies. Hitler, determined to prevent this as Hungarian oil was of vital importance for the German war effort, invited Horthy to the Palace of Klessheim, near Salzburg, on 15 March, in order to keep Horthy out of the country, thereby leaving the Hungarian Army without orders. The talks continued for three days, but as Horthy boarded his train to return to Budapest, German forces were already marching across the border from Austria into Hungary, with orders to capture critical Hungarian facilities. Mother's reference to 'Black Sunday' is apt: 19 March 1944 – the date of the German occupation of Hungary – effectively sealed the fate of some 565,000 Hungarian Jews.